CW01369795

Machines for Better Woodwork

By the same author

Modern Woodturning
Woodturning for Pleasure

Machines for Better Woodwork

Gordon Stokes

Evans Brothers Limited

Published by Evans Brothers Limited
Montague House, Russell Square,
London WC1

First published 1980

Text © 1980 Gordon Stokes
Line illustrations © 1980 Evans Brothers Limited

Illustrations by V. J. Taylor

All Rights Reserved. No part of this publication
may be reproduced, stored in a retrieval system, or
transmitted, in any form or by any means, electronic,
mechanical, photocopying, recording or otherwise,
without the prior permission of Evans Brothers Limited.

British Library Cataloguing in Publication Data

Stokes, Gordon
   Machines for better woodwork.
   1. Woodworking machinery
   I. Title
   621.9   TS850

ISBN 0–237–44931–5

Set in 10 on 11 Univers by Northampton Phototypesetters Ltd
Printed in Great Britain by Hazell, Watson & Viney Ltd, Aylesbury, Bucks.

ISBN 0 237 44931 5   PRA 6847

Contents

The Sawbench	7
Radial Arm Saws	35
Bandsaws	47
Electric Drills and Portable Power Tools	64
The Pillar Drill	77
The Portable Router	85
Spindle Moulders and Disc Sanders	96
Planers	105
Combination Machines	112
The Woodturning Lathe	126
Workshop Layout	135
Grinding and Sharpening	138

Acknowledgments

For permission to reproduce photographs the publishers are indebted to the following:

Bosch Ltd   pages 68, 71 (right)
Clico Sheffield Ltd   pages 81, 116
The Coronet Tool Co Ltd   pages 17, 32, 34 (left), 61, 72, 101, 107, 109, 121, 122, 123, 125, 134 (bottom left)
De Walt Ltd   pages 34, 35, 43, 44, 45, 60, 137
Elu Machinery Ltd   pages 72 (bottom right), 73 (bottom right), 75, 85, 94
Kity (UK) Ltd   pages 11, 104, 111, 115, 117
Mafell Ltd   page 7
Myford Ltd   pages 126, 134 (bottom right)
Stanley Tools Ltd   pages 64, 65, 67, 70, 72 (left), 73 (bottom left), 86, 87, 93
Startrite Machine Tool Co Ltd   pages 77, 78, 105
Sumaco Machinery and Tools Ltd   pages 10, 12, 53, 58, 65, 134 (top right)
Wadkin Ltd   pages 8, 13, 15, 102
Willow Ltd   pages 18, 103 (left)
Wolf Electric Tools Ltd   pages 69, 71 (left), 72 (top right), 73 (top left and right), 74, 84, 141
Zinken Ltd   page 112

Chapter one

The Sawbench

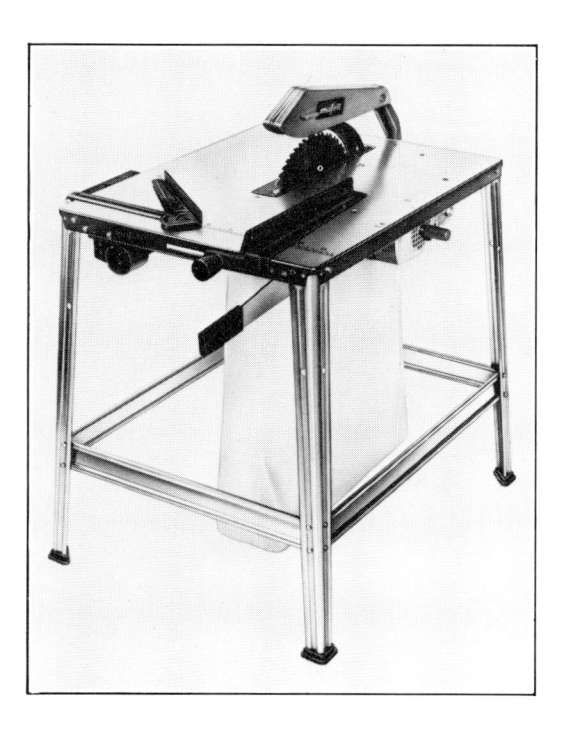

If an order of priority is to be established for the purchase of woodworking machinery, it will vary remarkably little across the great range of woodworkers. There can be little doubt that in the majority of cases the most important machine, and the machine which will be bought first, is a powered saw of some kind. In recent years the radial arm saw has come very much to the fore, and has rather taken the place of the circular saw in the minds of many woodworkers. This is due to its remarkable versatility, its extreme accuracy, and the ease with which it can be set up and used. In spite of this, however, there are still large numbers of people who would prefer to use a sawbench as such, and this is the machine which we will consider first.

It should be noted that in the case of the circular sawbench, apart from the quite obvious fact that the blade rotates, it remains in other respects stationary, the timber itself being moved. A radial arm saw performs most of its operations with the wood stationary and the blade moving through it.

On the face of it, a sawbench would appear to be an extremely simple device, consisting of a flat table through which the circular saw blade itself projects. The projection of the saw blade through the table can be varied by the operator, and the machine is normally provided with a rip fence, to guide the timber when cutting along its length, and a mitre guide which is designed for cutting across the grain and to give accuracy in the cutting of specific angles.

When one begins to study the various

A powerful saw from the continent with rise and fall and tilt facilities, widely used by home workers and small contractors.

makes of circular saw bench, however, it becomes obvious that there are many differences and these differences will have varying values for individual operators, according to the type of work which they propose to undertake.

Sawbenches, like many other machines, are available either for bench mounting or as floor standing units. In the former case the sawbench can be positioned on the worker's own wooden bench in the workshop, whereas in the latter it is mounted on a metal cabinet. The cost of these metal cabinets appears to be excessively high due very largely to the high cost of steel. Timber, however, is also expensive, so it may be as well to go into the costings carefully before building a bench to take a

A heavy-duty sawbench by Wadkin capable of continuous use.

machine of this kind. The prime prerequisite is a high degree of stability and a bench which is lightly constructed will be a nuisance, or even dangerous. The machine which will be mounted on it is quite heavy, and before it has been used for very long it is likely that movement will develop in the joints of a wooden bench, which will begin to rack or sway from side to side. A satisfactory bench for a machine of this kind requires legs about 75mm (3in) square, and the amount of timber which will be needed to make a really solid bench is quite surprising. There is the minor consideration, of course, that the manufacturer's metal stand, painted in the same colour as the sawbench itself, does make the machine look a great deal more impressive. Most woodworkers however, do not buy machines in order to impress anyone and the accent should always be on safety and efficiency in use. The decision as to whether the machine is to be mounted on a wooden home-made bench or upon a steel cabinet as provided by the manufacturer, is of course one for the individual.

Another point which seems to cause a certain amount of controversy is the table itself. There is still a very large band of enthusiasts which insists on a cast-iron top to a sawbench. The reason for this is that a cast table-top, which has been machined after casting, should remain completely flat throughout its lifetime. In this age of hurried manufacture, however, this may or may not be the case, since the casting needs to be 'weathered'. This consists of leaving it out in the open for a considerable period of time after it has been manufactured so that any movement which takes place within the metal will have ceased before the machining itself is undertaken. It would appear nowadays that many cast-iron tables are not, in fact, weathered or at least not weathered sufficiently and it is not uncommon to find that they are slightly warped. Cast iron is, of course, brittle and will break if it receives a really hard blow, but it is possible that throughout the long lifetime of a good circular saw bench no such hard blow will be delivered, and so perhaps the point is a trifle academic.

An alternative to a cast-iron table-top which has been machined is a top made from some form of aluminium alloy, which is a great deal lighter and, of course, softer. Such table-tops are, however, quite satisfactory and much more pleasing in appearance. The drawback lies in the fact that the softness of the metal is such that hard objects rubbed across it can cause considerable scratching. This can be avoided by careful use.

The third type of table used on circular saws is the sheet metal variety. Tables of this nature are normally cheaper, but are frowned upon by some woodworkers. A well-made machine with a sheet metal top can be extremely efficient and entirely satisfactory, provided the thickness of the metal is adequate. In some cases it is really very thick and braced to give it extra strength and rigidity.

A further point regarding tables for sawbenches is that those engaged in cabinet-making and the finer forms of woodwork, as distinct from the bulk ripping and cross-cutting of heavy sections of timber, will make constant use of a mitre guide. This particular device, which is discussed fully on page 00, has beneath it a strip of metal designed to fit into a slot in the surface of the table, and which can be slid back and forth. It is important that the fit of this strip in the slot should be exact but not so tight as to render the use of the device difficult. On the best saws there is a mitre guide slot both on the left and right-hand sides of the blade; it is not vital that this should be so, but one of the advantages is that many woodworkers like to make wooden jigs for various purposes, some of which are discussed on page 00. Such jigs are far more accurate if they carry two mitre guide runners which fit both of the slots in the table.

Another item which should be inspected carefully, but must be considered in relation to the available capital, is the rip fence. The rip fence runs parallel to the blade and can be adjusted to a desired distance from it. It is used when cutting timber along its length, the wood being placed firmly against the rip fence and moved along it into the blade, contact being maintained between the fence and timber throughout the operation. This produces a perfectly straight cut. Ideally the rip fence should run right across the table to the rear, where it is secured by means of a clamp just as it is at the front. A rip fence designed in this manner is, to some extent, safer than one which does not reach right across the table, but there is another important point to be considered. When heavy pieces of timber are being ripped, a fence which is secured only at the front of the table is likely to bend slightly away from the saw blade under the pressure of the timber as the cut progresses. If this happens, inaccuracy will obviously result. There are ways of overcoming this drawback on machines which are so constructed, such as attaching a length of wood to the rip fence, with a small block at its far end which can be clamped to the table, thus providing a wooden rip fence which runs right to the rear of the table and is rigidly secured.

A low-priced sawbench unit which is light and portable.

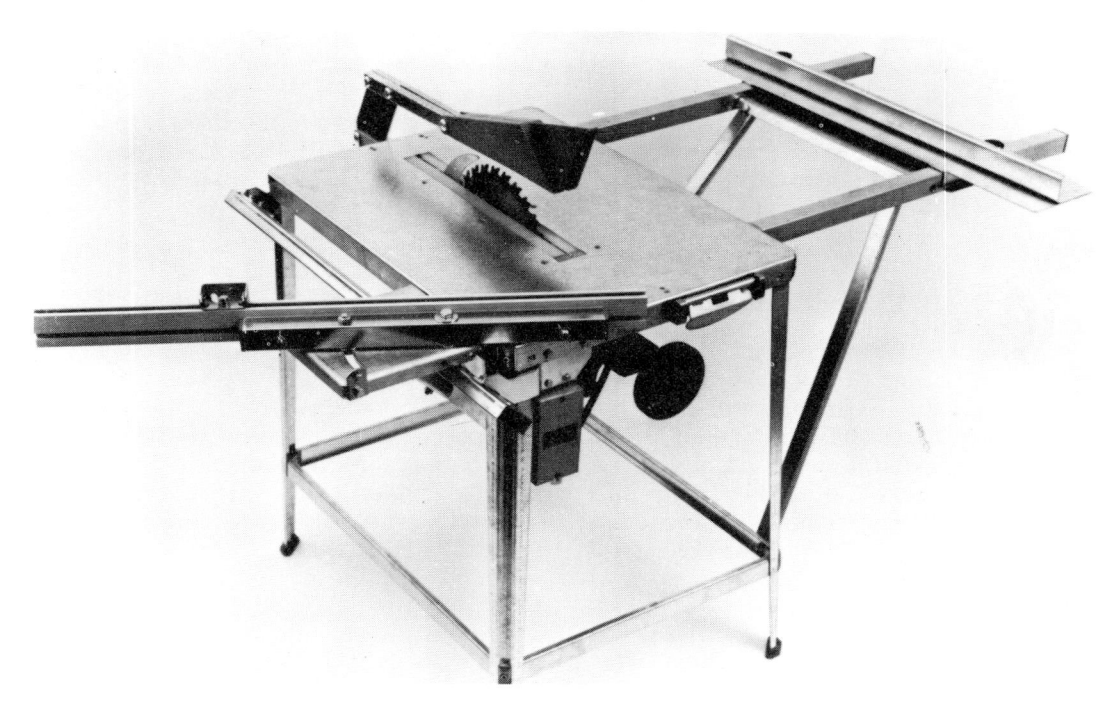

Those who have studied catalogues of circular saws may have come across the expression 'rise and fall, tilt arbor'. On many relatively cheap machines the depth of cut is adjusted by raising or lowering the table itself, the spindle which carries the blade remaining stationary. This works quite well, but there is one slight drawback in that the operator cannot establish an exact table height to suit him and maintain it. The height of the table will vary each time the depth of cut is adjusted. Allied to the point I am now making is the fact that many workers frequently need to make angled cuts in which the angle between the circular saw blade and the table is other than 90°. The type of bench where the table is raised or lowered to vary the depth of cut is usually designed to cater for angled cutting by tilting the table itself, the blade remaining vertical. For much of the work which the average woodworker is likely to undertake, this will be quite satisfactory, but there are occasions when it is a nuisance. One obvious reason is that the wood has a tendency to slide sideways if the table has been tilted, which must be effectively countered by some means. In addition, if one is trying to cross-cut a piece of timber which is fairly long with the table tilted, the end of the timber may strike the workshop floor, rendering the operation impossible.

The alternative to a tilting table machine, in which the depth of cut is adjusted by raising or lowering the table, is the tilting arbor variety. By virtue of this design, the table remains at exactly the same height, and horizontal, at all times. It is the circular saw blade itself which is raised or lowered

Kity 617 circular saw with provision for rise and fall and blade tilt. Rip fence, metal guide and adjustable stop for cross-cutting are all provided and a table extension is available.

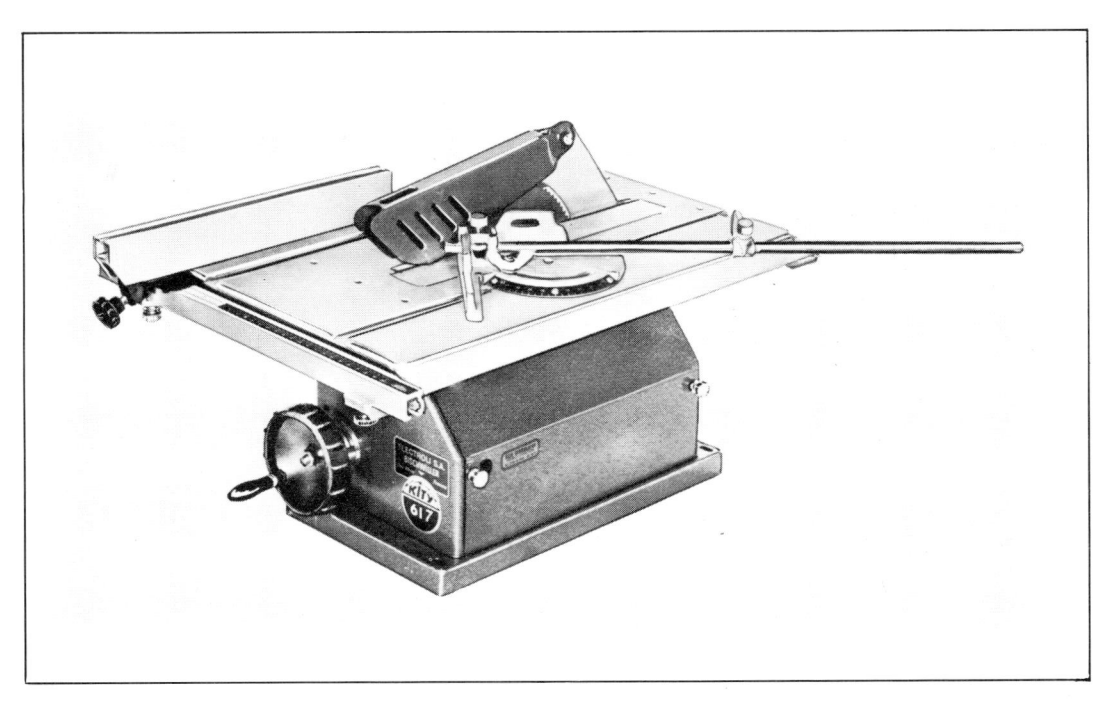

and tilted. Unfortunately, this involves the provision of fairly complicated mechanism which can be rather expensive. Such machines are, however, a delight to use and may well be worth a little more money in terms of satisfaction over a long period of use.

In looking around machinery showrooms, this type of machine can generally be picked out fairly easily because it will have two control wheels. One of these raises or lowers the spindle which carries the circular saw in order to alter the depth of cut, whilst the other will tilt the spindle in order to provide for angled cutting. Normally, of course, if the spindle is designed to tilt, the drive mechanism of the machine will require the motor itself to move also. If this is the case the sawbench will need to be made from fairly heavy metal, since the weight of an electric motor large enough to drive a circular saw is considerable.

The size of the table is also to be considered when purchasing a sawbench. However large the table, there will always be times when it is too small, just as the largest of workshops never seems quite large enough. The sensible thing is to select a machine with a table adequate for most purposes, but which has provision for the addition of support rails at either side. This is quite a common feature in many good sawbenches and these support rails or tables can be purchased at a later stage when they become necessary. They are extremely useful in handling large pieces of wood, such as panels for cabinet construction. It is difficult, and to some extent dangerous, for a person working alone to handle large pieces of timber of this nature on a small sawbench. If the supporting tables or rails are fitted, and if they are of robust construction and accurately engineered, they will prove to be a very valuable adjunct to the bench itself.

One must also give some thought to the amount of power which will be available to drive the blade. Those whose woodwork is of a very light nature may be able to manage with only a half horsepower motor. Others who need to rip and cross-cut hardwoods up to 75mm (3in) in thickness, will require a one horsepower motor. If a saw with a small motor is used for heavy work over long periods, the life of the motor will be drastically reduced. As with other forms of woodworking machinery, the totally enclosed type of electric motor is most suitable, since it will not fill up with sawdust. Anyone who feels that the half horsepower motor will be enough and that the depth of cut likely to be required most of the time will not exceed 50mm (2in), will find quite a wide range of benches fall into this category. A saw which will cut 50mm (2in) deep can handle timber of 100mm (4in) thickness, if a cut is made into one side and the timber inverted for a second cut, but unless the opposing faces of the material are exactly parallel, the sawn face which results from cutting in this manner will not be flat.

On some sawbenches it may be found that there is sufficient clearance for the fitting of a larger blade than that provided by the manufacturer, thus producing a greater depth of cut. This is not normally advisable, since sufficient power may not be available to drive the blade. A sawbench has to work extremely hard in most workshops, and should always be fitted with some form of thermal overload cut-out to prevent the motor from becoming overheated. It should also be borne in mind that whilst considerable power is needed when using a sharp circular saw blade in hardwood at its full depth of cut, an

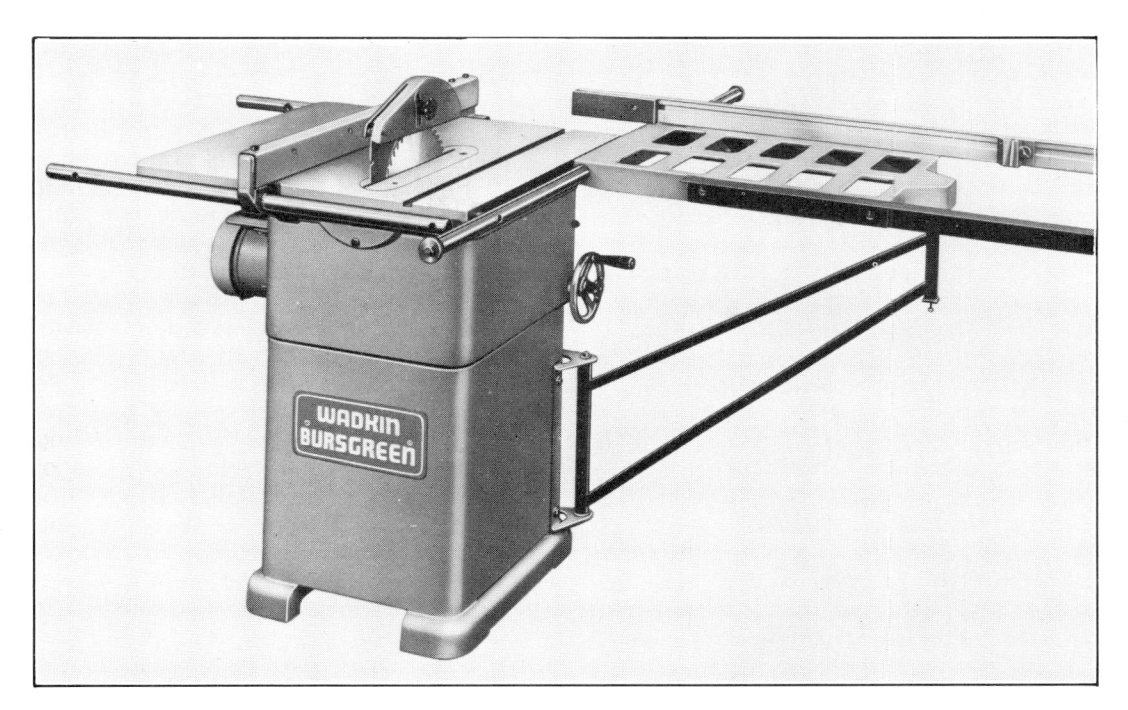

Industrial sawbench fitted with an attachment for cutting panels.

even greater amount of power is needed when making a similar cut with a blade which is becoming blunt. For this reason circular saw blades must be kept very sharp at all times.

Since the sawbench is still by far the most common type of circular saw, we will consider first the various aspects of its use. The most important basic functions of any circular saw are the cross-cutting of wood to a given length, and the ripping of timber to a given width. The prime requisite in both cases is, of course, accuracy. These are operations which, when carried out with hand saws, are very difficult for a beginner. The skill required in the proper use of hand saws is greater than many people realise. Circular saws take the hard work out of such operations and have, if well serviced and properly adjusted, a very high degree of accuracy built in. This accuracy must be jealously guarded. A circular sawbench should have its settings regularly checked, and adjustments should be carried out immediately if all is not as it should be.

Before going further into the practical aspects of using a circular sawbench, I would like to try to dispel one myth which is rather discouraging to beginners. Dreadful tales are told about circular sawbenches and the injuries which they have inflicted. Certainly it is true that many people have injured themselves badly on circular saws, just as it is true that many are killed or injured by wandering carelessly into the traffic. The matter must be viewed in perspective, however. Once a circular saw is switched on the operator can, if he so desires, settle himself comfortably in a chair and watch it for months on end,

13

without the slightest danger. In order to be injured he must leave his chair, cross the room to the saw and place his hand in close proximity to the blade. My point, of course, is that it is not normally the circular saw which is dangerous, it is the individual who is using it who is dangerous. There is no need for a woodworker to fear a circular saw, but he must respect it, since serious injuries can result from careless use. It is most important, having purchased a new circular saw and established it in the workshop, to study the instruction book in depth, before attempting to use the machine. Lack of knowledge can easily lead to accidents.

Setting up the saw table
Machines, if properly set and correctly used, will give a great deal of accuracy and safety, vastly reducing the amount of time required to complete a given project. A machine which is not correctly set cannot be expected to produce accurate work, may well give rise to accidents, and will not greatly reduce the amount of time needed for a project, since considerable time will be taken in correcting the errors at a later stage. It is, therefore, of extreme importance that sawbenches, together with other woodworking machines, should be correctly set when received from the manufacturer and that this setting should be checked as necessary throughout the life of the machine. It is not safe to assume that because the machine is brand new, everything is in order. It may well be that on leaving the factory it was thoroughly tested, inspected, and found to be correctly set, but the settings may well have been altered by jolts and bumps in transit so the whole thing should be checked through thoroughly before it is used. This checking should be done in conjunction with the manufacturer's handbook, since one machine may vary in minor respects from others. The settings are a matter of establishing that the relationships between various parts of the machine are as they should be; a typical example being that where a 90° cut is required there is in fact an exact 90° angle between the vertical side of the saw blade and the horizontal surface of the table. Having checked the settings on the machine, and thoroughly studied the handbook, it should be safe to go ahead with some cutting. Do not assume, however, that because the settings have been checked once they will remain correct. After a period of use, depending on the amount of timber which is passed through the machine, the checks should be repeated, and the settings will sometimes be found to have altered slightly. Powered woodworking machinery is inherently accurate and must be given every opportunity to remain so.

The method of setting a circular saw bench is explained here in the manner which I adopt myself. There are other ways of achieving the same result, but this method has the merit of simplicity and can be entirely relied upon.

From the point of view of setting, the most important thing is that the saw blade runs exactly parallel to the slot in the surface of the table and to the rip fence. If the saw blade is out of line with either there will be difficulties of one kind or another. Setting up a saw in the manner described here takes remarkably little time, once the operator is familiar with the procedure. First set the rip fence close to the mitre guide slot in the table using the coarse adjustment on the rip fence to do so. The micrometer adjuster can then be employed to make the final adjustment to bring the rip fence precisely to the edge of the slot. If the fence is not parallel to the table slot this will immediately be apparent and the fence must be adjusted so that it runs exactly along the edge of the machined recess.

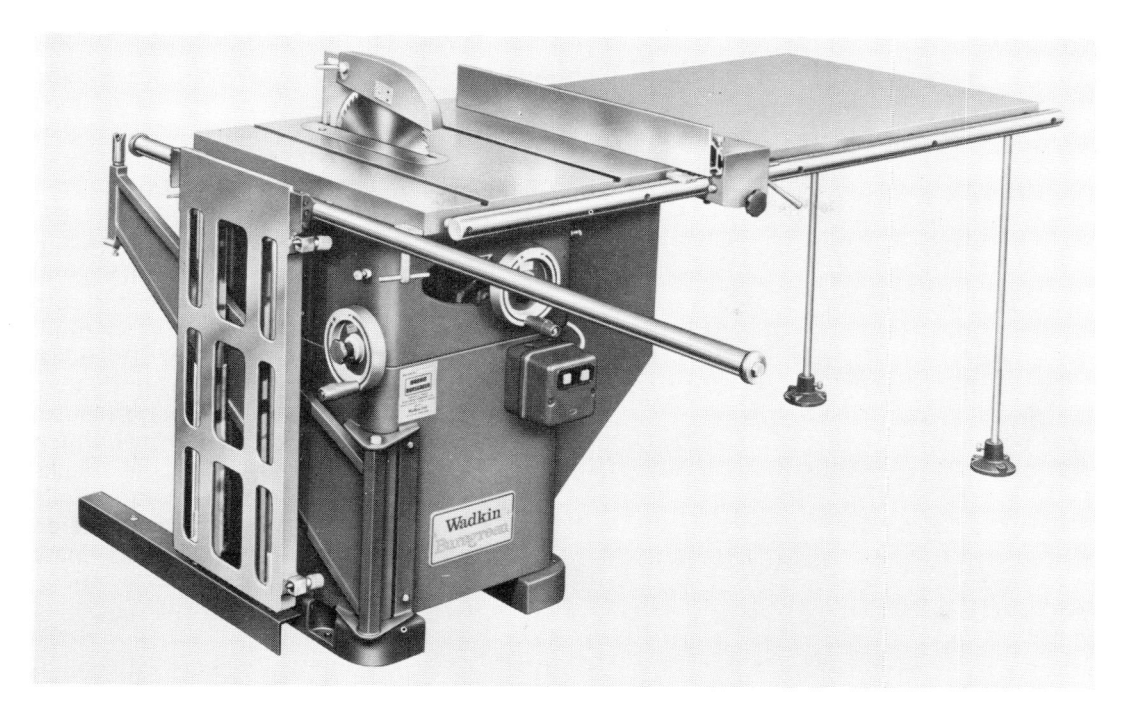

Provision is made on all good saw benches for this adjustment of the rip fence and though it may vary slightly from one model to another, it is in principle always the same. The adjusting nuts or screws should be slackened slightly, but not completely, then the rip fence can be tapped with the side of the hand until it is lying in exactly the right place, whereupon the adjusting nuts are re-tightened.

Since we now know that the rip fence is in line with the table slot, it only remains to make certain that the rip fence is also in line with the saw blade. In order to achieve this the saw blade is given its full projection through the table and the rip fence is moved over towards it to a point where there is a gap between blade and fence a little greater than the width of any

Professional sawbench fitted with extension table. Note panel cutting attachment in retracted position on the left.

coin which the operator may have in his pocket. When this has been done and the coarse adjusting clamp has been tightened, the coin is placed between blade and fence at the end closest to the operator, and the micrometer adjuster is used to bring the fence across finally so that it just lightly nips the coin between itself and the blade. Make sure when doing this that the coin is not touching an inward-leaning tooth of the saw. When this has been set up, it should be possible to slide the coin along the full length of the blade without any tendency for it to jam, or for a gap to appear. If either of these things occurs the table itself must be moved slightly so that the situation is corrected. There are always nuts on any

15

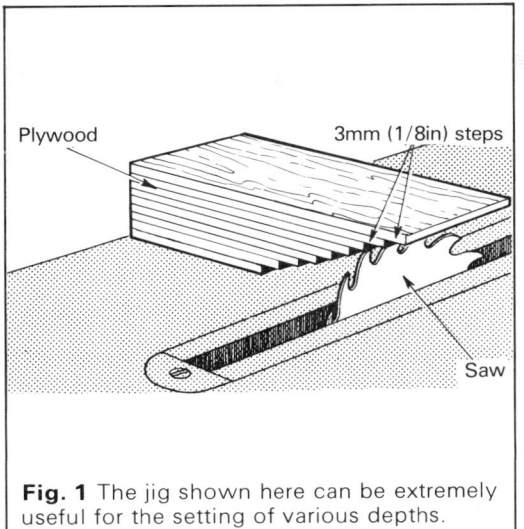

Fig. 1 The jig shown here can be extremely useful for the setting of various depths.

sawbench which will permit this kind of adjustment and the manufacturer's instructions should be referred to. It is not advisable to loosen the nuts completely, since the table will then swing about and make the adjustment rather difficult. They should be slackened slightly, and the further side of the table can be tapped as required until the coin slides evenly. When this has been done, the nuts should be re-tightened and the check should be made once more.

For normal cross-cutting purposes, and in fact for general ripping, the saw blade is usually required to be at 90° to the surface of the table. This should be checked by means of an accurate carpenter's square, making sure that the top edge of the square passes an outward-leaning tooth. If the angle is found to be anything other than 90°, this can be adjusted quite easily by means of the table tilt mechanism, and the pointer should be re-aligned on the scale to read zero. This process is relatively simple and it is important that it is carried out at regular intervals since heavy use, or the occasional knock, can easily put things slightly out of alignment and make the saw inefficient. Maintenance of the circular saw bench, apart from the obvious necessity for re-sharpening the blades, really consists of carrying out adjustments like the one described above, having an occasional run round the entire machine to check the tightness of nuts, and taking some protective measures against rust. Too much oil will cause a build-up of sawdust and is not really desirable.

The bearings on modern sawbenches are sealed for life and do not require greasing, but the bright parts do need some attention. Wiping over with a light film of oil is generally all that is needed and many people use the aerosol lubricants now on the market. These are very good and just a drop or two will do the job. They have the advantage of being able to reach the parts of the machine which are otherwise difficult to attend to.

Having stated that ripping and cross-cutting are the two basic functions of circular saws, I should perhaps point out that many of the more sophisticated operations carried out on them are, in fact, variations on these two themes.

Ripping on a circular saw
The term ripping describes the process in which a piece of timber is cut along its length — or in other words with the direction of the grain. This is a simple operation when performed on a machine which has been correctly set by an operator who knows what he is doing. It is also an operation which holds problems and traps for the unwary and inexperienced operator. The timber which is to be ripped should

be checked through for nails or any other foreign bodies which might damage the saw blade. An examination should also be carried out to ensure that the surface which is to be placed upon the table of the machine is free from any kind of projection which might catch on the table. Accidents have happened through this, when the forward progress of the timber has been halted temporarily, extra pressure has been added to overcome the difficulty and the wood has suddenly moved forward quite rapidly taking the operator's hand with it into the blade. Such things, of course, are the fault of the operator who must be wary. One very good habit which the new owner of a circular saw should develop is the hooking of one or more fingers of the hand which is closest to the saw blade over the rip fence itself. This provides an anchor for the hand and, should anything untoward occur, it may well prevent it from being brought into contact with the teeth of the saw. A ripping cut should be completed by means of a push stick, which is simply a piece of wood with a notch in the end which can be used to push the wood towards the saw so it is not necessary for the operator's hand to pass anywhere near the blade. If the push stick should slip and be nicked by the saw, it is a matter of a few moments to make another, which is not the case with fingers.

Let us assume that we have a board which is 150mm (6in) wide which must be reduced to a width of 100mm (4in). The depth of cut must be set correctly, and this is done first with the machine switched off. The timber is placed against the blade and parallel to it; the projection of the

Ripping a long board on a Coronet Major machine. Note the use of the out-feed roller, lower left.

17

blade from the table is then adjusted so that the saw blade will emerge through the top of the timber to the depth of a gullet. Put another way, this means that the teeth will come through the top of the timber, but none of the blade will do so. There is obviously no virtue in having more blade coming through the timber than is strictly necessary.

Once the depth of cut has been set, the next step will be the positioning of the rip fence to produce precisely the width of timber required. Most saw blades in general use have what is known as set. This simply means that alternate teeth are bent slightly to left and right, so that the kerf, or cut, produced by the saw blade will be slightly wider than the thickness of the blade itself. This allows the blade free passage in the wood, preventing friction which would waste power and cause the blade to become hot. The fact that the blade has this set must be borne in mind when setting up a rip fence.

Some machines have scales across the front of the table which will enable the rip fence to be positioned at a pre-determined distance from the blade and, provided the blade in use is one to which this scale has been set, these are very accurate indeed. It is easy to forget that when a blade is changed and a different type is used the thickness of the kerf may vary. If it does, the accuracy of the scale on the front of the machine is destroyed.

When a blade is changed, the setting of the scale and pointer must be checked and reset as required. Most workers position the rip fence by measuring from the fence to the blade. Such measurements must be taken from the fence to a tooth which is leaning towards the fence. If the measurement is taken to a tooth which is leaning the other way the cut will be inaccurate. I have seen people hook the end of a steel rule around the blade and then measure to the fence. This will also produce an inaccurate result since the width of the timber will then be less the width of the kerf.

Almost all rip fences are provided with coarse and fine adjustments; the coarse adjustment being provided by means of a small clamping lever which when released will permit the rip fence to be moved easily along the bar which carries it. The correct procedure is to move the fence to approximately the position desired, and to make the final fine adjustment by means of the micrometer adjuster. This is a little device which will move very slowly indeed as the knob is turned. Once the operator is satisfied that the rip fence is in exactly the right position, the adjuster can be locked so that the fence cannot move while the machine is in use. When all this has been done the saw can be started, the timber placed on the table firmly against the fence, and the cut can begin. The wood should be moved forward slowly and steadily to the blade, keeping both hands well clear of the teeth, and it can be pushed forward until its end reaches the front edge of the table; from this point onwards a push stick should be used to guide it and to propel it forward. The hand which is not engaged with the push stick will be occupied in holding the timber to the fence and, as mentioned before, one or more fingers should be hooked round the fence itself to prevent accidents. The guard provided for the saw blade must be used.

A point which has not been mentioned so far is that for purposes of ripping timber a riving knife is provided. The riving knife prevents the timber from closing up behind the saw blade. Some timber will not do this, it may even want to open out behind the saw blade, but in many cases there will be a tendency for the wood to close up. If the machine was being used without its guard in position, which of course it should not be, and the riving knife was not in use, the timber might well close up and pinch on the back of the blade and it could be thrown up and forward at the operator. This is unlikely on small saws but it might very well happen on large ones.

In addition to the safety factor, the use of the riving knife is essential for those who are using their sawbenches for sophisticated precision work. When very fine-toothed saw blades are used, or blades with tungsten carbide teeth, extremely good surface finishes can be produced provided that the settings of the machine are as accurate as they should be. If, however, the timber is allowed to close up and so contact the teeth of the saw at the back, the surface, which was cut smoothly as it passed the front of the blade, will be roughed up and ruined by the teeth at the rear. The precise positioning of the riving knife, which can normally be adjusted slightly, is important in that it must be directly behind the saw blade, not slightly to one side or the other.

Another most important point is that the riving knife provided with the machine when it is delivered is suitable for the blade provided by the manufacturer at the time. There are, however, a number of types of blades for circular saws and many woodworkers change them frequently for specific jobs. If a blade which is considerably thinner than the one originally provided is used, it may be that the riving knife will jam in the kerf. On the other hand, if a blade which is thicker than the riving knife should be used, the knife itself will be quite valueless. The knife is now thinner than the blade and the wood can still close up and contact the teeth at the rear.

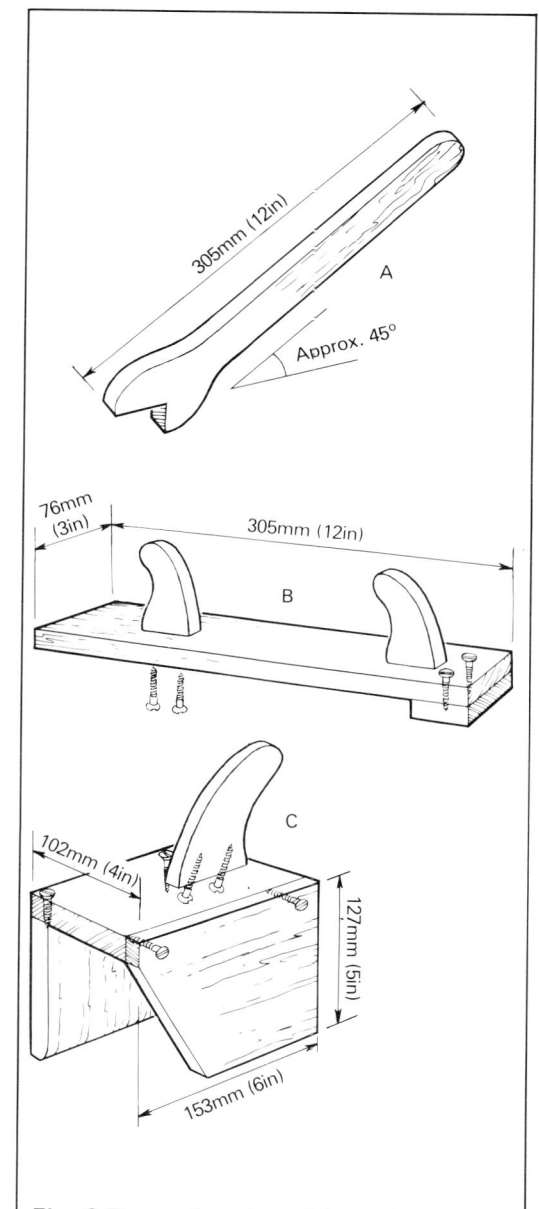

Fig. 3 Types of pusher sticks and pusher block useful in conjunction with sawbenches. The one shown at **C** is used astride the ripping fence.

Problems and faults

There are a number of faults which may arise when a circular saw is being used for ripping. In the early days of using a circular saw many people find that the wood will either jam between the blade and the rip fence, or will tend to drift away from the rip fence as the cut proceeds. The cause of this is misalignment between the rip fence and the blade and it is absolutely essential that the face of the rip fence and the face of the blade are precisely parallel. If the machine is checked and found to be correctly aligned, then the timber itself should be inspected to make sure that the edge which is being run against the rip fence is absolutely straight. If it is not then problems might well arise.

An inexperienced operator can create problems by not feeding the work properly; once he has allowed it to drift away from the fence it is very difficult to get it back again. Practise, of course, will make perfect, in this respect.

Sometimes when a piece of timber has been ripped there may be a smell of burning and the surface of the timber will be seen to be brown and to have suffered from the effects of considerable heat. This is commonly caused by the use of a blade which is far too blunt to be serviceable. Circular saw blades must be kept sharp at all times.

Another factor which has to be taken into consideration, particularly when timber from coniferous trees is being sawn, is the build-up of resin on the teeth. If this happens, the saw becomes very inefficient and burning may easily result. Such deposits of resin can be removed by means of various solvents, or carefully scraped away with a knife.

If the wood which is being sawn is unusually hard or tough it may be advisable to run the saw a little slower; most saws do have provision for more than one speed, and if this is the case then the lower speed should be selected. The rate of feed should also be considered. This should be steady and should not cause any apparent reduction in motor speed. Reduction in motor speed is generally noticeable by a drop in the pitch of the sound produced. If the cause is, in fact, a blunt blade this may well be indicated by a tendency for the timber to climb up the blade as it is pushed forward.

It is not unusual for a worker to set the rip fence with great care and to find when the cut has been completed that the timber is a little narrower than it should be; this, of course, relates to the point I made earlier about the manner in which the measurement between the blade and the fence is carried out. If the width of the blade has been included in the measuring, by hooking the end of the steel rule round the blade, then the work will show this.

When a piece of timber has been ripped in the normal ripping position which is intended to produce a 90° cut, this cut should be checked by means of a carpenter's square. If it is found that the angle produced is other than 90°, even though the blade itself is completely square to the table, the timber should be checked. It may be found that there is some degree of warp in the wood and this will make the cut inaccurate. The solution is to put any timber which is likely to warp, or be warped already, through a thicknesser before it is ripped. (See page 109.)

When long pieces of timber have to be ripped by an operator working alone, there is a problem in that he is unable to support the timber on the far side of the machine.

Support devices can easily be made in the workshop for this purpose and these are mentioned on page 00. However, if in a situation like this the timber is pushed through the saw until a certain amount of it projects behind the saw, the operator can walk to the rear of the machine and complete the cut by pulling on the timber. Great care must be taken to see that the wood remains firmly against the fence until the cut is completed. The process may feel a little strange at first, but is a perfectly safe and efficient method of completing the cut, under these circumstances.

There may be occasions when it is desirable to rip very thin strips from the edge of boards. If these strips are 2mm ($\frac{1}{16}$in) or so in thickness the saw blade may catch them and drag them down through the slot in the table, smashing them as it does so. If this should occur there is a simple and extremely efficient remedy. The insert in the table surface, which surrounds the blade, should be removed and replaced by a piece of plywood or hardboard. To do this the blade is lowered below the surface of the table, the hardboard is cut to fit the open area, secured in place by means of the normal retaining screws, and then the machine is started and the blade brought back up so that it cuts its way through the plywood or hardboard. This will mean that the work when ripped will be supported right up to the blade itself and there will be no chance of it being damaged.

Odd jobs crop up in relation to circular saws from time to time, and it may be that an operator wishes to rip round stock along its length. This is not an operation to be carried out without some form of assistance in the shape of a jig, since it can be quite dangerous. What is required is a piece of wood in which a suitable V-shaped groove has been cut lengthwise. This piece of wood is placed against the fence and pushed forward into the rotating saw blade so that the saw cuts exactly along the bottom of the V groove. When the jig reaches the back of the table it can be clamped to the rip fence or to the table top. Round stock can now be placed in the V groove and pushed forward with a push stick. This will be found to be a safe and effective way of getting round the problem.

Cross-cutting

Cross-cutting means cutting a board or piece of timber across the grain. If it is simply a matter of cutting a piece off the end of a board without any requirement for accuracy, many workers will hold the wood with one hand each side of the blade and simply push it forward, not making use of a mitre guide. This will work perfectly well, but care must be taken to see that as the wood is pushed forward and the cuts take place, the hands are not pushing the wood in such a manner as to cause it to pinch the blade. A little practice on cuts of this nature will soon show what is meant here, in fact the hands, whilst pushing the wood forward, are endeavouring to open the kerf and give clearance. Most cross-cutting is, however, carried out with the assistance of the mitre guide and if this is used the job will become considerably easier.

Mitre guides are, in general, rather poorly made and the marks upon them, which are designed to allow the operator to set up specific angles, are of little or no value. The marks themselves are far too thick; the line with which they are designed to register is also too thick; so that any really precise or accurate work is out of the question. The reason for this is unknown to me, but there are one or two makes of circular saw which provide extremely good mitre guides, one of these being Startrite. The mitre guides provided for its machines are really magnificent pieces of work and it might well be worth purchasing one and altering the strip which slides in the table groove to make it fit another machine.

The first step in the cross-cut operation is to place the material which is to be cut firmly against the mitre guide, moving it into the required position so that the saw will cut in the right place, then moving both timber and guide forward together so that the cut is completed. Many saw tables have two mitre guide slots, either of which can be used according to the cut which is being made and the preference of the operator. At this point it should perhaps be observed that most mitre guides are not really satisfactory if used as supplied, unless the timber is of very small dimensions. It will be found much more satisfactory to fit a wooden sub-fence to the mitre guide. This can be cut from rectangular hardwood of suitable dimensions for the machine and screwed firmly in position. It is necessary to make sure that the height of this wooden sub-fence is such that it will not be completely severed by the saw blade. It is also extremely important that the timber used for the fence has been accurately planed. If it has not, then the opposing faces of the timber may be out of parallel, causing inaccuracy. Whilst the necessity to use a piece of wood which is wide enough to permit the saw to pass through it without severing it completely will be fairly obvious, the height of the fence can, if desired, be reduced on the section which runs along the mitre guide itself so that the thing is not too difficult to control with the hands. The work should be held firmly against the mitre guide as the cut is performed, and most operators use both hands. It is not, however, advisable to hold the section of timber which is to be cut off. Both hands should be employed to hold the wood against the mitre fence. Pieces of wood which have been cut off in this manner should not be removed from the saw table by means of the fingers whilst the blade is rotating. They can be pushed into a safer area by a piece of wood, or the machine can be switched off and allowed to stop before they are touched.

A normal cross-cut operation involves taking the mitre guide forward together with the timber, until the saw has severed the material, then bringing back the mitre guide and timber to their original starting point. Inaccurate work can result if the timber is inadvertently allowed to move even slightly toward the saw blade before it is drawn back, and most people make a habit of moving it a short distance away from the blade before this is done.

It must be noted that cross-cutting on very short pieces of wood is always rather dangerous, except when done by experienced workers. Those who are not accustomed to the use of a circular saw will be well advised to keep away from the cross-cutting of very short pieces of timber until they become familiar with the machine and the processes involved.

One very important point must be raised whenever the question of cross-cutting on a circular saw bench is discussed and this is the unfortunate habit which some workers have of using the rip fence as a stop when cross-cutting. To explain this, let us consider a situation in which it is desired to cut off a number of fairly short pieces of wood, all the same length. At first glance it would appear to be quite logical and reasonable to position the rip fence the required distance away from the blade on the opposite side to the mitre guide, place the wood against the mitre

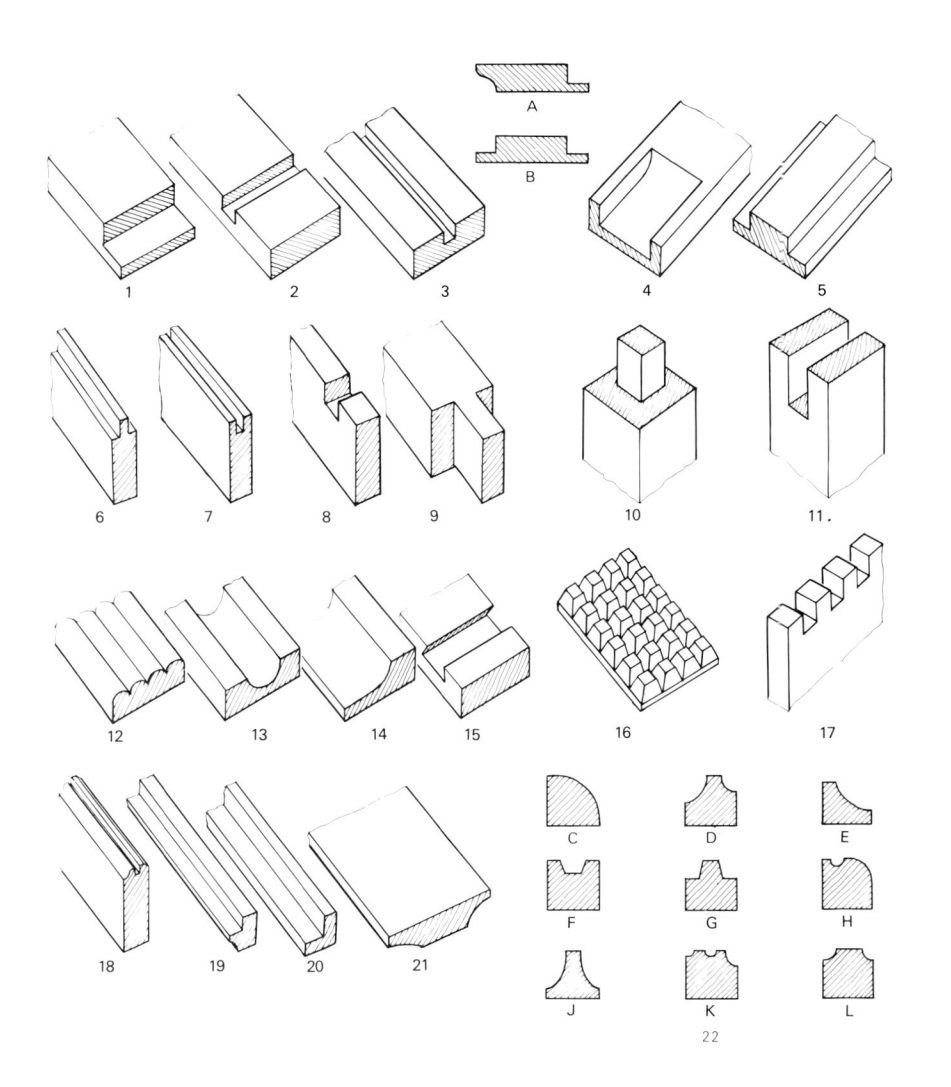

Fig. 2 Some of these cuts may require slight attention with hand tools to remove radius left by curve of blade. **A–K** shows sections of the various mouldings. **1** Rebate **2** Dado **3** Groove **4** Hollowing **5** Edge rebate **6 & 7** Tongue and groove **8** Notching **9** Square tenon **10** Slot **11** True tenon **12** Through slot **13** Surface cuts **14** Coving **15** Edge coving **16** Butter pat cutting **17** Dovetail **18** Box combing **19** Edge mould **20** Coved edge **21 & 22** Ripped mouldings

fence, slide it across until it touches the rip fence and then push it forward until the cut is completed. If this were done, time after time, the pieces which were severed would be precisely the same length.

While what I have said so far is quite true, there is an underlying danger in this procedure which all workers should be aware of. There is no problem whatsoever until the moment when the short piece of wood is severed from the main stock. When this happens it is possible for it to twist slightly and become jammed between the rip fence and the saw blade. This can give rise to a very ferocious kick-back of the timber, the severed section being hurled with quite remarkable force to the rear. If the operator is in line with this at the time a very serious injury can result.

The problem can be overcome quite simply by attaching a small piece of scrap wood to the end of the rip fence which is closest to the front of the table. If the face of this piece of wood is now used to position the timber for each cut, it will be seen that there is a gap between the end of the severed section of timber and the rip fence, permitting the offcut to twist or to move sideways without any danger whatsoever. Most workers, of course, are aware of this, but in a book of this nature one is very conscious of safety as it relates to beginners.

In considering the cross-cutting of a piece of timber which is not much wider than the saw table itself, there is no need to worry about any form of kick-back unless it is as a result of the method described above. On occasions, however, it will be necessary to cross-cut quite long pieces of timber which overhang the saw table by some distance and may be of fairly heavy section. In a case like this, when the cut nears its completion there will be a tendency for the ends of the timber to drop, causing the wood to pinch the saw blade and produce a kick-back. This type of kick-back is not anything like as serious as the one described earlier. It is unlikely to cause an accident but it may give the operator a nasty moment if he is not prepared for it. This can be avoided by providing some sort of support for the ends of the timber so that the sagging does not occur.

Some people appear to be bothered over the apparent difficulty in relation to the cross-cutting of a wide board. Some pieces may be of such a width as to prohibit the use of the mitre fence since the forward edge of the timber is overhanging the table before the cut is commenced. This can be dealt with by reversing the mitre guide in the table slot so that its face is towards the operator, placing the timber against it and making the cut to the point where the mitre guide reaches the far end of the table. The machine is then stopped and the mitre guide brought round into its normal position in front of the timber. The machine is then restarted and the cut completed.

On timber which is too wide even for this method it will be necessary to scribe an accurate line with a dark pencil and to follow it by eye without using the mitre guide. There is no danger in this procedure, even though the mitre guide is not used, provided that the timber is not twisted during the cut and that pressure is not applied to both sides of the timber at the end of the cut, so pinching the wood on to the back of the blade.

It will be noted that when a wooden sub-fence has been correctly made for the mitre guide, the saw projected through the table to its fullest extent and the guide, together with sub-fence, pushed forward once over the saw blade and returned to the starting position, there will be a saw kerf in the mitre guide sub-fence. The edge of this saw kerf nearest to the mitre guide is an accurate mark from which measurements can be made. In other words, if the front of the timber which runs along the mitre guide is marked off in centimetres or inches, measuring accurately from the saw kerf, the marks can be used for cross-cutting small pieces to length.

The timber is positioned so that one end lines up with, say, the 15cm (6in) mark, the cut is made in the normal manner and the piece which remains in contact with the mitre guide after the completion of the cut will be 15cm (6in) in length. This can be taken a stage further by using a small block of scrap wood clamped to the fence at the required point so that the wood is pushed up firmly against this. The cut can then be made without the necessity for peering over the guide to line the wood up with a mark.

A further refinement is to run a slot right through this part of the mitre guide sub-fence so that a block can be attached by means of a small recessed bolt with a wing nut. It is then a simple matter to slide it to any particular mark, tighten up the wing nut and use the equipment as described.

When stop blocks of this kind are used on woodworking machines it is advisable to ensure that they do not rest on the saw table, there should be a 5mm–10mm ($\frac{1}{4}$in–$\frac{3}{8}$in) gap so that any scraps of sawdust or chips of timber can escape from under the block rather than becoming trapped in a corner where their presence would adversely affect the accuracy of the cut.

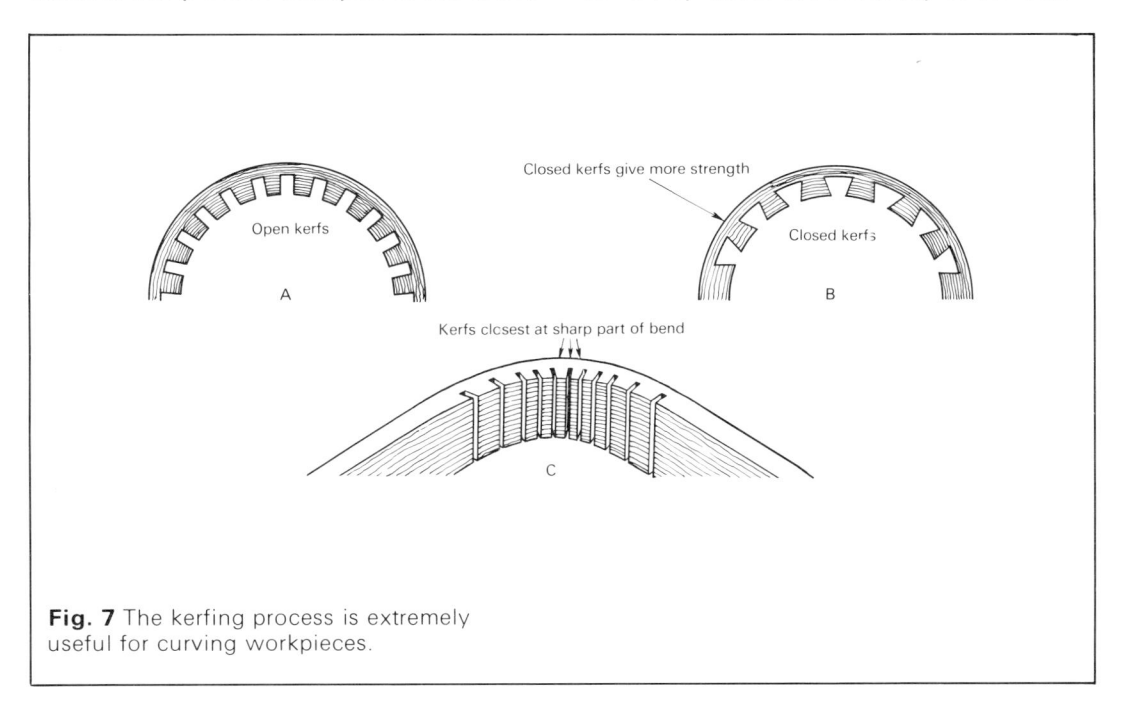

Fig. 7 The kerfing process is extremely useful for curving workpieces.

Some mitre guides, like those supplied for Kity machines, are equipped with devices which assist the operator in cutting to length. These, if used as intended, are accurate and are a great help.

Another method often used is the clamping of a short block of wood by means of a G cramp to the table, rather than to the rip fence as described earlier. The timber is placed against the mitre guide, slid across the table until it touches the clamped block, then taken forward to complete the cut. Hundreds of pieces of wood of precisely the same length can be cut in this manner without any difficulty whatsoever. In this case, as before, there should be a rebate of some kind along the edge of the stop block which will allow sawdust and chips to escape. When this type of cross-cutting length stop is used it should not hold the free end of the wood. It will be seen that if it does, the same danger exists as was described in the reference to using the rip fence as a length stop.

A frequent operation which comes under the heading of cross-cutting is the trimming of a piece of wood to length after it has been marked off with a pencil. This is quite simple since it is only necessary to line up the pencil mark with the edge of the saw kerf in the mitre guide sub-fence, then make the cut in the normal way. It is often possible when working with thin pieces of wood to cut several at once, placing them one above the other.

Cross-cutting at angles other than 90°
The most common example is the cutting of a mitre, as would be required in the making of a picture frame. Most woodworkers know how difficult the production of really accurate mitres can be unless the right equipment is available. It might at first glance appear to be quite a simple matter to set a mitre guide to 45°, place the wood against it and make the cut. The likelihood of complete accuracy is remote unless the matter is studied in greater depth.

The scale provided on most of the mitre guides is unsuitable for the production of really accurate angles. The line which is used to set against the scale has thickness, the marks on the scale itself have thickness, and it is quite possible for some form of parallax error to creep in according to the position of the operator when reading the scale.

Work of this kind requires the production of wooden or metal templates, which can be checked for accuracy and kept in the workshop for use at any time. The template is simply a flat piece of material which has the requisite angle between two of its sides. It is placed against the mitre guide with the machine switched off; the clamping nut of the mitre guide is loosened and the guide is swung until the template is firmly in contact with the face of the mitre guide and with the saw blade. At this point the mitre guide clamping screw should be tightened, and preferably given a little extra twist with a pair of grips to make sure that it will not become loose during the cutting. This procedure should produce accurate angles.

Certain precautions should be taken, however, against a phenomenon known as creep. When timber is cut at an angle it has an undesirable tendency to move along the mitre fence slightly as it is cut. A really firm grip with the fingers may prevent this and it can certainly be prevented by clamping the wood to the mitre fence with a suitable clamp. Many workers overcome the difficulty by facing the wooden sub-fence of the mitre guide with a fairly coarse glasspaper which prevents any movement of the timber.

Compound mitre cuts, which are required for the production of picture frames with angled sides and sometimes referred to as shadow frames, are made with the mitre guide set at 45° and the saw, or the blade, tilted to the same angle. Work of this kind requires considerable care and, in fact, all mitring operations and the cutting of precise angles can be carried out much more safely and with greater accuracy on radial arm machines.

The choice of saw blade for use in cutting mitres is important. A well-made mitre should fit without leaving any obvious glue line. This will not be the case if a coarse blade has been used to produce it, unless the faces of the mitre are subsequently sanded. It may well be that although a mitre was cut with complete accuracy in the first place this accuracy is lost in the sanding process. It is preferable, therefore, to use a sharp, fine-toothed blade to cut the mitres so that a very smooth end grain surface is produced. A tungsten carbide tipped saw blade, which is intended for cross-cut purposes and has somewhere in the region of sixty teeth, will produce a very good sawn surface for mitres. Another type of blade which can be successfully used is the hollow ground variety, and in fact the thin rimmed plywood one is my usual choice.

Cutting rebates

Most rebate work on a production basis is now done by means of a spindle moulder, a machine which is considered on page 27. It is also possible to produce good rebates by means of a small jointer or surface planer, though this operation cannot be carried out on combined planer/thicknessers. Large rebates are still

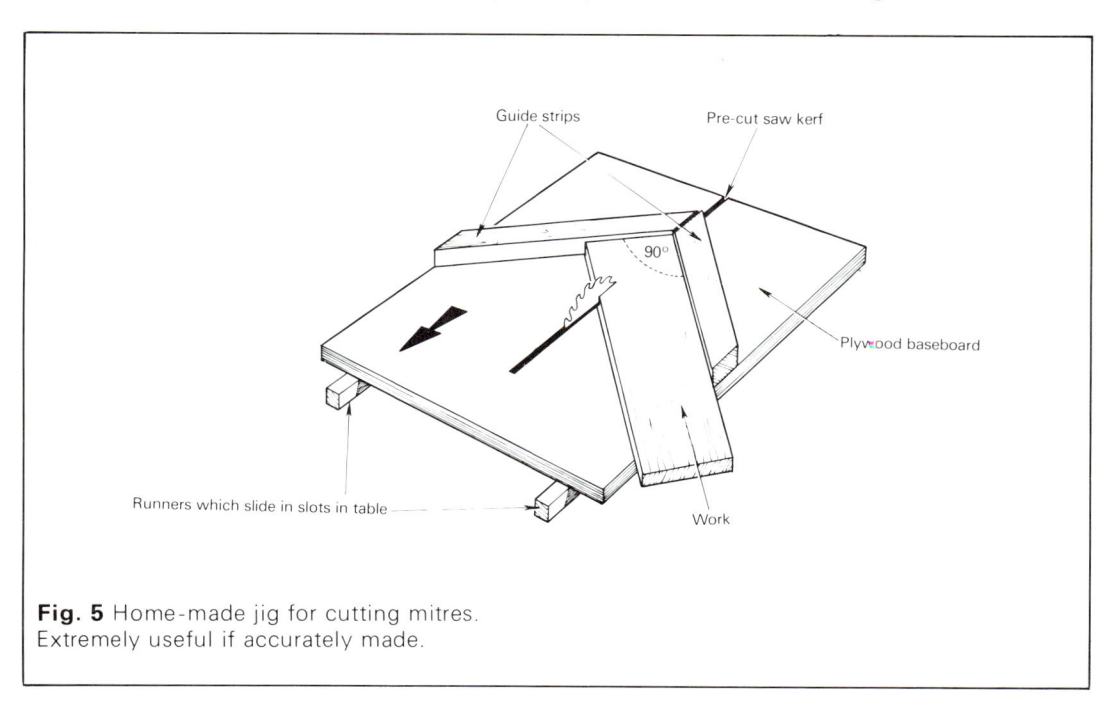

Fig. 5 Home-made jig for cutting mitres. Extremely useful if accurately made.

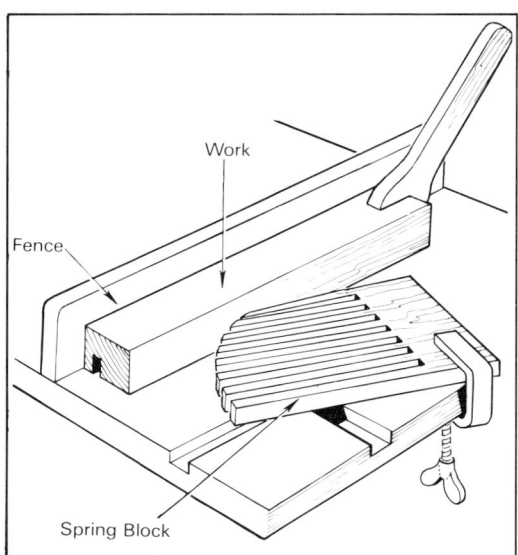

Fig. 6 Wooden spring block made from scrap timber and used to hold the material against rip fence.

best performed on a circular saw and most other rebating operations can be carried out successfully on such a machine in the absence of other equipment.

In the production of normal rebates a square or rectangular strip is removed from the edge of a board. In order to do this two ripping cuts are required, these being positioned to remove precisely the amount of wood which is called for, and the setting of the machine provides for the second cut to meet the bottom of the first one exactly. It will be noted that in cutting a rebate along the edge of a board one of the ripping cuts must be made with the board on edge and this is the more difficult of the two cuts. The rebate is marked out on one end of the board and it is normal, though not essential, to make the cut in which the board is on edge first. It is not necessary for the saw blade to be set quite to the full depth for this cut, since in making the second cut the corner of the rebate will be cleaned by the teeth of the saw.

Reference is made in this book to the use of home-made wooden springs for holding timber which is being processed and this is an operation where the use of such a spring may be useful. By using something of this nature to keep the wood firmly against the fence of the machine it is possible to feed the material over the blade by means of a push stick, keeping the hands well clear. It should be noted that when the second cut is completed there is every likelihood of the timber which has been removed being flung back quite violently. It is unlikely that this would cause any serious injury, but it could startle the operator who might perhaps have an accident as a result. It is quite easy to stand slightly out of line with this piece of wood, so that it can simply be thrown back behind the machine without any trouble.

Producing thin boards from thick ones

This operation is sometimes referred to as re-sawing, and is not recommended for those who have little experience with saws. It is probably one of the most potentially dangerous of the standard cuts, and so must be treated with respect. Having said that, I should point out that it is also a very important cut indeed since there are many occasions where boards need to be reduced in thickness by cutting through the centre. It should be noted that, although this is a ripping operation, neither the riving knife nor the saw guard can normally be used. It is not possible to use the riving knife because the cut will not pass right through the material, and on many machines it is not possible to use the guard either since this is often mounted above the riving knife.

The projection of the saw through the table should be set to a little more than half the width of the timber and the first cut is a straightforward ripping operation. From a safety point of view it is as well to use some sort of spring clamped to the table which will hold the work against the fence.

If the machine is of the variety where the depth of cut is set by raising or lowering the table, care should be taken to see that the clamp which fixes the table in its desired position is firmly tightened. When the first cut has been completed the timber is reversed, keeping the same side against the fence, and the second cut is made. Provided reasonable care is taken in operations of this nature there need be no real danger. Those who are inexperienced, or perhaps of a nervous disposition, may like to leave about 10mm–20mm ($\frac{1}{2}$in–$\frac{3}{4}$in) of timber uncut at the centre, finishing the job off with a hand saw, or on a bandsaw.

Some beginners do not like cutting timber on a circular saw bench without the use of either the mitre guide or the rip fence. In some situations, however, it is necessary to work in this manner. For instance, when there are wany edges on both sides of the plank a straight edge must be established along one side before the timber can be ripped as required against the rip fence. It will be found that a clear, black line ruled on the timber can be followed quite easily and provided no sudden swings are made, causing the blade to buckle, there should be no trouble at all. It is perhaps best in situations like this to cut to a little more than half-way through the board, then reverse it and complete the operation.

Tapers

The cutting of tapers on a sawbench is not difficult and there are two forms of jig which can be manufactured in the workshop for the purpose. One of them will give a fixed taper, whereas the other is adjustable. The timber should be prepared carefully so that it is perfectly square and cut exactly to the required length.

The construction of the first form of jig, which provides for a fixed taper, can be followed fairly easily from Fig. 4. The jig consists of a board with a piece of wood attached at one end in which are cut two notches. The board must, of course, have a perfectly straight side which will run against the rip fence. The work is placed in the first notch of the jig, which is then placed against the rip fence, and the work and jig are pushed forward together so that one side of the workpiece is tapered. The workpiece can now be turned through 90° and the process repeated. The remaining two sides are cut with the work positioned in the second notch, in the manner described above.

The adjustable jig is a slightly different proposition but is well worth making up since it can be used for any project. It is made from two boards, and in use these boards will be on edge. It is necessary for the width of them to be greater than the height of the rip fence, or the slide adjuster will foul the top of the fence.

The length of the boards can be such as to suit a particular saw bench, having a thickness of 12mm ($\frac{1}{2}$in) or so. They are connected at one end by means of a hinge and a line is marked across the top surface of each board at a distance of 305mm (12in) from the hinge centre. The idea is to be able to open and close the jig as required and to be able to lock it in the given position. This is best accomplished by means of a thin piece of wood

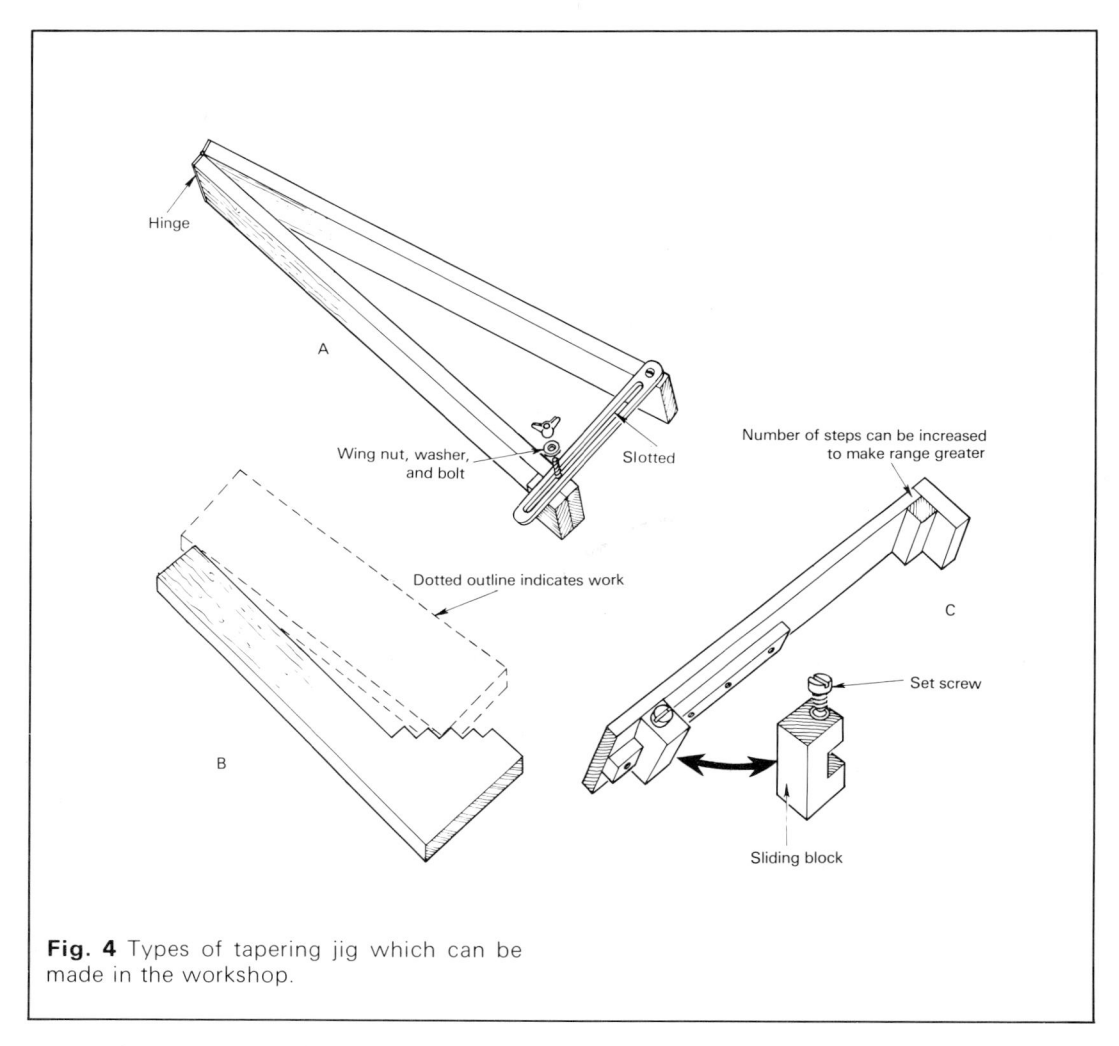

Fig. 4 Types of tapering jig which can be made in the workshop.

or metal which has a slot along it through which a small screw or bolt and wing nut can be passed.

In most operations the required taper is worked out on a basis of a given distance per metre in centimetres or per foot in inches, and it will be seen that if, for example, the required taper per foot is half an inch, the jig will be opened so that there is the distance of exactly half an inch between the two marks, and then locked.

A stop block can be fitted on the outside of the board which runs closest to the saw blade at its rear end, nearest the operator, to support the wood while the cut is being made. When the wood has been placed in position against the face of the jig, supported by the stop block, the jig itself is used in the same manner as the one described earlier. Both these home-made jigs work extremely well.

Jigs and Fixtures
Many home woodworkers manufacture odd items which are extremely useful from a safety point of view, or for producing guaranteed accuracy. Returning for a moment to the question of cutting mitres, one of the most important jigs for sawbench work is the mitre cutter. This is a relatively simple thing to make and it will prove most useful. The basis of it is a rectangular piece of plywood, blockboard or similar material, to one side of which, parallel to the short sides, are fixed strips of metal or hardwood. These are positioned to run freely in the mitre guide slots of the table.

Jigs of this nature are very much more efficient when used on saw tables which have two mitre guide slots, though they can be used in tables which have only a single slot provided that the fit of the runner in the guide slot is exact and care is taken in using the jig. It is vital that the two strips which are attached to the underside of the jig are precisely parallel and exactly located, or the jig will be extremely difficult to move.

One of the easiest ways to achieve this is to make the runners very slightly thicker than required, position them in the mitre guide slots, coat them with adhesive, then lay the jig on top of them with a weight upon it and allow the whole thing to set. A carpenter's square should be used to check that the leading edge of the jig is, in fact, at 90° to the mitre guide slot. When the adhesive has dried sufficiently, so that there is no question of the runners moving, the jig can be taken to the work bench and a few small brads can be tapped home to make sure of the security of the construction.

At this stage we have a jig which we know to have its front edge at right angles to the blade and its runners precisely positioned to slide in the table slots. The next operation will be to start the machine, place the jig on the table and push it forward until the saw blade has cut about two-thirds of the way through the jig.

The machine is switched off and the operation which follows must be carried out with extreme care and precision. Now mark two fine lines at precisely 45° to the saw kerf which has been made in the jig, or at 45° to the leading edge of the jig, whichever way you care to look at it. It is important that these lines are marked precisely otherwise the whole purpose of the jig will be defeated.

When making up anything of this nature I prefer to use an impact adhesive to fix the little guide strips in position so that if there is the slightest inaccuracy in the lines I can try the jig out, using it gently, and check the resulting cut for accuracy. If it is not quite right the rubbery nature of the adhesive used will allow the guide strip to be moved very slightly and finally fixed with brads.

Fig. 5 will make this jig quite clear and it can be used by placing the timber to be cut inside or outside the small guide strips, which are normally made from square section material about 20mm ($\frac{3}{4}$in) thick. Hardwood is the best material for the purpose. If the wood is square at the ends it can be placed behind one of the guide runners so that its end is flush against the other. If there is any doubt about the angle across the end of the wood being true it can be placed against the outside of one of the guide runners, but it must in any case be held firmly on the jig while the cut is made. The rate of feed should be slow.

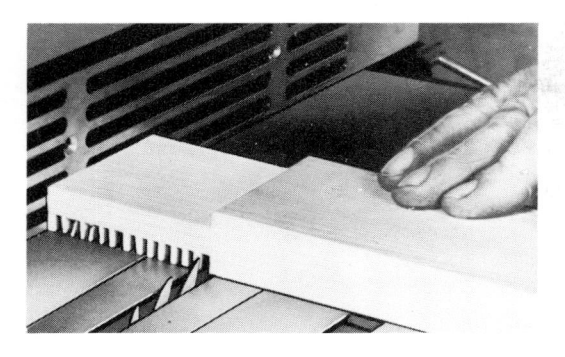

First stage in the cutting of a tenon on a saw table. The small fingers of wood which are left can be broken away quite easily when the cut is complete.

Second stage of the tenon cut procedure. The surface of the tenon is cleaned by sliding the material backwards and forwards across the rotating blade.

In cuts of this nature it is important for the teeth of the saw blade to be really sharp, the feed rate to be steady and every precaution taken to prevent the wood from moving along the guide strip, producing creep as was described earlier. If one of these jigs is made really accurately it will produce perfect mitres every time after a little practice.

I am frequently asked to explain the most satisfactory method of cutting tenons on a circular saw. A tenon can be described as a rebate across both sides of the end of a board; a rectangular section is cut away from each side of the end of the board, leaving the tenon projecting. It follows, therefore, that this sort of thing could be done in the same way as a rebate along the edge of the board by making one cut with the material horizontal on the table, then resetting the machine to make another cut with the wood vertical. This would remove the required amount of timber, but although the vertical cuts and those where the timber is horizontal can be performed in sequence there are, of necessity, two saw settings to be made for any tenon which is cut in this manner.

Anyone with access to a planer/thicknesser will find this provides a far better system, but if not it may well pay to buy the timber for a given project where there are a number of tenons which have to be cut, and to have it thicknessed by the supplier. If there is a variation in the thickness of the various strips of timber, then this method of cutting rebates on the circular saw will result in variations in the thickness of the tenons themselves, and since the size of mortise which is cut with a modern mortiser will not vary at all, there will be some difficulty in assembling the final project.

The method of cutting tenons, if a thicknesser has been used on the material, is really extremely simple. It can be done with an ordinary circular saw blade, as I am about to describe, or it can be done with a dado head or a wobble saw, both of which are attachments for the circular saw. Let us assume that we have a piece of 25mm × 50mm (1in × 2in) timber which is to have a 50mm × 20mm (2in × $\frac{3}{4}$in) area removed from both sides of its ends to leave a tenon to fit the mortise. A piece of scrap timber from the same stock which is to be used on the project will be useful for setting the machine.

The first operation is to set the projection of the saw through the table so that it equals the thickness of the timber to be removed in cutting the mortise, in this case 6mm ($\frac{1}{4}$in). The tenon length is 50mm (2in), so that a small block of wood firmly clamped to the end of the rip fence which is nearest to the operator, in the manner described earlier for cutting off short lengths of timber, can be used to position the workpiece.

The timber is placed against the mitre guide and its end slid along to touch the small wooden block clamped to the rip fence. The saw cut made in the wood by pushing forward will be 50mm (2in) from the end of the timber. The width of the saw kerf must, of course, be included in this 50mm (2in) measurement.

The cutting of tenons is now a very simple operation. The timber to be tenoned is placed against the mitre guide and slid along until it touches the wooden block, held firmly against the mitre guide and pushed forward. It is then brought back and moved slightly along the mitre fence. This process is repeated until, by means of a number of cuts, the rebate is formed.

It will not matter if some small thin sections of timber have been missed in the process, they can be broken away with the thumb and the rough surface so produced will be a help rather than a hindrance when the tenon is glued up. When this stage has been reached the timber is turned over and the process is repeated on the other side, so completing the tenon.

Reference to page 46, the section which deals with wobble saws and dado heads,

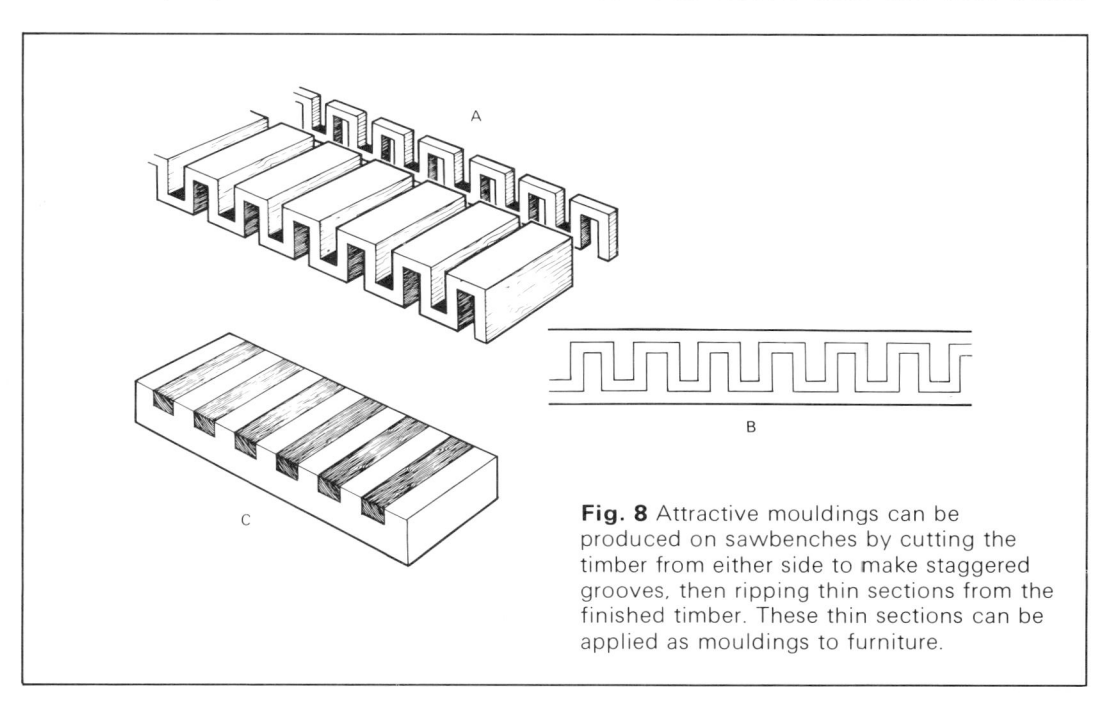

Fig. 8 Attractive mouldings can be produced on sawbenches by cutting the timber from either side to make staggered grooves, then ripping thin sections from the finished timber. These thin sections can be applied as mouldings to furniture.

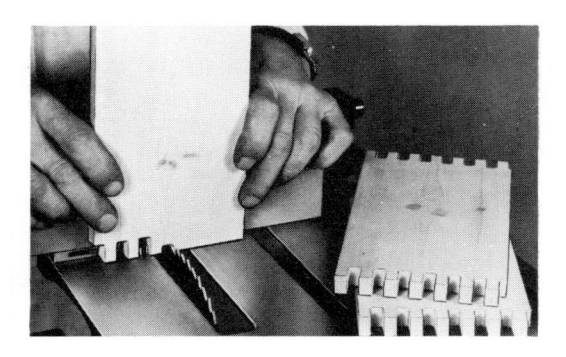

Box combing on a Coronet saw table using a wobble saw. Very attractive joints can be produced by this method.

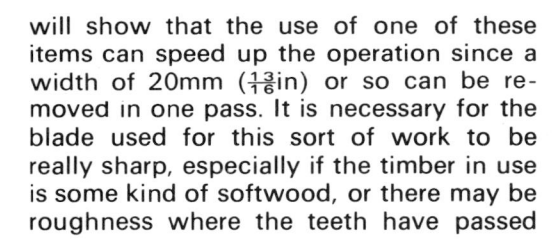

The DeWalt 'snipper' saw designed for accurate cross-cutting of angles. Ripping cannot be carried out on this type of machine.

will show that the use of one of these items can speed up the operation since a width of 20mm ($1\frac{3}{16}$in) or so can be removed in one pass. It is necessary for the blade used for this sort of work to be really sharp, especially if the timber in use is some kind of softwood, or there may be roughness where the teeth have passed across the grain.

There is one big advantage when long pieces of timber have to be tenoned. In this particular method the timber is horizontal all the time and if it is particularly long, the far end of it can quite easily be supported on some home-made device.

Chapter two

Radial Arm Saws

In my own view the radial arm saw is both safer and more accurate than the sawbench, particularly for home workshop use. It is also a very great deal more versatile. A complete book could be written on radial arm saws, routers and the various uses to which they can be put. This chapter will have to serve as an introduction and the interested reader will immediately perceive the possibilities. I have selected the DeWalt and the Susemihl radial arm saws to explain the necessary points. They are in many ways similar, though in other ways entirely different, but both of them have the virtues of safety, versatility and accuracy.

There are few woodworking machines more difficult to describe to anyone who has not seen them, than radial arm saws. This is a very complex machine which has gained considerable popularity in recent years, yet is still unknown in detail to large numbers of woodworkers. The trend, however, is obvious and sales show quite clearly the rapidly rising popularity of the radial saw. Numerous types of radial arm saw are available for the home woodworker but the DeWalt is undoubtedly the most popular. The model which is currently available at the lower end of the price scale will do all that is likely to be required of it by the average home worker or small commercial user. There are quite a large number of models in the range, some of them being extremely expensive and designed for heavy commercial applications. The type featured in this chapter is the DeWalt 110 but it should be borne in mind that the remarks made about it will refer in broad principle to any other radial arm saw.

The Susemihl is a smaller machine, equally

The DeWalt 110 radial arm saw has a reputation for reliability and accuracy.

accurate, extremely safe, and one which I like very much. One should perhaps point out, however, that it is unreasonable to describe the Susemihl as a radial arm saw. The reason for this is that with the Susemihl the table itself pivots, rather than the arm, so that it is best described as a radial bed saw. I pointed out this fact to the agents and they did in fact change the description!

The basic principle of a radial arm saw, from which it gets its name, is that saw and motor are carried on a heavy duty horizontal arm which pivots about a column mounted at the rear of the machine. The blade of a radial arm saw is mounted directly on to the end of the motor spindle and the motor is held in a yoke. This yoke is attached to the horizontal overhead arm by means of roller bearings and so can be moved back and forth along the arm. Provision is also made for locking it at any desired point.

The newcomer to radial arm saws frequently has great difficulty in working out just exactly what they will do. When their available movement has been worked out, he can sometimes get the saw into a situation where he will have difficulty in remembering just what he did to get it there in the first place. Do not be put off by this, since a few weeks work with a radial arm saw will soon convince any user that he has a tool really worth buying. The problem from my point of view is the difficulty of describing clearly the functions and various movements incorporated in the design.

Component parts

Radial arm saws of the DeWalt type are available with metal leg stands, which although useful are not absolutely necessary since the machine can, in fact, be mounted on the user's own bench. The saw has a metal sub-frame which forms a base. Mounted on top of this metal sub-frame is the saw table itself, normally composed of a number of pieces of chipboard. The complete table is in four parts, the first section at the front nearest the operator is a fairly large piece of chipboard running back to the saw fence which is a piece of 50mm × 25mm (2in × 1in) chipboard placed on edge across the machine. The fence is sandwiched in between the main table and the remaining two parts by means of clamps which can be operated from the rear of the machine. It will be seen, therefore, that the rip fence can be moved from its normal position towards the rear of the machine. The instructions which accompany new radial arm saws should be followed closely by the user and it is important that the relationship between the table and the blade must be kept correct at all times. The saw table

The Alpha model R460 radial arm saw.

should be completely level so that when the blade is moved across it will touch the table surface at all points. Levelling mechanisms are built into radial arm saws and it is not difficult to keep the table as it should be. Unfortunately, one does sometimes experience problems with warping or twisting of the table-top and if this is severe there is little alternative other than to make up a new table. The column of the radial arm saw is a stout steel tube which fits into a circular casting attached to the rear of the machine. It is very important that this should be kept adjusted so that no play is present between the two components. The radial arm itself which carries the saw and motor is attached to the top of the column and can be raised and lowered by means of an elevating control. On most machines one complete turn of this control will raise or lower the arm by 3mm ($\frac{1}{8}$in). It is possible, therefore, to make extremely accurate adjustments to the depth of cut.

The motor of a radial arm saw is suspended from the radial arm itself by means of bearings running along special tracks. The adjustment of these bearings is important to the satisfactory performance of the machine and they should be kept adjusted so that all of them revolve when the saw is pushed along the arm. The saw is mounted in a metal yoke which is in turn attached to the arm. This system permits the motor to be rotated under the arm or tilted as required.

The saw blade of a radial saw is attached to the shaft of the motor, not driven by means of a belt as is the case with most saws, therefore there is no power loss through belt slip but protection has to be provided for the motor by means of a thermal over-load cut-out switch. This switch will operate if the motor reaches a set temperature and when the temperature

A detail from the De Walt 110 radial arm saw.

has dropped sufficiently a re-set button can be operated so that the machine is once again ready for use

The various movements which are incorporated in this machine are controlled by means of latches and clamps. The first and perhaps most obvious requirement is for the swinging of the radial arm about the column. The latch at the rear of the arm is lifted, the clamping lever is released and the arm can be swung to left or right. At the 45° position in either direction the latch can be dropped into a slot and the clamp tightened giving a perfect 45° angle. On some radial arm saws the elevating control is mounted at the front, close to the operator. This may at first sight appear to be a highly desirable location for this control but there are certain drawbacks. It is then necessary to provide a threaded rod, running under the machine to the back, and some form of gearing. It is not

37

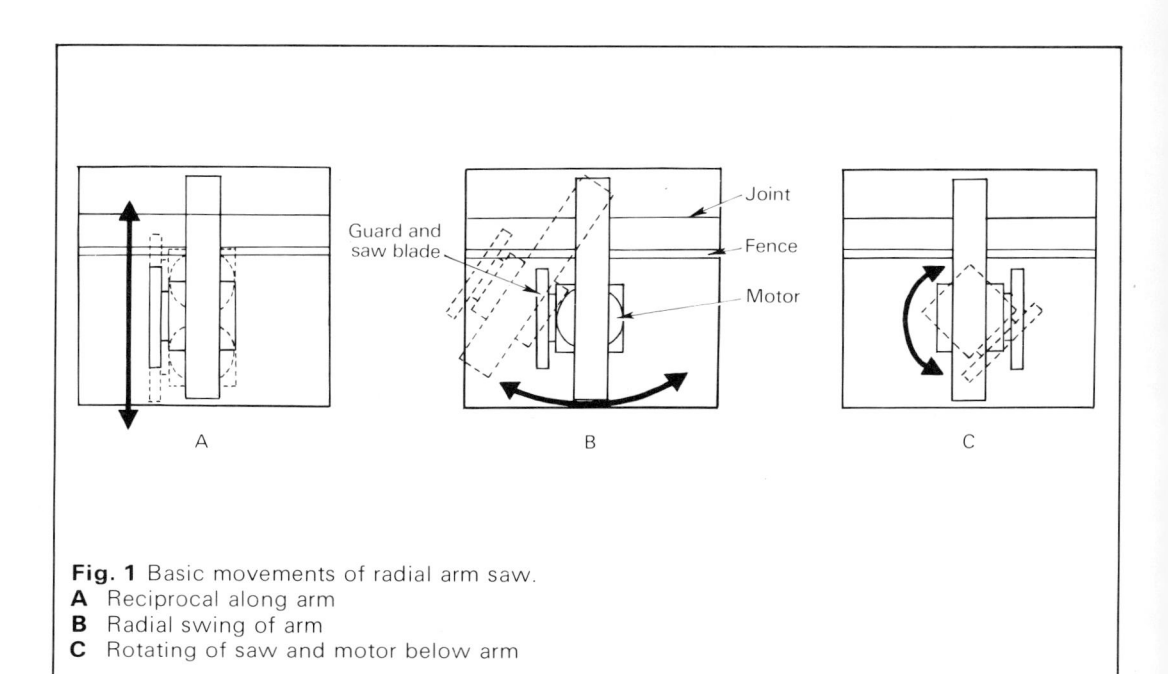

Fig. 1 Basic movements of radial arm saw.
A Reciprocal along arm
B Radial swing of arm
C Rotating of saw and motor below arm

unusual for serious problems to arise because of this construction and most workers are prepared to accept the slightly inconvenient position for the elevating control, on top of the arm itself at the rear.

The movements we have, therefore, are the swing of the radial arm about the column, the rotation of the motor below the arm, the tilting of the motor in its yoke and the rise and fall of the arm itself. The swing of the radial arm and the two movements of the motor relative to the arm can be accurately set by means of the scales and pointers provided on the machine.

Cross-cutting

For satisfactory cross-cut work with a radial arm saw it is necessary for the blade to be at exactly 90° to the surface of the table so that the cut will be vertical, and for the path of the blade, as it is pulled through the wood, to be at precisely 90° to the table fence. This should be checked and established before the machine is used. Before going on to describe cross-cutting in detail, I should perhaps point out one of the main advantages of the radial arm saw, which is that it can be positioned against the wall of the workshop, preferably in the centre, with a clear space at either side. Long timbers can be handled for cross-cutting or ripping in such a situation with no difficulty. In the case of an ordinary type of saw bench it is necessary to position the machine in the middle of the workshop floor in order to cope with material of this nature. The reasons for this will become apparent as we proceed. In a cross-cutting operation the rotation of the blade is such as to cause the teeth to pull the material in towards the fence of the machine, holding it firmly in place. This is quite important since it means that small pieces of timber can be cut safely, simply by placing them in position and pulling the saw through, without the need to hold them by hand. The normal procedure for cross-cutting is to place the material against the fence and to pull the saw steadily through. This works very well on fairly light sections of wood, but is not a satisfactory way of tackling the matter in the case of thick pieces of hardwood. It is better, with material of this kind, to pull the saw to the forward end of the arm, place the material against the fence, then push the saw through the wood. The reason for this is that the saw will perform quite well on light timbers which are not too thick, but may try to 'walk' through the wood on large and heavy materials. This tendency is removed if the blade is pushed rather than pulled. It may appear that this process would cause the rotating teeth to lift the material from the table, but this is not the case and if the material is held firmly the method works extremely well. It is interesting to note that the instruction book provided with the Susemihl radial arm saw does in fact suggest that the saw should be pushed through the timber in all forms of cross-cut work.

In order to achieve complete accuracy in cross-cutting with a radial saw it is necessary to ensure at all times that sawdust and chips are not allowed to collect between the material and the fence. Wood which is to be cut must be in contact with the fence all the way along and if any chips are allowed to get between the two there is likely to be a small error.

In setting for cross-cutting the motor is started and the arm is lowered by means of the elevating crank until the teeth of the saw blade just mark the top of the table.

At this point we come to one of the safety aspects of radial arm saws which must be borne in mind at all times. A cross-cut operation consists of pulling the motor and saw blade through the timber, then pushing it back *to its full extent* so that the blade is *behind* the table fence. The importance of this cannot be over emphasised, since if the blade is left forward of the fence, even by a small amount, there is danger of the next piece of timber being grabbed by the blade as it is being placed in position. The operator of a radial arm should train himself from the very beginning to pull the blade through the timber and then return it to the furthermost position along the arm. As I pointed out earlier, the rip fence can be moved further back across the table and some workers do have a bad habit of leaving it in this position after use. It will be found that when it is positioned in this way it is not possible to have the blade behind the fence, and the danger is obvious. The actual process of cross-cutting is perfectly simple and entails holding the timber firmly against the fence while the blade is pulled through it. It will be seen, of course, that if a number of fairly narrow pieces of wood are to be cross-cut it is quite possible to place them all on the table and draw the blade through them in one pass. This is known as gang cutting and is a very useful method.

The usual purpose of cross-cutting is the production of precisely square ends to pieces of timber, or the cutting of workpieces to an exact length. The kerf which the saw blade will cut in the rip fence can, if correctly used, be extremely useful in setting up material for cross-cutting. It will be seen that if a new fence has been fitted to a saw, the first cross-cut operation will leave a kerf in the fence and clear marks should be made on the table surface, lining up exactly with each side of this kerf. These marks can, if desired, be brought right across the table to the front edge, and will serve to position timber for cross-cutting. If for any reason the fence has to be disturbed and later replaced it will be a simple matter to ensure that it is put back exactly where it came from. One of the big advantages of cross-cut operations with a radial arm saw, as against a saw bench, is that any layout marking will be uppermost on the timber and in clear view of the operator throughout the proceedings. Such marks have to be downwards when a saw bench is used and this does make things rather difficult.

It is often necessary to cut a number of pieces of wood to precisely the same length and the system employed here is the use of a stop block which is attached to the table fence by means of a small cramp. The block should not touch the table surface, but have a gap of about 10mm–12mm ($\frac{3}{8}$in–$\frac{1}{2}$in). This will permit any chips and accumulations of sawdust to pass under the stop block rather than become trapped against it, thus causing inaccuracy in the length cutting. Once the block has been accurately positioned it is a simple matter to slide the workpiece along the fence until it touches the block and then pull the saw through and return it to its original position. If the job is done properly there will be no variation whatever in the length of the cutoffs.

Radial saws are provided with positive lock positions for 45° cross-cut work and the cutting of mitres plays a large part in workshop activities. If the radial arm saw has been correctly set up according to the manufacturer's instructions this will be found to be a very precise and simple operation. Anyone who has tried to cut mitres for picture frames by hand will be only too well aware of the problems involved. Working with a radial arm saw which is correctly set will give a cut which is at 90° to the table surface and precisely at 45° to the fence. Provided the workpiece is secured sufficiently, so that no creep is present, the results should be entirely satisfactory every time. Some discussion of saw blades appears on page 140 but it should be noted that for the cutting of mitres, particularly for picture frames, the use of a very sharp saw blade with fine teeth is recommended.

In connection with the cutting of mitres, some workers who do a lot of this work have a special fence which they place in position purely for use on such occasions. This fence will have a number of very sharp brad points projecting from its face by about 3mm ($\frac{1}{8}$in). The workpiece is pressed firmly against these, and there is no chance of creep.

Ripping
Ripping, of course, is cutting a board along the direction of its grain. With radial arm saws the difference between ripping and cross-cutting is that in the cross-cutting operation it is the saw blade which moves through the material, whereas in the ripping operation the saw blade remains stationary, other than in respect to its rotation, whilst the material is pushed along the fence.

Some people seem to have the idea that radial arm saws are not particularly suitable for ripping, the setting up procedure being considered too complicated. Such opinions are normally voiced by those who have not had a great deal of experience with these tools since in fact the setting up of such a machine for ripping is perfectly simple and straightforward and the ripping procedure itself is entirely satisfactory. Those who are used to it can set a machine up to rip timber in a few moments, but unfortunately the process does sound complicated when described in print and may appear so to a new owner for some little while. The first steps in preparing for ripping operations are the setting of the radial arm in the normal 90° cross-cut position and the rotation of the motor below the arm so that the saw blade runs parallel to the rip fence. Description of the process is complicated by the fact that there are two specific positions of the saw blade for ripping, these being known as in rip and out rip. The in rip position is used where narrow pieces of timber are to be ripped from a board, the motor being swung so that the saw blade is away from the operator and towards the rip fence. In the out rip position the motor is swung the opposite way so that the blade is nearer to the operator than to the rip fence, this position being used for wider timber. When it is desired to rip timber which is too wide to be accommodated in the normal situation of the saw the rip fence can be moved back closer to the column.

Most radial arm saws are provided with rip scales, these often being marked both in centimetres and in inches. The idea is to read off from the rip scale the exact distance of the saw blade from the fence but for practical purposes I always find it best to measure it by means of a steel tape. Provided only one type of saw blade is ever used in the machine, the rip scale will be perfectly accurate and can be used without any problems at all. It is, however, the custom of most radial saw operators to change blades quite frequently for different operations and it should be noted that the thickness of these blades will vary, so rendering the rip scale inaccurate. Those who wish to use the scale will, of course, have to adjust it accurately each time a blade is changed. The use of a steel tape means that the work will be accurate at all times but the measurement must be made from the fence to a tooth which is set towards the fence. If this measurement is done accurately a perfectly

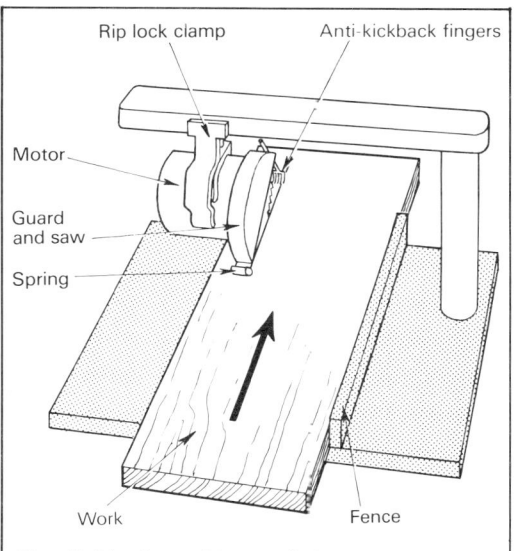

Fig. 3 Ripping with a radial arm saw. Feed direction shown by arrow. Spring and anti-kickback fingers must be correctly set.

satisfactory result will be produced. Once the measuring has been done the rip clamp should be tightened. This will lock the carriage at the precise position required on the arm so that there is no chance of it moving during the cutting.

Taking the DeWalt 110 as an example, attention must be paid to the saw guard and the fittings which are attached to it. These are for the purpose of ripping and must be correctly set.

At one end of the guard there is a small steel spring and at the other a rod which carries a number of curved steel fingers. To set up correctly for ripping the rotating saw should be lowered until its teeth just touch the table-top and switched off. A piece of the material to be ripped is then placed on the table below the small steel spring, the clamping screw for the guard is slackened and the guard is swung so that

Fig. 4 Plan view of radial arm saw showing 'in rip' and 'out rip' positions.

(A) IN-RIP
Guard and saw blade
Motor

(B) OUT-RIP
Motor
Guard and saw blade

action of the saw blade, and the anti-kickback fingers are designed to prevent the timber from being thrown back at the operator. If these two items are set properly the process of ripping on the radial saw will be found to be perfectly safe and entirely accurate. It should be noted that, as with other types of circular saw, the ripping of very short pieces of wood is not recommended and can be rather dangerous.

In all ripping operations on machines of this type a push stick should be used to complete the cut. The ripping operation itself is perfectly simple but it must be remembered that whether the saw is in the in rip or the out rip position, the timber must always be fed from the end of the saw guard which carries the spring. Under *no* circumstances should timber be fed to the saw from the anti-kickback finger end.

When ripping boards care must be taken to see that the timber remains in contact with the fence throughout the operation and it is essential for the material being ripped to have a perfectly straight edge to run against the fence. If this is not the case, as perhaps with a wany-edged board, a pencil line should be drawn down the timber and the first rip cut done by eye, without the use of the fence. This will provide a straight edge for subsequent cuts which can be carried out in the normal manner.

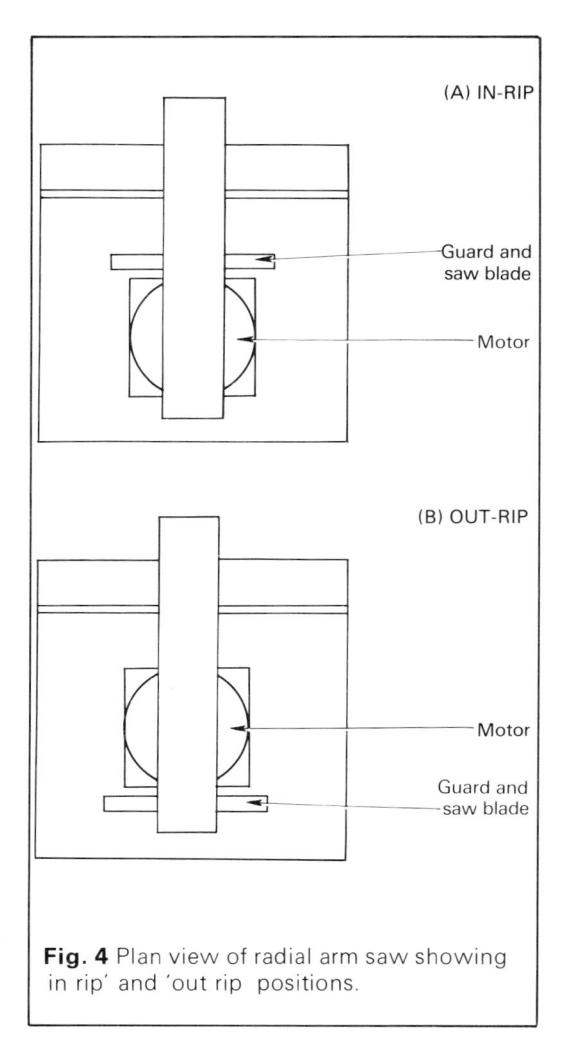

the spring touches the timber. The clamping screw is then re-tightened. The timber can now be taken from the spring and positioned at the other end of the guard so that the anti-kickback fingers can be lowered until they lie on the surface of the timber.

The function of the steel spring is to hold the wood down on the table while it is being cut so that it cannot be lifted by the

Some operators are not entirely happy about ripping to a pencil line by eye on a radial saw and for those who feel nervous about this sort of operation there is a possible alternative. A batten with a straight edge can be clamped to the underside of the boards or secured with small nails. Provided that the front edge of the table is parallel to the rip fence, as it should be, the board can now be slid along the table

A specially designed wobble saw being used to cut wide grooves in timber. This type of cutter is efficient and has a wide range of uses.

board overlapping the fence, the ripping cut being taken along the edge of the board which is nearest to the front of the table. Again, when this has been done, the two pieces can be separated and the rest of the ripping operation can be carried out normally.

Bevel cutting
Bevel cutting consists of cutting completely through the material with the saw blade set at an angle other than at right-angles to the table surface. This can be subdivided into bevel ripping or bevel cross-cutting. Apart from the fact that the saw blade is tilted in relation to the table, the operations are as described previously. Before the motor can be tilted to produce a bevel cut it is necessary to elevate the arm sufficiently to allow the blade to swing without its movement being obstructed by the table-top. Once this has been done the motor is started and the arm is lowered until its teeth just touch the table. Angle cutting of this kind can be done in the normal 90° cross-cut position, in the out rip or in the in rip position, or with the radial arm positioned at 45°, or some other intermediate angle. It is important to note that when alterations in the configuration of the machine have been made, such as tilting the motor or swinging the arm, the clamps must be re-tightened before the machine is used. If we consider a situation in which the radial arm has been swung to 45° and the motor has been tilted to 45°, we have the classic compound 45° angle cut, which will give a cut of 45° to the rip fence and at 45° to the top of the table simultaneously. This particular cut is commonly used in the making of picture frames.

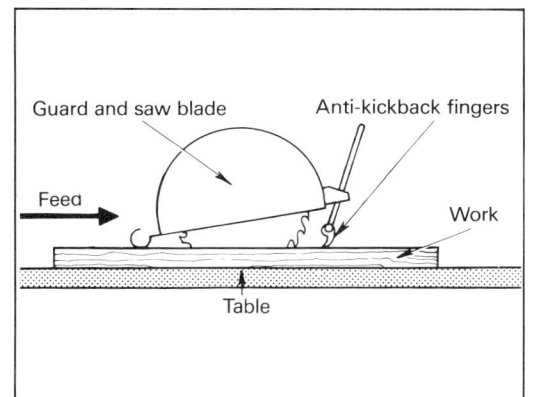

Fig. 5 Correct setting for ripping with a radial arm saw.

with the batten running against the table edge. This will provide a straight cut along the further side of the board, after which the batten can be removed and the remainder of the ripping carried out in the normal manner. Another system which can be used is to take a flat board with straight edges and secure the piece of wood to be ripped to the top of it. The lower board will then be run along the rip fence, with the curved or irregular edge of the upper

Joint cutting

Most woodworking joints can be cut very successfully by means of the radial arm saw though the process is, in most cases, considerably speeded up by the use of a wobble saw or dado head. In the absence of these attachments joints can be cut using an ordinary saw blade and a high standard of accuracy can be achieved.

Successful joint cutting of the type described here requires the use of a planer/thicknesser. If all the timber is of exactly the same thickness the joints will be accurate and will fit together perfectly. Perhaps the most obvious application of the saw in joint cutting is in the production of tenons. A tenon is a projection on the end of a length of wood which is produced, in effect, by rebating across the grain on opposing faces. Normally, of course, a number of tenons of the same size will be required, so the length of the tenon can be set by positioning a stop-block against the fence of the machine so that the timber can be pushed up against the block to position the first cut, which will determine the exact location of the shoulder of the tenon. The next job is to set the depth of cut to remove precisely the required amount of wood. This can be done quite easily by lowering the arm of the machine, with the motor switched off and the timber in place, until the saw teeth just lightly brush the surface of the material. The exact depth of cut can now be set by working from the number of turns of the elevating control which gives 3mm ($\frac{1}{8}$in) movement, up or down, per full rotation. The timber can be taken away from the fence, and if, for example, the depth of tenon required is 6mm ($\frac{1}{4}$in) two complete turns of the elevating control in the correct direction will lower the blade by this amount. The saw is then pushed to the rear of the arm and started and the timber is placed against the fence in contact with

Above: A geared chuck can be obtained for the DeWalt saw for use in drilling operations as illustrated.

Below: Disc sander unit fitted to the radial arm saw. Angle sanding, as illustrated here, becomes a simple matter. The sanding disc can be moved relative to the timber or the disc can be locked in position and the timber passed along it.

the stop block. The saw is now drawn forward and returned to its position, the timber is moved along about 3mm ($\frac{1}{8}$in) and the process is repeated, continuing until the final cut removes the last little piece of wood at the extreme end. The timber can now be turned over and the whole process repeated which will produce a tenon of the required length and depth.

The procedure is greatly speeded up by using a dado head which will remove up to 20mm ($1\frac{3}{8}$in) of timber in one pass. It

DeWalt 110 radial arm saw with motor swung to the vertical position and cutter block fitted; note the use of the special guard. Excellent mouldings can be produced in this way.

DeWalt 110 radial arm saw fitted with a jigsaw attachment.

will be seen that in the cutting of a halving joint the procedure is almost exactly the same as described for the cutting of a tenon, though here it may be necessary to mark the exact position of the halving joint and to cut to the marks. In the cutting of any kind of joint on a saw bench or a radial arm saw, the setting of the machine should be checked by producing a joint in scrap timber of the same dimensions as those which are to be used in the project.

Any final minute adjustments can then be carried out and complete accuracy will be ensured. It will be found that the movement of the timber along the fence by about 3mm ($\frac{1}{8}$in) after each cut becomes instinctive and almost automatic with practice

and if small slivers of wood should happen to be left behind these can safely be ignored and brushed away with the fingers when the job is completed. Numerous other joints can be cut on a radial saw just as they can on a saw bench and some of these can be studied in more detail in the section about woodworking joints on page 33.

Tapers
The normal method employed for cutting tapers on a circular saw, described on page 29, can be used equally well on a radial arm. A tapering jig can be constructed quite quickly and simply by the home worker and is run along the rip fence of the machine, just as it would be on a saw bench, with the saw correctly positioned.

45

The dado head
There is no doubt that two of the most useful accessories for the radial arm saw are the tungsten carbide tipped saw blade and the dado head. Neither is cheap but both are extremely useful, and almost indispensable to anyone engaged in production work.

Chapter three

Bandsaws

Bandsaws have increased in popularity in recent years, but care must be exercised in the selection of a machine of this nature. There are now quite a number of different models available to the home user and the small business and it is essential to establish, before paying out the considerable sum of money which will be required, that the machine in question is suitable for the work envisaged.

There are several small bandsaws on the market which are excellent for those who wish to do light woodwork. These machines are not, however, satisfactory if they are to be used for the cutting of hardwoods of any reasonable thickness. If they are so employed they are likely to be a source of constant trouble and irritation. Numerous larger machines are available for selection if the intention is to carry out production work in joinery or cabinet-making.

The bandsaw, as its name implies, carries a blade which is a continuous loop of metal with teeth cut along one edge. Its purpose is the cutting of shapes, which means that it is extremely efficient in cutting curves of any kind, but it must be remembered that it is not by any means as efficient as the circular saw when it comes to cutting straight lines.

Bandsaws fall into two categories, the two-wheeled and three-wheeled varieties. Two-wheeled bandsaws normally have fairly large wheels and are preferred by many workers because it is possible to fit them with blades of a fairly heavy gauge metal which will stand up to the biggest enemy of the bandsaw — metal fatigue. The wheels of a good bandsaw are fitted

The Willow wide throat bandsaw. This single-speed machine is designed for cutting wood but a multi-speed model is available for use with a wide variety of materials.

47

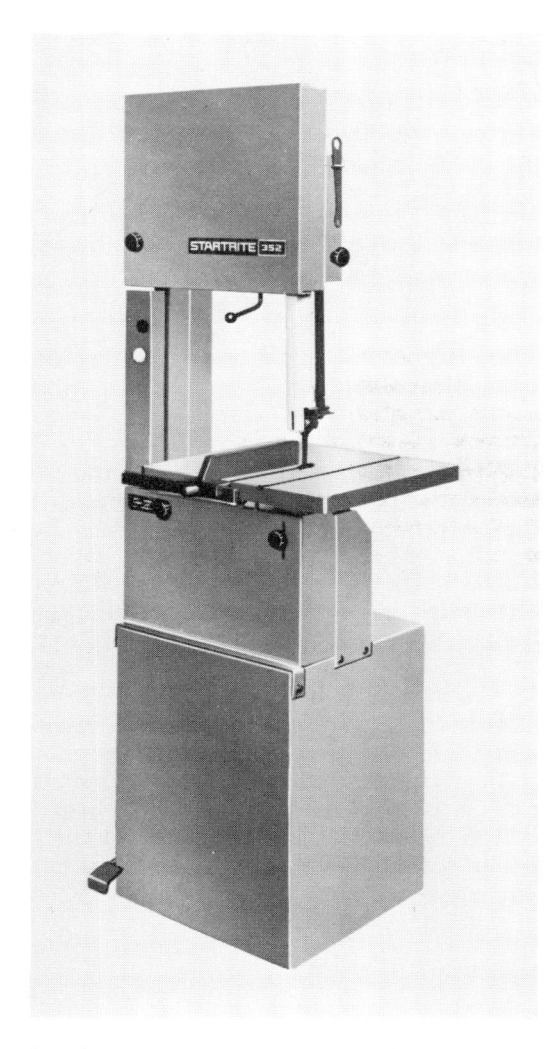

Bandsaw shown here is suitable for home workshop and light industrial use.

with rubber tyres which have a slight convexity, or crown, which helps in tracking the blade. On good bandsaws the tracking is easily adjusted and it is possible to make the blade run in precisely the required position on the wheels without any difficulty at all. On cheaper models it can be extremely difficult to achieve this

and the blade is likely to come off the wheels at frequent intervals in the case of the two-wheeled bandsaw, and quite often on the three-wheeled bandsaw as well. The upper wheel is fitted with a mechanism which enables it to be raised or lowered, so that the desired amount of tension can be put upon the blade. It is important that the tension used on the blade of a bandsaw is not too great since this does very little to improve the cutting efficiency of the machine and leads to early blade breakage. The tension required on a bandsaw is that which is sufficient to prevent the blade from slipping on the wheels whilst cutting.

Another important feature of any bandsaw is the system of guides and thrust rollers which is employed. These are explained in full detail on page 50 later in this chapter, but the function of these devices is to prevent the blade from twisting during the cut. If the guides are well-designed and well-made, they will do their job extremely well. If they are of poor design and poor manufacture, they will render the machine extremely difficult to use satisfactorily. Note also that guides and rollers should be fitted not only above the table of the bandsaw but also below it.

It may well be that for certain workers it is a matter of importance that the bandsaw table should be capable of tilting. Most good bandsaws have a table which will tilt, but the provision of this facility does of course cost money. If it is felt that the facility will be little used it may be as well to buy a cheaper machine which does not provide this.

At one time it was customary to describe a bandsaw in terms of the diameter of the wheels. This has now been discontinued and the measurement given in the description of a bandsaw normally refers to the

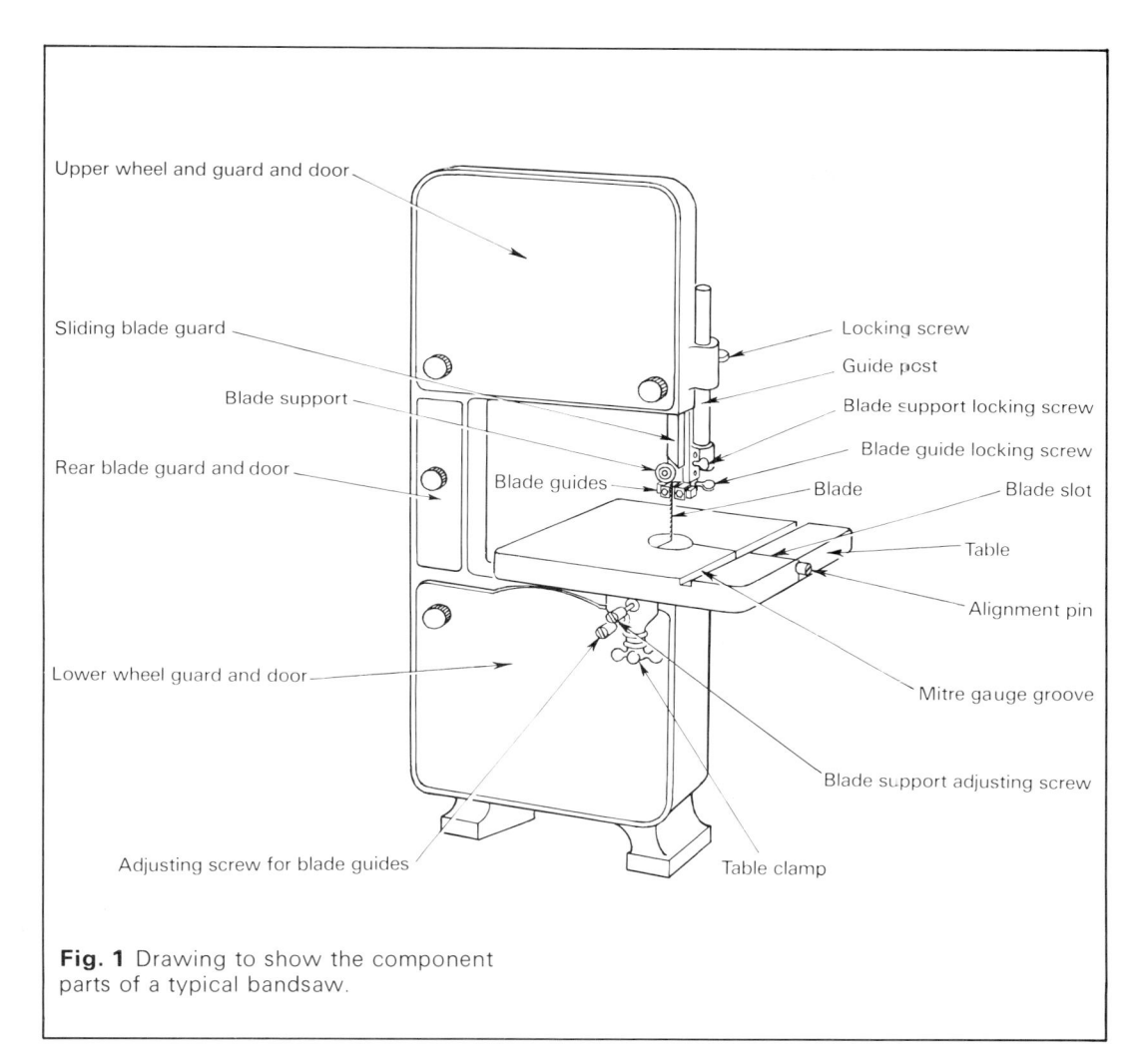

Fig. 1 Drawing to show the component parts of a typical bandsaw.

throat, which is the distance between the blade and the vertical part of the casing. A 380mm (15in) bandsaw will, therefore, accept a 380mm (15in) long piece of timber between the upright part of the column and the blade itself.

Some bandsaws are provided with metal cases or cabinets which are quite useful though extremely expensive. A workable alternative is a home-built chipboard cabinet mounted on industrial castors. When a bandsaw is used the amount of feed pressure required is very small compared with a circular saw and the bandsaw can be used quite satisfactorily standing on castors. This means that it can be kept in a suitable corner of the workshop and brought out into the room when it is required.

For the purposes of cutting wood, and it

49

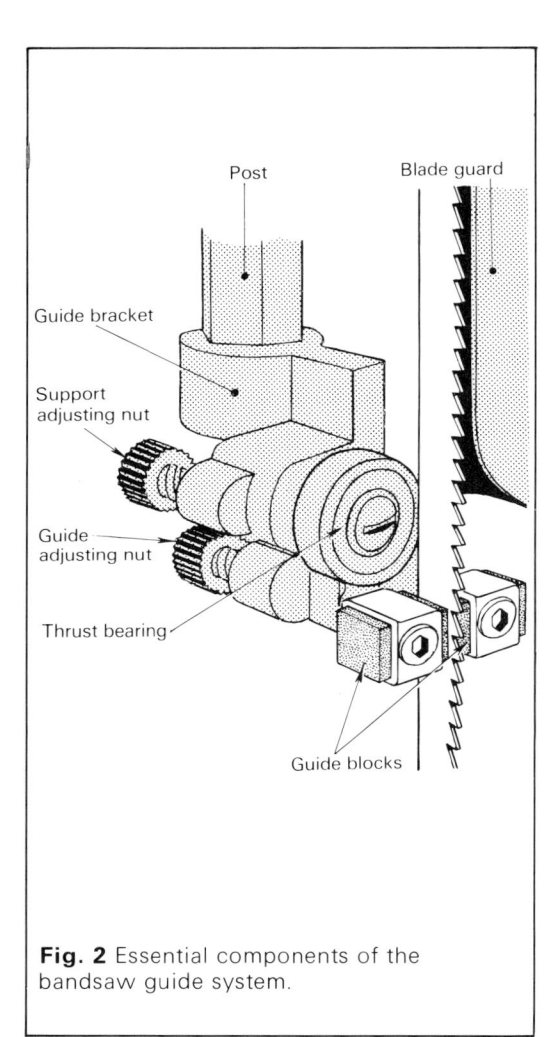

Fig. 2 Essential components of the bandsaw guide system.

must be remembered that bandsaws are available with speeds for cutting a very wide variety of other materials, a speed of 2,000 to 3,000 rpm will be quite satisfactory. The power of the motor is not critical but a half horsepower should be regarded as minimum on a machine which is expected to cut up to 75mm (3in) hardwoods.

Most machines are now fitted with front covers made of fibreglass. This reduces the weight and cost of the machine and is perfectly satisfactory, since the function of the front cover is simply to prevent the blade from flying out and injuring the operator if it should break in use.

Guides and thrust rollers
The guides which are fitted to bandsaws today may be of metal, wood or even some form of plastic. They should not rub the blade when it is running free, a slight gap being left between the ends of the guides and the blade itself. It is also important that the guides are so positioned as to run behind the gullets so that they do not contact the teeth. The thrust roller is provided to prevent the blade from being pushed off the wheels by the timber during the cut. Good machines have a thrust roller both above and below the table and the blade should not be allowed to contact this roller, except when the machine is cutting. When it is running free there should be a small gap between the back of the blade and the roller itself, usually about 1·5mm ($\frac{1}{16}$in).

One of the most important factors, if efficient working is to be achieved, is the setting up of the bandsaw. This can, perhaps, best be examined in the light of the fitting of a new blade. Assuming that a blade has broken, the first step is to switch off the machine and to remove the plug from the mains. Remove the front cover of the machine and extract the broken blade. Take this opportunity to thoroughly clean out the interior of the bandsaw using some form of workshop suction device. A piece of stick, or something similar, will be required to poke the dust free from the various crevices. The amount of dust produced by a bandsaw over a period of time is quite phenomenal and the dust is extremely fine. Care should be taken that this is not unduly disturbed as it is removed or it will go everywhere. When the interior of the casing is completely clean, the wheels themselves should be examined to see whether or not there are deposits of resin and sawdust on the crowns of the tyres. If this is the case it must be removed, either by gentle scraping or the use of a solvent.

It is customary on most bandsaws for a small circular inset to be provided in the table itself at the point where the blade passes through. This must be extracted before a new blade can be fitted and normally it can be removed by pushing from below. There will also be a slot in the table through which the new blade has to be passed and most machines are fitted with a small locking plate below the table which connects across this slot. This plate is designed to prevent any twisting of the table and must be removed before the blade can be fitted.

Since we are discussing the situation in which a blade has broken and a new blade is being fitted, it will also be necessary to lower the upper wheel of the bandsaw. This will have been positioned to tension the previous blade and it will not be possible to fit a new one until it is lowered about 25mm (1in). The control for the tension is normally mounted on top of the bandsaw and is quite simple to operate.

Before fitting a new blade the guides and rollers should be slackened and moved back away from their normal position. This is done both above and below the table.

The new blade can now be placed in position noting that the direction of the teeth is important. They obviously must be pointing downward, toward the table, and it may well be that the new blade appears

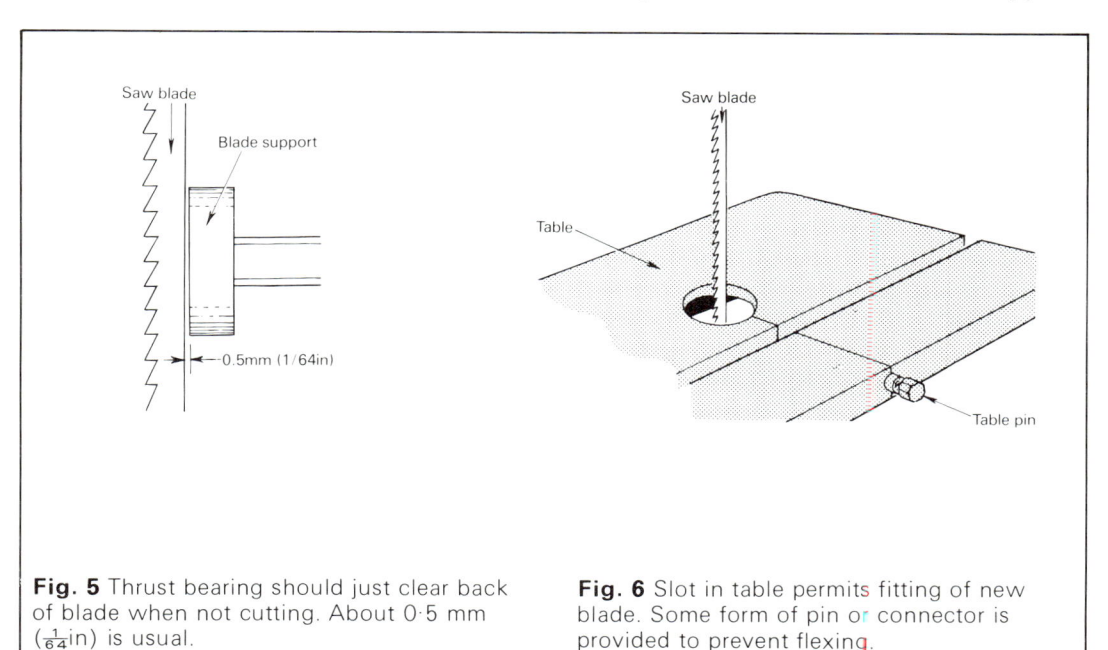

Fig. 5 Thrust bearing should just clear back of blade when not cutting. About 0·5 mm ($\frac{1}{64}$in) is usual.

Fig. 6 Slot in table permits fitting of new blade. Some form of pin or connector is provided to prevent flexing.

to have been wrongly cut because the teeth are pointing upwards. This has been known to confuse beginners but, in fact, if this is the case the blade can quite easily be turned inside-out whereupon the teeth will be pointing the right way.

The blade can now be slid through the table slot and positioned over the two or three wheels, as the case may be. It should be pushed into position so that it is sitting in the centre of the wheels and the tension control should be adjusted to apply some tension to the blade, *but not too much.* When this has been done the wheels of the bandsaw should be turned by hand in the direction in which they normally rotate. If they are turned a few times the position which the blade will adopt in relation to the surface of the rubber-tyred wheels will be quite clear. If this is not satisfactory, and the blade is running too far back or too far forward on the wheels, the situation can be remedied by operating the tracking control which is normally situated on the rear of the machine casing. This is likely to consist of two wheels, one of which clamps the mechanism, the other being the adjuster. The clamp is released and the adjuster is moved as the wheels are turned by hand until the blade has moved into the desired position, which is normally around the centre. When this has been done the clamp is, of course, re-tightened.

The tensioning can now be completed and the tracking is checked again to make sure that it has not been affected. With bandsaws of this size there is no hard and fast rule for specific adjustment which will allow the operator to apply a precise amount of tension to the blade. It is a matter of becoming used to the machine, but it is best to err on the side of a slack blade rather than an overtight one, since bandsaw blades are expensive and will break fairly quickly if run under extreme

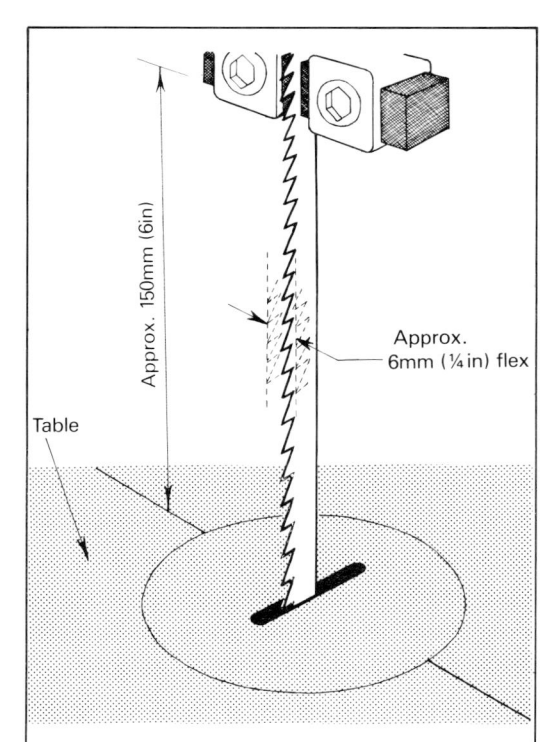

Fig. 8 Too much tension shortens blade life. Too little will permit blade to slip on wheels. Tension is arrived at by experience and 'feel'.

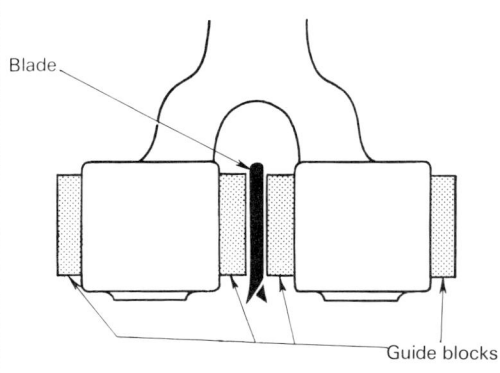

Fig. 4 Plan view of correctly set guide blocks. Note clearance between blade and blocks.

First position
(rear view)

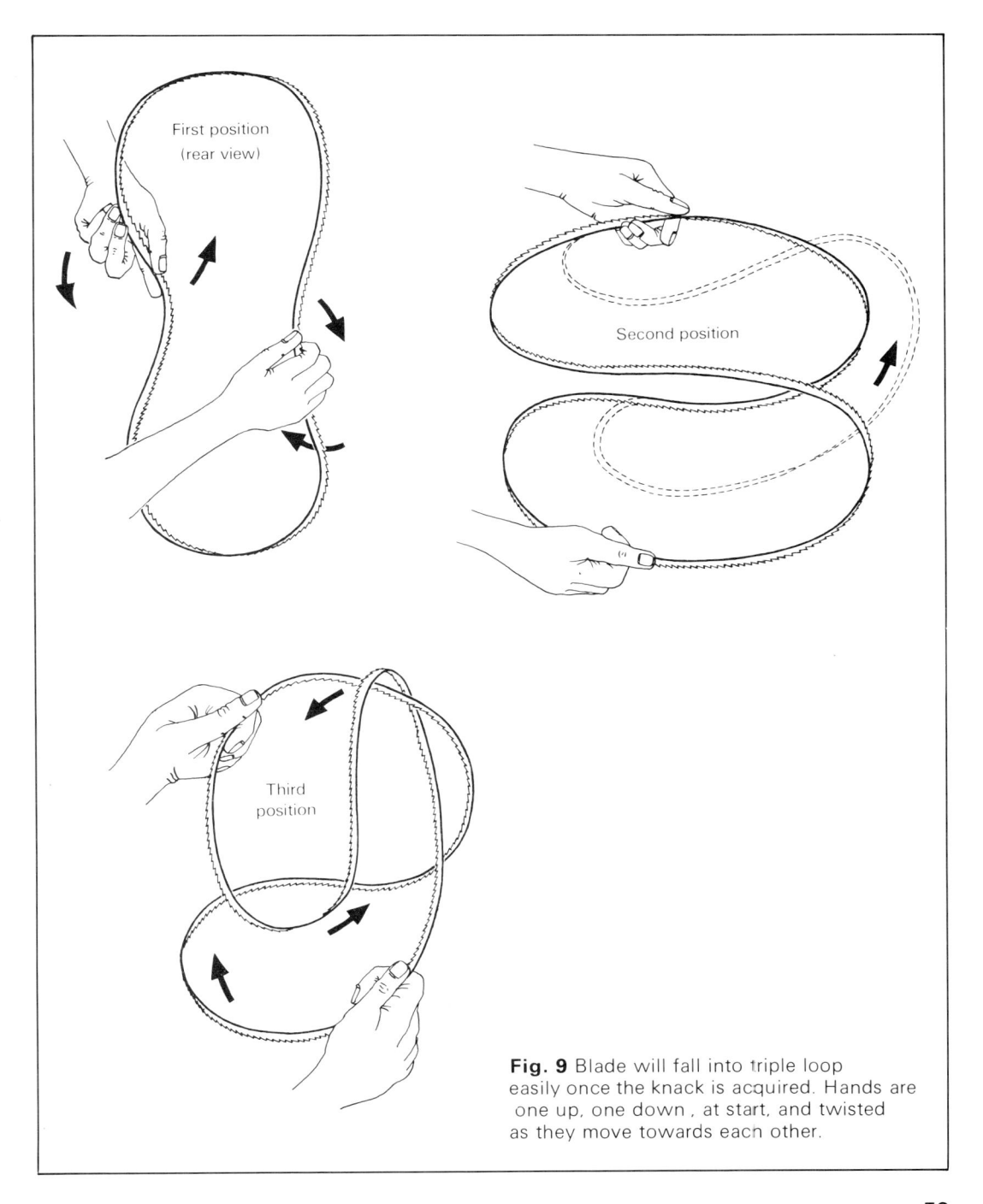

Second position

Third position

Fig. 9 Blade will fall into triple loop easily once the knack is acquired. Hands are one up, one down, at start, and twisted as they move towards each other.

53

tension. It is frequently suggested that the tension which has been placed upon the blade should be released overnight and readjusted the next time the machine is used. This may be a good idea but very few workers seem to bother about it. It would be a very necessary procedure if the blade was being run under too much tension, but once the operator has got the feel of the tool there should be no difficulty.

When all these stages have been completed the guides and rollers can be repositioned. The rollers are brought up so that they clear the back of the blade by about 1·5mm ($\frac{1}{16}$in) and the guides are positioned so that they almost, but not quite, touch the blade. Care must be taken when adjusting the guides to see that they are not allowed to push the blade out of line.

Bandsaws are, by nature, notoriously temperamental, but if the setting procedure is followed in the order described here it will become a matter of habit with the operator and there should be no difficulty whatsoever. It is usually a mistake to alter any one setting, since this may well affect others, and the best plan is to run through the whole thing in logical sequence.

A bandsaw is a very much safer machine for the beginner to use than a circular saw. It cannot kick back, or hurl pieces of wood at the worker, and provided he keeps his fingers well away from the blade at all times there is little chance of injury. It is, nevertheless, important to handle the tool with a reasonable amount of common sense, as is the case with any other form of woodworking machine. Accidents are possible but only if the operator is careless.

The actual sawing of a piece of wood is a very simple operation and does not place the worker under the same sort of mental stress as is common with newcomers to circular saws. The one point which should be watched at all times is that the upper guide and blade guard are always positioned just above the surface of the material being cut so that it is not possible for the operator's hand to reach the blade. The practice of using a bandsaw with the guard pushed right up is very dangerous indeed and it also means that the guides and thrust rollers are too far away from the timber to be serving any useful purposes.

When feeding timber on a bandsaw, the feed pressure should be sufficient to allow the saw blade to cut freely. Heavy feed pressure does not improve the cutting efficiency and will certainly reduce the life of the blade.

Ripping

Some people are disappointed when they have purchased a bandsaw which they intend to use for a considerable amount of ripping and find that the machine is not particularly efficient in this respect. A bandsaw does not perform very well in the ripping of timber since the blade itself is a mere ribbon of steel and will tend to wander in the grain of the wood to some extent. Another factor is that bandsaw blades always have what is known as 'lead'. This is because manufacturers are unable to obtain exactly the same amount of set on the teeth which lean to the left and to the right. As a result the blade will usually try to run off to the left or to the right if a piece of timber is fed across the table against a rip fence. This can be counteracted fairly easily if the rip fence is not used and the straight cut is made to a pencil line marked on the wood. The operator will automatically compensate for the lead by angling the timber slightly and the cut can usually be performed quite satisfactorily.

I have already noted that thrust rollers are provided on a bandsaw to support the blade as it is pushed forward by the wood during the cut, and so prevent it from being pushed off the wheels. There is, however, nothing to prevent the blade from coming off the wheels in a forward direction if sufficiently provoked and the normal cause of this is backing out of a cut. This should be avoided if at all possible since it is quite likely that it will cause such an occurrence. This fact is perhaps a little more significant than it may at first appear, having a considerable effect on the planning of work which is to be carried out on a bandsaw. All bandsaw work should be planned in such a way as to permit reasonably easy exit from the cut when it is completed. Badly-planned work may well result in the operator finding himself in a situation where he has no alternative but to back out of quite a long cut. A little foresight might well have avoided this situation, as will be shown by some of the diagrams.

There are a number of factors which make all the difference between a really good bandsaw operator and someone who just manages to cut up wood with the machine. In the main, like most of the expertise in using woodworking machines, these turn out to be little more than common sense. If one looks at the blade of a circular saw or of a hand saw, it will be seen that the set on the teeth, or in other words the outward lean which is given to alternate teeth, is designed to provide a saw kerf, or width of cut, which is greater than the thickness of the blade itself. This cuts down friction and renders the cutting operation a great deal easier than it otherwise might be. This is true of the bandsaw blade but the matter must be taken a stage further. If a bandsaw blade is to cut curves, some of which may be fairly tight, it is necessary for the kerf to be wide enough to permit

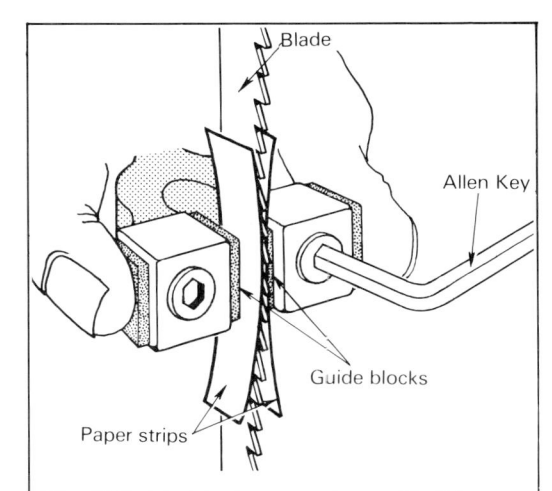

Fig. 3 Guide blocks are set up with thin card as shown to allow free movement of blade.

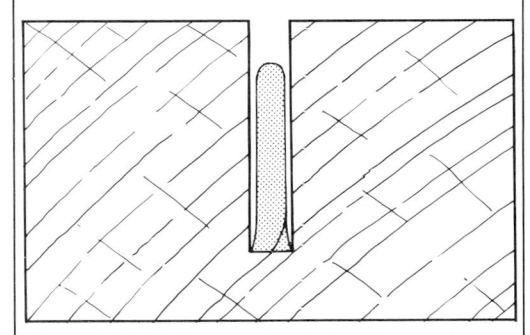

Fig. 10 Sufficient set is vital with bandsaw blades, to allow the blade to move in its kerf.

the blade to swing in it. For a blade of any given width there is a minimum diameter circle which can be cut and if any attempt is made to exceed this the blade will become over-heated and almost certainly break. It will be seen, therefore, that if the set of the teeth on a bandsaw blade should decrease for any reason, the efficiency of the blade will suffer a severe decline.

It may be difficult to see how the set on the

teeth of a machine can alter but in fact this frequently does happen. It can be caused by bad setting of the machine, which is running so that the teeth themselves are passing partly through the guides, but an even more frequent cause is the use of an inferior quality blade which is soft and unable to stand up to very much cutting of really hard timbers. It is axiomatic that a bandsaw can only be as good as the blade it carries and it is sad to see well-made and cleverly-designed machines being used with inferior blades. Good bandsaw blade is made by cutting and setting the teeth, then hardening them whilst leaving the rest of the blade relatively soft. This process is not carried out on cheap blades, nor is it possible on extremely thin ones. Some of the finest blade available, in my opinion, is Starrett or Milford, which can be purchased either as ready-made blade of a given length for a specific machine, or in rolls of about twenty metres or a hundred feet, packed in a plastic dispenser.

Up until a year or two ago it was uncommon to find amateurs using this type of blade and welding it up themselves. This has, however, become popular with the advent of small jigs which will hold the blade in position while it is welded. Various bandsaw welding jigs are available on the market, and, in fact, it is not difficult for an ingenious operator to make one up in the workshop. What is required is something which will hold the blade rigid, with both sections which are to be joined completely parallel. Small and quite simple jigs can be purchased and mounted in a vice in the workshop when required for use.

A length of blade is pulled from the dispenser, measured according to the requirement of the machine in use and cut from the roll by means of a pair of tin snips. A properly executed joint will include half a tooth on each end of the blade so that when the final joint is made there is no unpleasant gap. Next grind a small bevel on the ends of the cut length, so that when they are placed together they will give a reasonable soldering area. This can be done quite easily on a bench grinder and the angle produced on the end of the blade should be approximately 45°. Care must be taken to see that no undue pressure is applied on the blade against the grinder or it will be over-heated. Once these bevels have been ground they must not be touched with the fingers since any grease which is deposited on the surface will prevent the soldering process from being carried out correctly.

The blade is now placed carefully in the jig, the ground bevels are coated with a mixture of powdered flux and water and brought together so that they overlap correctly. At this point the jig is tightened up and heat is applied to the blade by means of a butane torch. Care must be taken to see that excessive heat is not applied, otherwise the metal will be crystallised and will rapidly break. The area around the joint should be heated to a dull cherry red and the solder applied. It should run through the joint quite freely, whereupon the heat is withdrawn and the metal allowed to cool. Being thin it cools extremely rapidly.

If the joint has taken correctly the blade can be removed from the jig and final cleaning up is carried out by means of a file or on the grinder. Blades which are welded up in this manner will sometimes run without any undue fault, but in general there is likely to be a slight bump as the joint passes through the guides. If this is only slight it need not concern the operator.

An advantage of this method of home welding of blades is that ready-made blades are rather expensive, and even they will sometimes break after only a few minutes use due to bad welding. The operator who is capable of welding up bandsaw blades can, of course, repair them as and when they break and is unlikely to be caught out over a weekend when no ready-made blades are to hand.

Bandsaws are very much affected by the direction of the grain of the timber. When cutting directly along the grain as in ripping, quite apart from any lead which may be present due to imperfect setting of the teeth, there will always be a tendency for the blade to wander from side to side in the grain. Very little can be done about this and it should be remembered that for straight rip cuts the circular saw is the correct tool and not the bandsaw. Reasonable results can, however, be obtained and the timber can be passed over a planer in order to true up the edge.

In cross-cutting directly across the grain the bandsaw will cut extremely well apart from a certain amount of blade lead. The worst situation is when passing from ripping, or cutting directly with the grain, to cross-cutting, or cutting directly across it, as when cutting out a circle from a plank, an occupation familiar to wood turners who cut up blanks for the turning of bowls. In cutting out a bowl blank, or a disc from a board, the different characteristics of the blade when cutting in various parts of the grain will immediately become apparent. The cross grain cutting is easy, the cutting directly with the grain is difficult, and great care has to be exercised when passing through what is referred to as the quarter grain end, or that part of the grain which lies between the two. With practice, it is possible to become expert at cutting out circles, and anyone who does a great deal of this will probably not even notice the difficulties referred to.

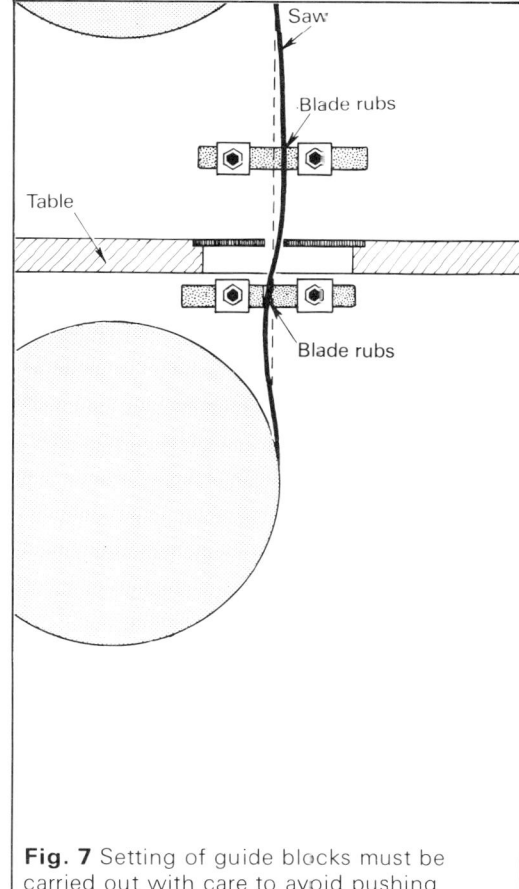

Fig. 7 Setting of guide blocks must be carried out with care to avoid pushing blade out of line. Blocks above and below table must be set accurately.

Hints for successful sawing
There are a number of tricks of the trade, for want of a better expression, which are well-known to experienced bandsawyers but which may not be discovered by an amateur for a long time unless they are pointed out. Some of these are dealt with here but unfortunately there is not sufficient space in a book of this size to go into every conceivable aspect of the use of a machine of this nature.

57

Reference to the accompanying sketches will make most of the points referred to quite clear. The making of two shelf brackets from one square piece of timber is a very common practice, but would be rather difficult to explain without the aid of Fig. 12. It will be seen that the curve which is cut from the corner of a square to the centre is repeated exactly from the centre to the other corner, but in a reverse direction; two identical pieces of timber will be produced and excellent brackets for small shelves can be made in this way. With a large and powerful bandsaw it may well be possible to cut four such squares, or even more, at once so manufacturing in one cut quite a large number of brackets.

A rather similar idea, which produces a bracket of a different shape suitable for larger shelves, is shown in Fig. 12.

Another old trick which can be useful is concerned with the production of curved pieces of wood from straight lengths without undue waste. Fig. 11 will make the principle fairly clear. The idea is to mark out the required curve on the straight strip of timber and make the first cut along the marked line. When this has been done the piece of wood which has the convex curve on it is glued to the top of the original piece, thus producing a curved length of wood. It is now necessary to mark the correct radius again on the bottom part of the timber and re-cut so that the waste involved will be seen to be very small indeed. These are not necessarily everyday cuts, but it can be very useful indeed to know of them when the need arises.

It is often necessary to cut shapes which have to be duplicated with a bandsaw. If the job is subsequently to be painted or treated in some similar manner the best approach very often is to take several pieces of timber, nail them together, mark out the desired shape, then treat the assembly as one piece of wood so producing a number of identical workpieces in one sawing operation. They should continue to be treated as one piece of wood for all sanding and trimming operations until the edges are considered to be satisfactory.

When timber of any reasonable length has to be cut consideration has to be given to the marking out in relation to the vertical column of the bandsaw. If the marking out is done on one side of the timber only it may not be possible to carry out the cuts at all since the column will obstruct the material. A typical case of this will be in the notching of a strip of timber, in other words the removal of a small square sectional piece from the corners at opposite ends. If the marking out for the removal of these sections is done on only one side of the timber, it will not be possible to make both cuts. The reason for this is that one cut can be made quite easily with the wood on the outside of the blade, but when it is turned round in order to make the second cut the column will effectively prevent it. It is necessary, therefore, to mark one corner cut out on one face of the timber and the other one on the opposite side. Points like this seem perfectly obvious when indicated but it is very easy to fall into a number of traps of this kind when using a bandsaw.

Safety in the use of all woodworking machines must be given due consideration. The bandsaw is, however, one of the safest forms of woodworking machine if used with reasonable common sense. There can be little doubt that the most usual cause of accident with a bandsaw is heavy pressure on the timber as it is being fed to the blade. If the blade should suddenly

Fig. 11

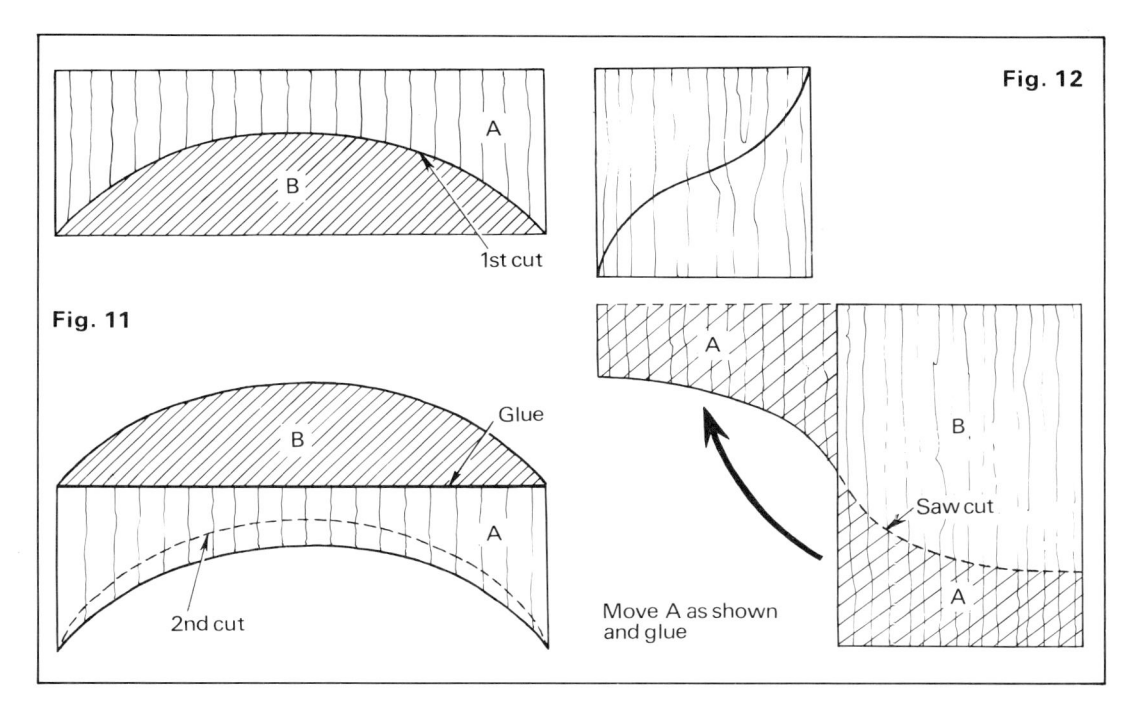

1st cut

2nd cut

Glue

Fig. 12

Move A as shown and glue

Saw cut

emerge from the side of the timber the hand can shoot forward and if the guard is incorrectly set a serious accident can result.

Sadly, another common cause of accident with bandsaws, though hardly credible, is the removal of small pieces of wood from the table with the fingers. Since there is very little trauma attached to the use of a bandsaw, which is a docile machine, some workers do become over-confident and it is quite possible to be lulled into such a mental condition, to flick pieces of wood vigorously from the table with the finger tips forgetting momentarily the blade itself. There are no second chances in such situations, one should remember that bandsaws are also used to cut up sides of beef!

Most bandsaws are available with rip fences, though in many cases these are optional extras. It is debatable whether the purchase of a rip fence is wise in view of the phenomenon of blade lead to which I referred earlier. Where a rip fence is provided for a bandsaw it should really have some provision incorporated for angling it in relation to the table. It is then possible to compensate for the blade lead by angling the fence slightly. Most workers, myself included, use a batten or strip of timber clamped across the table by means of a G cramp. If the timber is slid along this it works very well as a rip fence, and it is a simple matter to angle it in order to accommodate the lead.

The other item frequently provided for bandsaws is a mitre guide, similar to that provided for circular saws, and here again the efficacy of a mitre guide will be determined by the accuracy of the blade itself. It is unlikely that the accuracy obtained will in any way approach that of the circular saw, and for this reason the use of

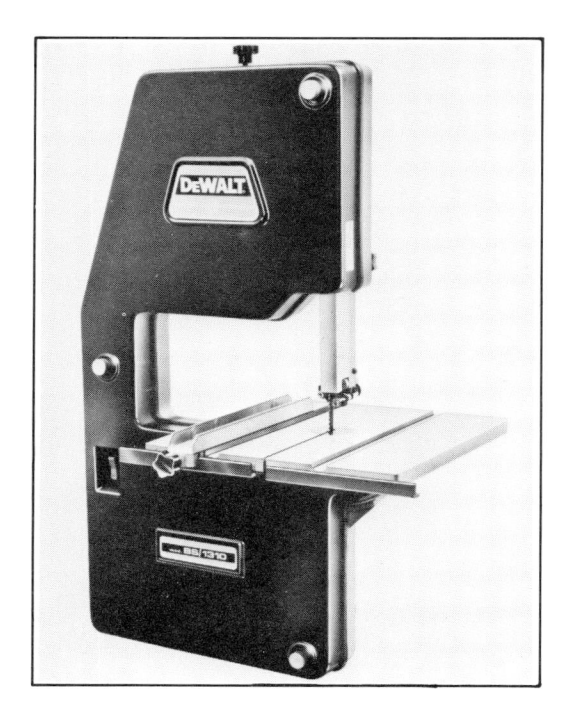

The DeWalt bandsaw. This machine is normally supplied with motor, on a metal stand.

a bandsaw for the cutting of mitres cannot be recommended. Sometimes a mitre fence is used in cross-cutting timber where a large number of lengths have to be produced but in view of the fact that a bandsaw does not tend to kick timber back at the operator, as a circular saw may do, there is no real reason why the timber cannot be fed to the blade by hand and in most cases this is the procedure adopted.

When a long piece of timber has to be cut through, somewhere near the centre, it will immediately be apparent this cannot be done on a bandsaw if the cross-cut is to be at right-angles to the edges of the board. In an emergency, however, it can be done provided some wastage of timber can be countenanced. The timber is placed on the bandsaw table with one edge against the column of the machine and is then pushed forward. A curved cut will result, and this will be allowed to continue to the centre of the board. The blade is then backtracked out of the cut, the board is turned over and the process is repeated. This will give a very roughly-shaped end to each piece, but the situation can be corrected by cross-cutting in the normal manner. In this connection it should perhaps be pointed out that if the width of the board does not exceed the available space between the upper guides and the table, the timber can be stood on edge and pivoted into the blade. In this case the amount of waste which occurs will be very slight and this procedure will be adopted by most workers wherever possible.

An operation which has been referred to in respect of circular saws is that of re-sawing (see page 28). Where the width of the board to be re-sawn does not exceed twice the available depth of cut of the circular saw blade, the circular saw will normally be employed for the job. Home workers do not, in most cases, possess large circular saws, 75mm (3in) depth of cut being about the norm.

If a 180mm–200mm (7in–8in) board is to be cut through the centre on edge this obviously cannot be done on the circular saw. Instead, a 75mm (3in) deep cut using the circular saw can be carried out from each side of the board, leaving a strip of uncut material at the centre. The board can then be passed through the bandsaw to separate the two pieces and the planer used to level the surface afterwards. Compound sawing is often required, particularly by woodcarvers, who may wish to take a fairly large square block of wood and mark it out on adjacent faces, so that band-sawing will remove a large quantity of waste before the carving is undertaken.

Another well-known compound sawing project is the manufacture of cabriole legs for furniture. In an operation of this kind the marking out must be done accurately on adjacent faces of the timber, which should be perfectly square. The sawing will be done working to the lines on one of the faces and keeping the waste to as few pieces as possible. When the bandsawing has been completed this waste will be replaced and held in position with transparent tape. The bandsawing procedure is then carried out again, this time working from the marks on the other faces of the timber. When this has been done the waste will fall away and the job will be seen to be complete in so far as the bandsaw is able to complete it. In the case of a cabriole leg, of course, a great deal of handwork is necessary to finish the project.

Some home workshop projects will call for the smooth and even bending of lengths of timber. A common procedure adopted for purposes like these is that of kerfing, and this can be done on a circular saw. The saw kerf produced by a circular saw is, however, normally rather wide and for relatively small workpieces the bend produced is not as even as it might be. The very narrow kerf produced by a bandsaw blade lends itself to projects of this type since a far larger number of cuts, placed closer together, can be used producing a much more satisfactory curve.

It will be noted that in most cases the timber to be kerfed will be considerably longer than the throat of the bandsaw and it might be at first assumed that this would make the kerfing operation difficult. In fact it is not necessary for the kerfing cuts to be at right-angles to the face of the timber, so the wood can be placed against the column of the bandsaw and the mitre guide can be employed, this having been swivelled slightly to allow for the obstruction caused by the column. It is very important that the cuts should be of equal depth and that they should be carried through to within 1·5mm ($\frac{1}{16}$in) or so of the far side of the timber. In order to achieve this a stop block of scrap wood can be clamped to the table to stop the forward progress of the timber at the precise point required. The spacing of the cuts along the timber is a matter of trial and error on the part of the operator, but somewhere between 6mm–12mm ($\frac{1}{4}$in–$\frac{1}{2}$in) will work reasonably well for most jobs. Cuts should be equally spaced all along the workpiece. When a curved piece of timber has been produced by kerfing in this manner, the kerfs can be filled with a little glue when the bending is carried out and some workers like to mix the glue with fine sawdust. When the back of the curved workpiece is finally sanded it is not easy to see precisely what has been done to it.

The bending of the workpiece after it has been kerfed should be carried out carefully. It is best to partly bend the timber while in a dry state then to wet the outside surface with hot water whilst completing the bending. If the outer face is soaked in this manner the bend can be produced quite well and without great difficulty.

Compound bandsawing using a Coronet Imp.

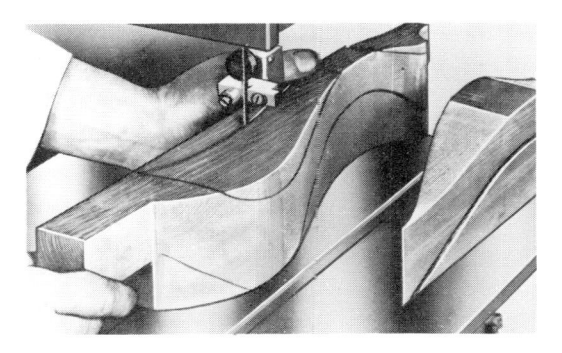

Pattern sawing is described in the chapter dealing with circular saws, page 7, but it is also a very useful technique when using a bandsaw to produce a number of identical shapes. Note that a pattern-sawn cut can only be produced when the cut can be taken through in an even operation. If any sharp corners are present it will not be possible to use this method. The idea is to mark out accurately a piece of wood of the desired shape and cut it carefully on the bandsaw. This piece is the master pattern for the production of the remainder. The underside of this pattern should have a number of small brads driven into it, evenly spaced over its surface. The heads of the brads are then cut off and filed to a point and should stick out from the surface of the pattern by about 3mm ($\frac{1}{8}$in). The points should be as sharp as possible.

It is also necessary to make up a pattern sawing jig in the form of a block of wood as described below. This is clamped firmly to the table and has a cut-out which permits the timber being sawn to pass beneath it. A small notch is cut in the curved end of this jig so that the bandsaw blade will fit into it. A piece of the stock to be sawn is then placed under the pattern which is pressed firmly down on to it, anchored by the small brads. Care should be taken when setting up a jig of this nature to see that the centre line of the jig is in line with the teeth of the blade. The workpiece, complete with pattern, can now be passed along the end of the jig and the blade will follow the contour. Since it is housed in the notch of the jig it will not cut into the pattern but will produce an identical workpiece.

Most people who buy bandsaws will have heard of the jig for cutting circles and most of them are anxious to try it out. In order to avoid disappointment, however, I should perhaps point out that such jigs are not normally satisfactory on thick timber. They are extremely useful for cutting out circles from plywood or softwood of about 25mm (1in) in thickness, but heavy pieces of hardwood are best dealt with by marking the circle accurately with a clearly visible pencil line and using normal free-hand methods. The cutting of such discs, as for the production of bowls in turning, is a knack which is quickly acquired and which will permit surprisingly accurate results.

The circle-cutting jig will only be as accurate as the marking and setting up has been so care should be taken in both respects. It is very simple and like most simple things it works. What is required is a small wooden sub-table which can be fitted on to the table of the bandsaw. This wooden sub-table will have a slot cut in it into which a hardwood strip can be fitted and the hardwood strip carries at one end a small, sharply-pointed brad protruding from its surface. This brad is the pivot pin upon which the timber, from which the circle is to be cut, will be rotated. Once the table has been clamped to the bandsaw table the pivot pin needs to be exactly in line with the teeth of the blade and directly to the side of it. The degree of lead which is present with the particular bandsaw blade in use must be taken into consideration and it may be found necessary to slightly alter the position of the sub-table after trial. Once it has been manoeuvred into the correct position, however, it will work very well indeed. Operation of the device is perfectly simple. A piece of wood large enough to produce the required circle is pressed down on to the pivot point, jig and work are advanced to the blade and the jig is firmly clamped in position. The saw can now be started and the wood can be rotated on the pivot pin. If the setting up is correct, a perfect circle will be produced.

Since a jig of this nature will be required for the production of circles of varying diameters it is advisable to provide it with a sliding strip carrying the pivot pin.

It is worth spending some time on the production of a good jig which will last for many years. If the sub-table is made from hardwood, the slot which is to accommodate the sliding strip can be cut out with a router and dovetail cutter or by hand with a sharp chisel, its edges being undercut at 45°. This will enable the strip to be made with matching 45° angled sides so that it can be slid into the board but cannot be lifted out. It is also necessary to provide some sort of clamping device in the form of a nut and washer so that once the desired position of the pivot point has been established the clamping device can be tightened, preventing the pivot from moving while the jig is in use.

I am giving basic ideas here, of course, and the individual worker may well adapt them to suit his own requirements.

Chapter four

Electric Drills and Portable Power Tools

The importance of the electric drill in power tool woodwork has changed considerably over the years. When first introduced, these tools were quite primitive and were used for the drilling of holes of various sizes in both timber and metal. Then came the heyday of the electric drill with attachments which could be used for almost every form of woodworking. The tendency then was for people taking up woodwork to acquire an electric drill with a range of attachments, and to use this until their devotion to the craft was established sufficiently, or until sufficient money had been saved, before going into the heavier types of powered tool. This is no longer such a common situation and there is no doubt that the average person has more money to spend, and the majority of hobbyists who enter into power tool woodwork now start with more specialised and expensive equipment.

There are certain obvious disadvantages in the use of an electric drill with a range of attachments, the principal one being the time involved in changing from one attachment to another. To fit the circular saw attachment to the drill in order to cut some timber, for example, can take ten or fifteen minutes and the worker may then find it necessary to dismantle the circular saw attachment in order to drill some holes or perhaps to fit a sander. Another disadvantage, of course, is that in many cases the use of attachments on an electric drill requires full power to be delivered by the drill itself. Electric drills designed for home use are not intended to be used for protracted periods on full power and if they are so treated, their life expectancy is reduced. The circular saw attachment is the worst offender in this respect, especially

Electric drills in carrying cases have become popular with professional users. The Stanley Topline kit is packed in a very robust case, and will be found extremely convenient.

when used on hardwoods. A great deal of power is required, even with a very sharp and correctly-set saw blade, but when these blades become blunt, which they do very quickly, and the set on the teeth begins to deteriorate, the power required is very high indeed and continuous use of a drill in this manner will rapidly result in the motor being burnt out.

Another contributory factor to the decline in popularity of the drill and its attachments has been the introduction and rise in favour of the independent portable electric tool. These are generally designed with sufficient power for their specific purpose and will prove to be much more satisfactory. The problem of changing over from one operation to another does not, of course, arise but the high cost of each individual unit needs to be given careful consideration. Some of these self-powered portable tools have firmly established themselves and one of the most obvious is the self-powered circular saw. This tool finds a place in most workshops since it has great value in its portability and in the fact that it can be taken to the work, rather than the work taken to the saw. In the cutting up of large and heavy sheets of material such as chipboard or plywood, for example, it is often far easier to use a portable power tool for the initial cutting and then to take the smaller pieces to sawbench for final accurate machining.

In essence an electric drill is simply an electric motor enclosed in a special casing. The end of the motor shaft carries a chuck to which may be fixed various cutters or drill bits and is usually designed with a form of pistol grip handle. It is always worth examining the shape of a handle on a drill before buying, bearing in mind that for correct use it is necessary to apply pressure along the axis of the tool. The design of some models makes this

The right tool for the job. Drilling in masonry calls for the use of an impact drill, often referred to as a rotating percussion drill which produces a hammering action as it rotates.

rather difficult and can result in the frequent snapping off of small drills, or cause considerable difficulty when a lot of pressure needs to be applied to the tool, as in the drilling of a very large hole.

Electric drills can be obtained as either single-speed, two-speed, four-speed, or infinitely variable. The single-speed version is obviously the cheapest and will be perfectly satisfactory if it is to be used only for the occasional drilling of holes in wood. A two-speed model will prove to be much more versatile and usually offers speeds of something like 3,000 and 900 rpm. Four-speed drills usually have a gear train inside the casing which can be engaged or disengaged by means of a sliding button from the outside. The trigger itself offers two positions, one high and one low. It will be seen, therefore, that with the gear train disengaged there will be two high speeds and that once it is engaged there will be a further two low speeds available. This becomes useful when a drill is to be used for a wide variety of purposes. Perhaps for driving a small lathe, drilling a very large, or very small hole, drilling into masonry and possibly for working in metal.

The infinitely variable speed type of drill

is not as popular with most workers but does offer advantages in specific situations. It is very useful for those who wish to drive a lathe attachment and it does enable the drill to be used as a screwdriver with a special bit fitted into the chuck. It is worth noting, however, that in most designs the available power decreases as the speed is lowered. The potential purchaser of an electric drill who is not fully aware of the various factors which affect their design is faced with a bewildering array. Tools designed for industrial use, where they are likely to be in use for several hours every day, are extremely expensive. At the other end of the scale is the consumer drill, designed for use in the home, which is relatively cheap. Most manufacturers design their particular models of electric drill to provide an estimated number of hours of working life at full power. In most cases the electric drill which is kept around the home is used at full power on very infrequent occasions, and then only for a few minutes at a time. If it has been provided with a motor which is expected to give between ten and twenty hours of full load life it may well last for five or six years in a situation where it is used infrequently. The cost of manufacturing a motor which will give a life many times greater than this, is, of course, much higher and industrial drills are not usually worth buying for home use. A further point here is that the industrial drills produced by a given company will not normally accept the attachments designed for the consumer range, and, in fact, the speeds provided for the industrial drills are not always suitable for this purpose. If a drill with attachments is being purchased with the intention of using it for a variety of purposes, then the consumer model is the one to be chosen.

No real maintenance is necessary on electric drills, other than to follow the instructions provided by the manufacturer which call for the replacement of the carbon brushes at fixed periods and an occasional service by the manufacturer's agents. When these tools are used in very dusty atmospheres, which is frequently the case, it is advisable to blow the dust out from the casing occasionally by means of a compressed air line. In doing this, however, it is as well to remember that compressed air often contains a very high level of moisture; so that when a drill has been cleaned in this manner it should be run until it becomes quite warm and any moisture which has been introduced will evaporate before it can do any harm.

When a drill is used on heavy work, where something approaching full power is being drawn from it, it will quickly heat up. For this reason it is not advisable to use a drill continuously on heavy work. It should be operated for a few minutes and then allowed to run with no load until it cools. A drill which is running with no load will cool down quite quickly through the action of the fan which is provided to blow air over the motor. If, having been brought to a high temperature by heavy woodwork, it is simply switched off and left on the bench to cool this will take some considerable time.

In most cases the attachments which are available for electric drills can be considered as very small versions of the power tools described in this book and the comments made about the larger ones will generally apply to the smaller ones.

When purchasing a good quality electric drill also consider acquiring a vertical drill stand which will accept it. These vary widely in quality and a heavy model which has a smooth action on its lever and spring return should be chosen. A power drill fitted into a vertical drill stand can be used with much more accuracy than when it is operated freehand and becomes an extremely useful item in the workshop. Attachments are also available for some electric drills which will enable them to be used as mortisers, and they are extremely efficient in operation. For the operator who wishes to cut mortises of reasonable size, such as would be expected in cabinet-making, such a tool will be well worth buying. If the intention is to manufacture gates out of oak, then something considerably stronger and more powerful will be necessary!

Time spent browsing in a good tool store will soon reveal to the newcomer a vast array of items, both large and small, which can be used in conjunction with electric drills. Very careful consideration should be given before purchasing some of these items and, if possible, discuss with other woodworkers the merits of the attachment since there are many almost useless gimmicks available. Most workshops, including my own, contain items purchased with considerable enthusiasm in years gone by which have been used not more than twice in the ensuing years.

On the other hand, of course, there are numerous items which will be extremely useful to the owner of an electric drill, particularly if he also has a vertical drill stand. Among these are the excellent Screwmate sets manufactured by Stanley Tools Ltd. When working on a project which requires numerous screws it can be a fairly laborious business to drill holes of suitable size for the shank, the thread and for the countersunk head. The Screwmates are manufactured in a range of sizes and will produce a hole for the screw, one for the shank and a countersink for the head in one operation, and to the correct

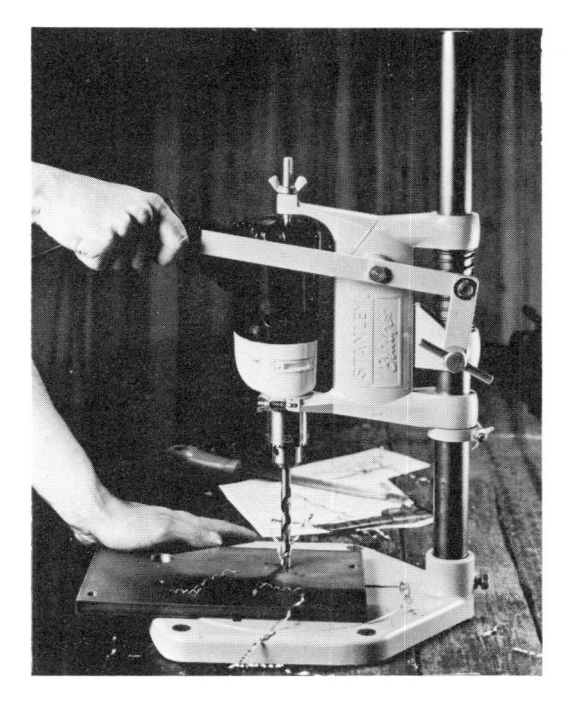

In the absence of a heavy duty drill press, excellent results can be produced using a unit such as the Stanley drill stand, shown here. A high level of accuracy can be achieved.

depth. I have found these to be of very great value over a good many years, and would not like to be without them.

The same company manufactures sets of plug cutters. These are small cutters in a range of sizes, designed to complement the Screwmate sets. Where screws are to be recessed into the surface of a piece of wood, and subsequently hidden, this method works very well indeed. Certain Screwmate sets can be obtained which will provide the necessary holes for the screw, but instead of a countersink will produce a hole of a specific size into which the screw will be recessed. By using a matching plug cutter small wooden plugs can be cut from a piece of wood

67

Bosch portable powered saw with guard retracted. The guard is spring loaded making the tool very safe in use.

and these will fit exactly into the hole made by the Screwmate. The important factor is that when plugs are made in this manner the grain of the wood runs across the plug rather than along its length so that normal face grain shows on top of the plug. This means that with care it is possible to cut a plug which will be almost undetectable when it is in position. It is best to cut these so that they will project very slightly above the surface of the workpiece, then plane them down and sand them carefully. If care is taken in matching the grain a very professional result can be achieved. It should be noted that the use of a plug cutter does require a vertical drill stand. It is very difficult indeed to cut plugs when using the drill freehand. If such a plug cutter is not available the only alternative is to use pieces of dowel, but in this case the grain runs lengthwise in the dowel and when any kind of finish is applied to the workpiece the end grain of the dowel will show up much darker than the surrounding wood. This will not matter if it is intended to make a feature of the plugs but in many situations it is undesirable.

Portable electric powered tools

The range of self-powered portable tools has now become very wide indeed and cannot be covered in depth in a book of this nature. I will, therefore, deal briefly with some of the more common types to give some idea of what is available. Such tools fall into two categories; the type of tool which is of considerable use to the home worker or hobbyist over quite a wide spectrum of woodworking operations, and the type of specialist tool, such as the Elu biscuit jointer, which is extremely efficient and almost essential to workers who are specializing in certain applications.

Portable power saws

The big labour-saving device in this category is the portable circular saw which, if correctly maintained and used, can be a very useful item in the workshop. It can also be very dangerous in the wrong hands and should always be treated with great respect. Many of the accidents which occur with portable power tools are complete unnecessary, and in some cases are so stupid as to be unbelievable. A typical example of this is the situation in which a worker is holding a piece of wood with his fingers underneath it and allows the blade to cut into his fingers.

Another situation which all too frequently causes accidents is where the guard on the machine has been either accidentally or purposely jammed in the open position. This is very dangerous indeed and must be avoided at all costs. Manufacturers go to considerable lengths to design machines which will protect the operator and it is foolhardy, to say the least, to jam a guard in the open position. The self-powered circular saw is a tool which has been designed specifically for a given purpose and is, in most cases, more efficient than a drill with attachments. The circular saw blade itself is carried on the end of the motor spindle and secured in position by a special washer with a nut. The other important part of the tool is the sole plate which corresponds to the table of a circular saw bench. This is hinged in two planes so that it can be moved up or down in relation to the blade giving greater or less projection, and can be tilted so that cuts can be made at an angle. There is usually a rip fence provided which can be adjusted so that the circular saw blade can be passed through a piece of timber at a fixed distance from its edge by running the rip fence against the edge of the board.

Although the motor has been designed for the tool's purpose and will provide sufficient power in normal circumstances, it is most important that due consideration be given to the set on the saw blade, the sharpness of the teeth and the rate of feed of the machine along the timber. The set on the saw blade is provided in order to give clearance for the blade itself. In other words the cut made by the blade is wider than the thickness of the blade itself, allowing free running. If, however, too much set is applied to a blade of this nature, a considerable amount of wood has to be removed and this may call for more power than the motor was designed for. If too little set exists on the teeth then the blade will rub in the cut, generating considerable heat and again demanding much more power than would be required under normal circumstances. It is important that the teeth should be kept sharp at

The great advantage of the Wolf saw is its portability, but home workers can easily construct a small table which will convert it into a circular saw bench.

all times with any form of saw, and using a machine of this kind with a blunt blade will effectively shorten its expectation of life.

Anyone who intends to use a portable electric power saw for cutting material such as chipboard, blockboard, plywood, etc. should invest in a tungsten-tipped sawblade. When such a blade is used the rate of feed of the machine along the timber should be reduced slightly, since the kerf is fairly wide and the motor may overheat if the wood is forced along too rapidly. With an ordinary steel blade two or three cuts through a large sheet of chipboard will effectively blunt the blade and, in fact, sparks can usually be seen coming

Above: The experienced operator will often use a portable circular saw in this way, starting the cut by balancing the machine on the forward edge of its sole, it is then slowly returned to its normal operating position so that the blade cuts its own way through the material. This process is *not* recommended for beginners.

Below: A portable saw being used to cross-cut a board to length. Note the use of the guide fence to ensure a square cut.

away from the underside of the material while the blade is cutting. A tungsten-tipped blade will, however, deal effectively with materials of this nature for very long periods before it requires sharpening. The sharpening of such a blade is outside the scope of the home worker, since it requires very expensive machinery, and such blades should be taken to the nearest saw doctor.

The jigsaw
This type of saw is also available as an attachment for an electric drill, but the purpose-built, self-powered version is a very different matter. These tools are extremely effective and are in use in many workshops. The Bosch jigsaw and the Wolf Sapphire are among the leaders and these will deal quite effectively with 50mm (2in) hardwood. For cutting out complicated shapes a really good quality jigsaw will be an excellent investment.

This tool has a sole plate, as does the circular saw, but the blade is secured at one end only and has a reciprocal action. Jigsaws, of course, are only 50% efficient since they must of necessity spend half the time, having executed a cut, in returning to the starting point before executing the next one. They cut, in other words, on the upstroke. Quite a wide variety of blades is available for jigsaws enabling them to cut very thin timber, quite thick hardwoods, plastics, metal and numerous other materials. Throughout this range of blade types there is also a very large number of tooth patterns and although a general purpose blade will serve very well indeed for hobby purposes, those who intend to use a powered jigsaw for commercial operations should ensure that the blade in use is the correct type.

Some modern jigsaws have a special action built into the movement of the blade which enables it to back off from the cut during the downward stroke. This alleviates wear on the blade itself, which would otherwise be rubbing to no purpose on its downward stroke and wasting power, and permits the sawdust to drop clear of the cut, so allowing the blade to cut much more rapidly and at a reduced temperature. Some jigsaws have a small lever on the casing which will enable this degree of orbital action to be varied according to the

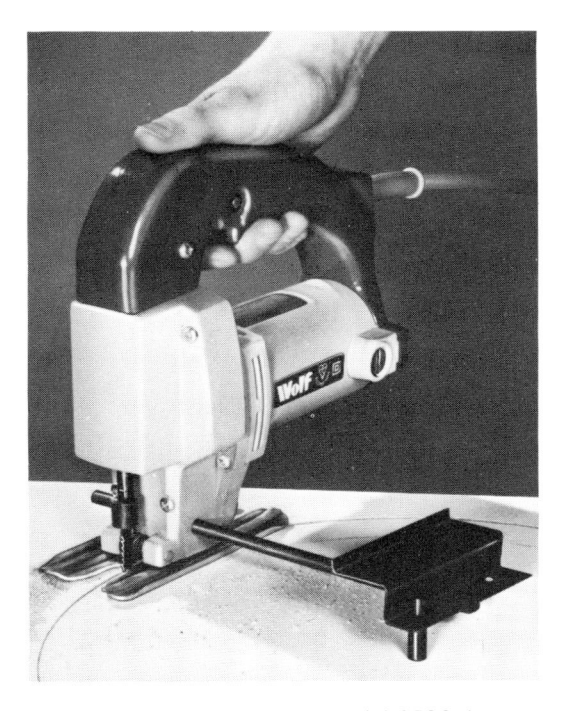

The Wolf Sapphire jigsaw, model 6528, in use with the circle cutting guide which is supplied as standard with each machine.

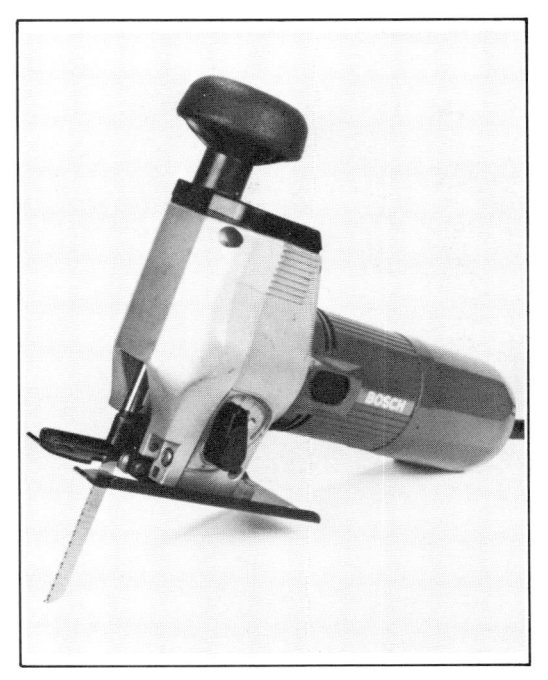

The Bosch heavy-duty jigsaw; these tools are aimed mainly at industry but have become popular with the domestic market.

material being cut. If a very smooth edge is required on the finished article the blade should be allowed to run vertically without any orbital action at all. If the objective is speed of cut without too much regard for the surface of the finished edge, then the full orbital action can be introduced. Obviously, the intervening positions can be utilised as required.

It is as well to make a habit from the very beginning of not placing the fingers below the workpiece being cut. It is quite possible in most situations to hold the timber without doing this, but if the fingers are placed below the workpiece there is every chance of a very serious accident.

Work which is being cut on a bench, or in a horizontal position on the floor of the workshop, must be blocked up with scrap timber so that it is above the floor or bench by more than the depth of cut of the jigsaw blade. If this is not done, the blade may strike the floor and break.

It will be noted that the action of the blade of a jigsaw tends to pull the sole plate of the machine down on to the material while it is operating. It is important that the sole plate be kept flat on the material at all times. Failure to observe this point will result in a high rate of blade breakage.

The jigsaw is an excellent machine for cutting to a marked line, particularly where numerous curves are required to be

71

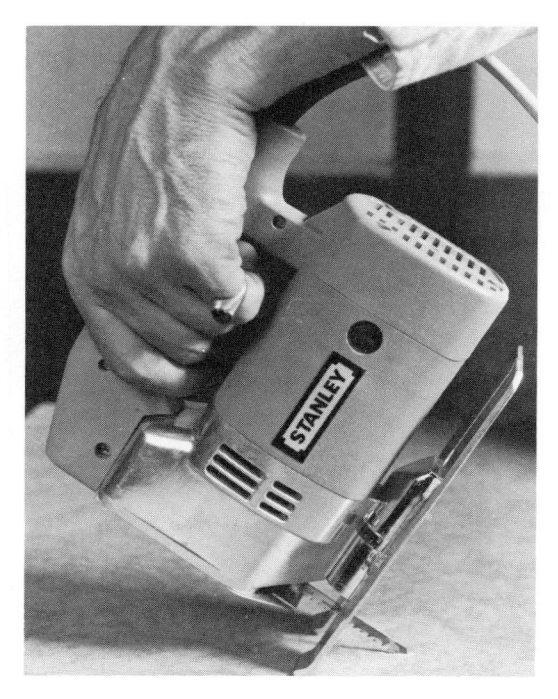

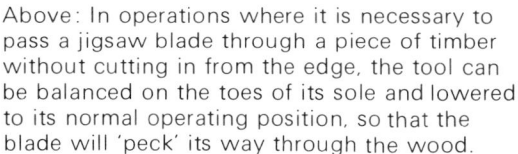

Above: In operations where it is necessary to pass a jigsaw blade through a piece of timber without cutting in from the edge, the tool can be balanced on the toes of its sole and lowered to its normal operating position, so that the blade will 'peck' its way through the wood.

Above right: The orbital sander is strictly a finishing tool and its use is not recommended for the rapid removal of timber. Excellent finishes can be produced with fine abrasive papers.

Below right: Orbital sander with dust extraction unit. Note brush round edge of sander base.

cut. It is not, however, the most efficient machine for straight line cutting which is, of course, the function of a circular saw. It is possible, provided that the blade in use has equal set on both ranges of teeth, to clamp a batten across a piece of timber and run the edge of the sole plate along the edge of the batten so producing a perfectly straight cut. This sounds easy, but if the set is unequal on the two ranges of teeth then the blade will lead to left or right which will result in the tool jamming against the fence or wandering away from it.

Sanders

Portable, self-powered sanders are described as orbital, disc or belt sanders. The disc sander is simply a rubber disc which is covered by a sheet of abrasive material and rotated at high speed. It is not by any means a finishing sander and is used mainly for the removal of paint, de-rusting ironwork and so on. The problem with a sander of this nature is that the abrasive grains must, of necessity, follow a circular path and so will be crossing the grain of the wood frequently. Unless a very fine grade of abrasive paper is used this will result in unsightly scratches on the surface of the work. It is also difficult to prevent

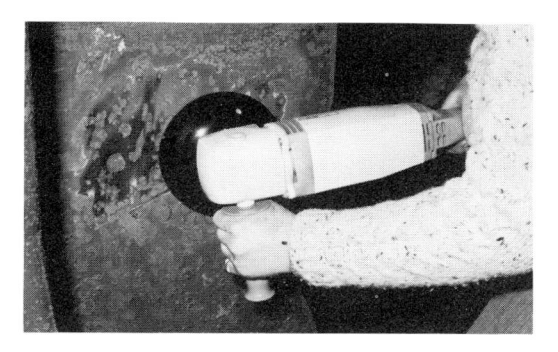

Above left: A Wolf heavy-duty disc sander being used to clean off corroded metalwork.

Below left: Stanley Swirlaway disc sander being used with electric drill. The ingenious ball joint which connects the sander to its arbor enables the disc to be kept flat on the material at all times.

Above right: The portable belt sander has considerable potential. Belts can be changed quickly and easily; a coarse belt will rapidly convert a rough surface to a smooth one and a fine belt will give a magnificent finish. Note the dust extractor bag.

Below right: Belt sander by Elu equipped with a special sub-frame to control the amount of wood being removed.

it from gouging into the wood in odd places.

Orbital sanders are finishing sanders; they do not remove wood rapidly but they can produce a very high quality finish. They have a rectangular base which is covered in thick rubber or similar material over which is stretched a sheet of abrasive paper. This rectangular unit rotates at very high speeds, sometimes in excess of 20,000 rpm, and the grains of the abrasive paper are in fact travelling in very tiny circles. Some sanders of this type have now become quite sophisticated having provision for dust extraction which is quite important for a tool of this kind. If no such provision is made, the dust cannot escape and it is necessary to lift the tool from the wood at frequent intervals in order to remove it. An orbital sander is not the tool to purchase when the rapid removal of timber is required as it is bound to result in considerable disappointment. The tool to be used in such circumstances is the belt sander.

Belt sanders are available as independent machines, mounted on either the bench or

73

The heavy-duty Wolf planer; model 8657, is ideal for reclaiming old timber. It has a 100mm (4in) wide blade and can cut up to 3mm ($\frac{1}{8}$in) deep at one pass.

on the floor so that the work can be passed over them. The portable belt sander also has an important part to play in many forms of woodwork particularly where the workpiece itself is large. The sanding belt on a machine of this kind is of the endless variety and travels over two drums, one of which is powered by the motor. The tool can be used across the grain, at an angle to the grain or in line with the grain. This means that when the object is to remove wood as rapidly as possible a coarse belt is used across the grain and this will reduce the surface of an uneven board very quickly indeed. When it is required to finish the surface of the board the tool will be turned so that the path of the grains is along the

Portable hand planers are excellent for certain applications in joinery. They do not, however, produce entirely satisfactory results when used to plane boards which are wider than the length of the cutter block.

grain of the wood and a fine belt fitted. Excellent surfaces can be produced with powered belt sanders once the operator has acquired the knack of using them. In most cases it is not advisable to allow the belt sander to stop, even for a brief period, on the surface of the wood since it does cut the material away quite quickly and will, therefore, begin to sink into the surface of the timber creating small ridges. Some models have a frame around the underside which prevents the tool from sinking into the wood more than a minute amount. A belt sander, as I have said, removes timber at a phenomenal rate and, therefore, produces a very large quantity of dust. Most portable belt sanders now have some form of dust extraction, usually consisting of a bag attached to the machine into which the dust is drawn by suction.

Unfortunately, this system is not usually entirely efficient and if a machine of this nature is to be used for protracted periods it is advisable to have an alternative dust extraction system, such as are described on page 103.

Portable power planers
The portable power planer is not a particularly popular tool with home woodworkers, although it does have its applications for specialist work. One of the most common of these is the shooting of the bottoms of doors. Since the cutter block is usually not much more than 50mm (2in) in width it performs this function very well indeed but has limited use in the home workshop. It is not uncommon for a powered portable planer to be purchased when the intention is to plane boards of considerable width. This tends

The Elu biscuit jointer. A most unusual and ingenious tool. Used for the accurate joining of man-made materials.

to lead to disappointment since it is not possible to obtain a smooth surface across a wide board with a small planer and ridges will be formed between successive cuts. Although the tool can be used in this manner for the overall levelling of a rough board, a large portable belt sander will be required in the final stages to bring the whole surface to a suitable level condition. Operations which can be performed satisfactorily, however, include rebating and the cleaning up of small workpieces. The power available is quite small compared with that of a large bench planer and it is important when using a machine of this kind to ensure that the rate of feed along the timber is not excessive. If the tool is fed too fast there will be a drastic reduction in the rpm overloading the motor and resulting in a poor surface finish.

Just as a small portable power saw works in the same way as a large saw bench, so the small powered planer works along the same lines as the large bench planer. In both cases the portable tool can be considered in the light of the larger bench machine, operating upside down. Depth of cut on a bench planer is varied by adjusting the height of the feed table and the same principle applies to the small hand machine. As with a bench planer, a number of light cuts will produce better results than one heavy one and bearing in mind the small power available it is obviously essential for the knives to be kept razor sharp at all times. Most portable powered planers are supplied with a honing jig and in some cases a special oilstone so that the knives can be slipped out of the block and honed up frequently. Failure to follow this practice will result in dull edges and this will cause the motor

Angled planing of board edge with portable powered planer. Note use of fence.

to be overloaded and shorten the life of the machine.

A point which is frequently overlooked is that when timber is passed across the table of a bench-mounted planing machine it is supported fully by those tables. When the situation is reversed and a portable planer, which is fairly heavy, is passed across the timber care must be taken to ensure that the weight of the planer does not cause the timber to bend so producing inaccuracy in the cut.

Unlikely though it may seem, far too many accidents occur with portable electric planers because of the manner in which hand smoothing planes are frequently used. A person who is accustomed to using a hand plane will frequently place his fingers below the plane, resting on its sole, particularly when running along the edge of a board. Old habits, unfortunately, die hard — and it is unpleasant to consider the results of this practice when applied to a powered machine. Conversely, those who have been properly trained in the use of hand planes will always place them on the bench on their sides rather than sole downwards. This practice may well be applied to a powered planer since it is equally undesirable for the cutters to come into contact with the surface of the bench. As is the case with other powered machinery, the cutter block should be allowed to stop before the machine is laid down. It is very dangerous to put a machine down while it is still rotating at a fairly high speed, even though it is switched off.

The setting of the cutters in a portable power planer is along the same lines as that for a bench machine. In both cases the setting must be done accurately and checked from time to time and it is bad practice to change one cutter without changing the other; they should be used in pairs in order to keep the cutter block correctly in balance. One further point which is often the cause of shortening the life of these machines is that they are allowed to run for relatively long periods when they are not, in fact, cutting and it is as well to make a point of switching them off when they are not in use.

Elu biscuit jointer

This is a fascinating portable tool which is of tremendous value to those who are engaged in construction from such materials as chipboard or plywood. It has many specialist uses and can produce strong joints in a very short space of time.

It is a fairly expensive tool, but for commercial application this is a minor consideration since it is capable of recovering its cost quite quickly. For the home workshop it is perhaps a little too expensive since it is a single purpose tool likely to spend most of its time in a cupboard or drawer. The idea is very ingenious and I must confess to having been very favourably impressed when I first tried the machine out. Basically, it consists of a powerful motor, contained in a small cylindrical body, driving a special saw blade. There is a sole plate which equates to that used on a portable power saw and a fence which can be adjusted to vary the position of the saw cut in relation to the edge of the timber. The machine can be used for the cutting of grooves and housings in addition to its normal function.

Small 'biscuits' manufactured from compressed timber are used in the jointing, these being elliptical in shape. The machine works on the principle that when plunged into the wood it produces a curved slot which will accept one half of a biscuit. The success of a joint made with this machine will depend on the accuracy with which it has been set initially, but assuming correct setting, first-class joints can be produced. The biscuits are coated in glue before the joint is assembled and this soaks into the compressed timber causing it to swell and the strength of the joint is quite surprising. Datum marks are provided on the machine so that they can be lined up with marks on the wood to ensure accuracy and when the machine has been used a few times the production of good joints becomes a very simple matter. In fact, an effective joint between, for example, two pieces of chipboard can be effected in an amazingly short time.

Chapter five

The Pillar Drill

I am always surprised at the relatively low popularity of pillar drills and this may be due to general ignorance of the versatility and usefulness of this machine among amateur workers. In listing machinery in order of priority to set up a workshop I would place a pillar drill very high on the list, quite close to the circular saw and planer/thicknesser. Machines of this kind are to be found in almost every metal-working shop, yet they are also of tremendous value to a woodworker, and those who have had access to one for any length of time will fully appreciate its worth.

A pillar drill can be divided into four basic parts, the base, the column, the table and the head. The base should be heavy, of sufficient size to afford reasonable stability and provided with bolt holes for securing it to the floor. In most cases it also forms a working table for use when very long workpieces have to be drilled. The term head refers to the motor, drilling spindle, pulley guard, operating levers, clamps, etc. The head is attached to the upper end of the column and can normally be moved up or down. The table can also be moved up or down the column and can be pivoted about the column if necessary. On most machines currently available the table is not capable of being tilted which is

Heavy-duty drilling machine shown here with a short pillar for bench mounting.

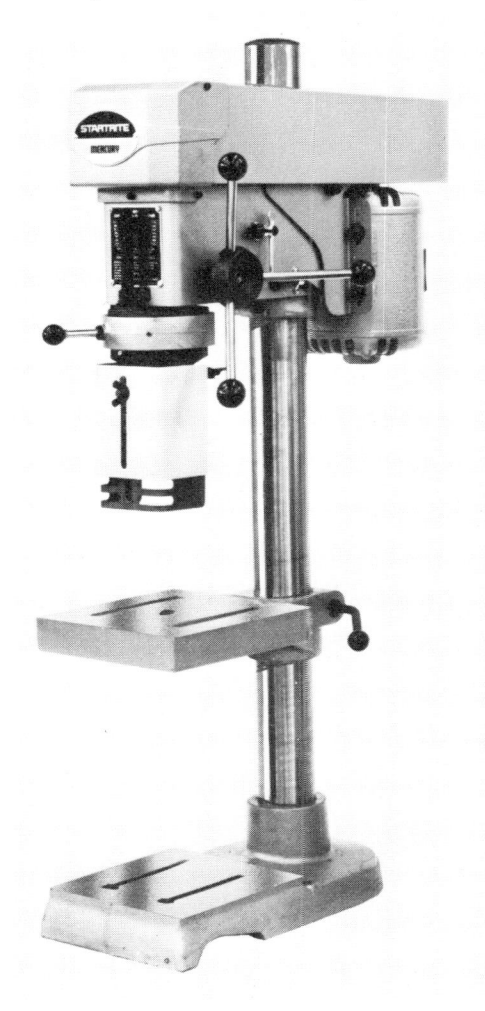

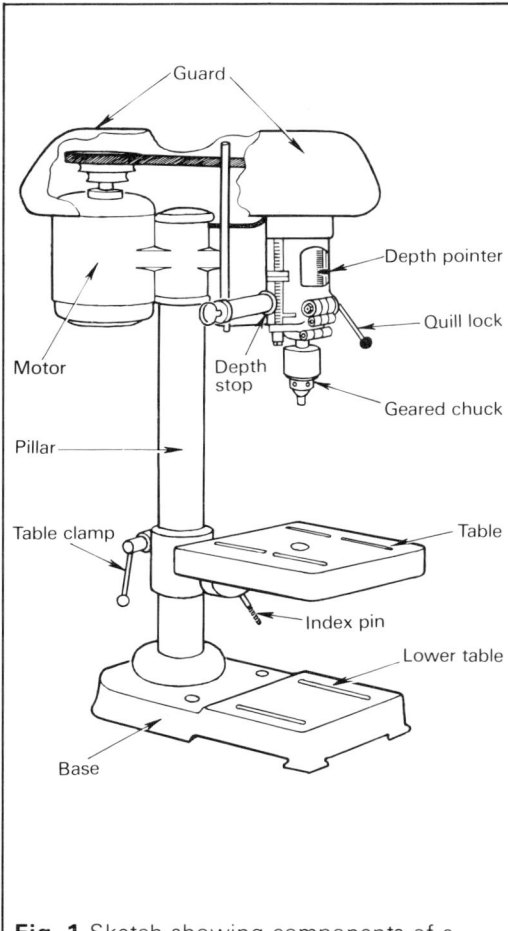

Fig. 1 Sketch showing components of a typical pillar drill.

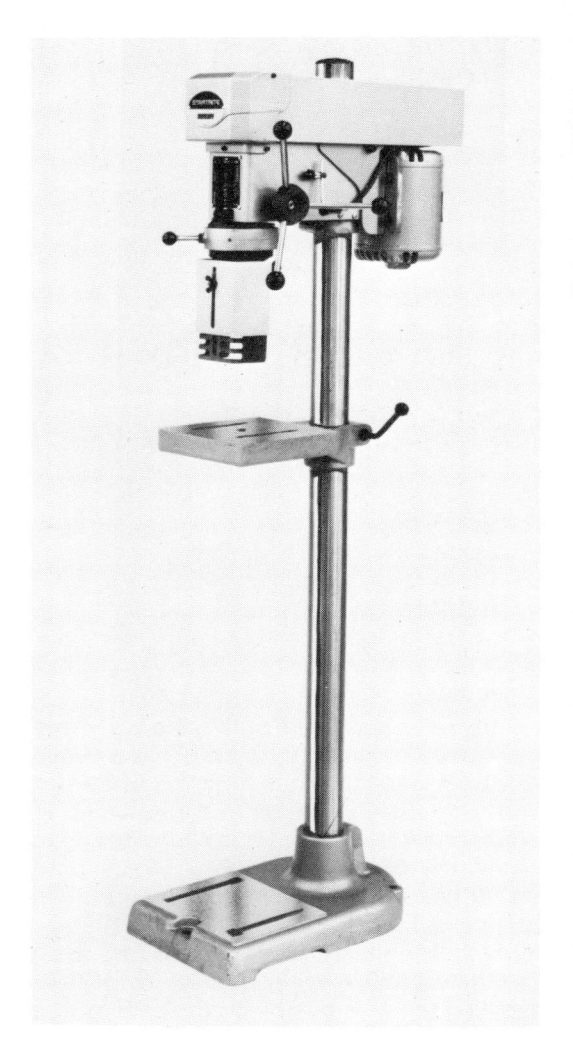

Floor standing pillar drill for heavy-duty operations.

unfortunate since a tilting table is of great value for angled drilling.

The important part of a pillar drill is the vertical spindle which rotates about its vertical axis and carries at its lower end a geared chuck, which is similar to the type fitted to electric drills but a great deal larger. This chuck, like that on the drill, is tightened or loosened by means of a key. The spindle carrier can be moved up or down by means of a lever and is spring loaded so that it will return to its normal position when the lever is released. An adjustable depth stop is normally provided with two nuts which can be tightened to lock it in position to ensure accurate drilling to a required depth. Most pillar drills now run with either a half or three quarter horsepower motor which is certainly adequate for woodworking purposes.

Pillar drills are available as floor standing models, with a long column, or for bench mounting, in which case the column is considerably shorter. There is remarkably little difference in the price of the two and the floor standing model is preferable if space permits. The tension of the belt on a machine of this kind is not by any means critical but it should be adjusted so that the belt does not slip under normal loads. Tensioning is effected by moving the motor closer to, or further away from the column.

The table of a pillar drill has a hole at the centre and in use this hole is normally positioned so that the drill, when passing right through a workpiece, can be passed through the hole without damaging itself or the metal of the table. Slots are also provided in the table to be used when it is necessary to clamp workpieces securely in position.

On most models the return spring which takes the feed lever back to its original position is adjustable, and full instructions for adjustment are provided in the manufacturer's handbook.

Most pillar drills have a drive system which has four or five available speeds. The slow speeds are used when large cutters such as saw tooth bits or Forstner pattern bits are employed, whereas when using spade bits, or flat bits as they are sometimes called, a high speed is desirable. The speed is changed by moving the drive belt from one pair of pulleys to another.

Some other types of cutter which are likely to be of use to the woodworker are the solid centre bit, the machine spur bit, the hollow spiral bit with either single or double fluted configuration and the double spur

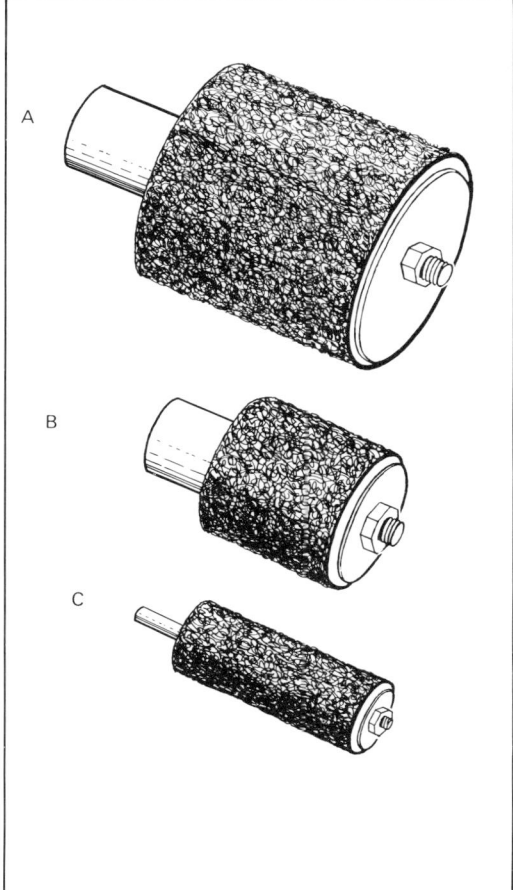

Fig. 4 Rubber sanding drum for use on drill press. When in use rubber expands so holding sanding belt firmly.

bit which has a solid centre. The multi spur bit is another name for the saw tooth pattern and some people refer to flat bits as centre bits. All these cutters can be sharpened by the home worker by means of small files. It is important to keep all drill bits clean and free from deposits of resin and dust which can cause them to become overheated.

Another application of the pillar drill is the

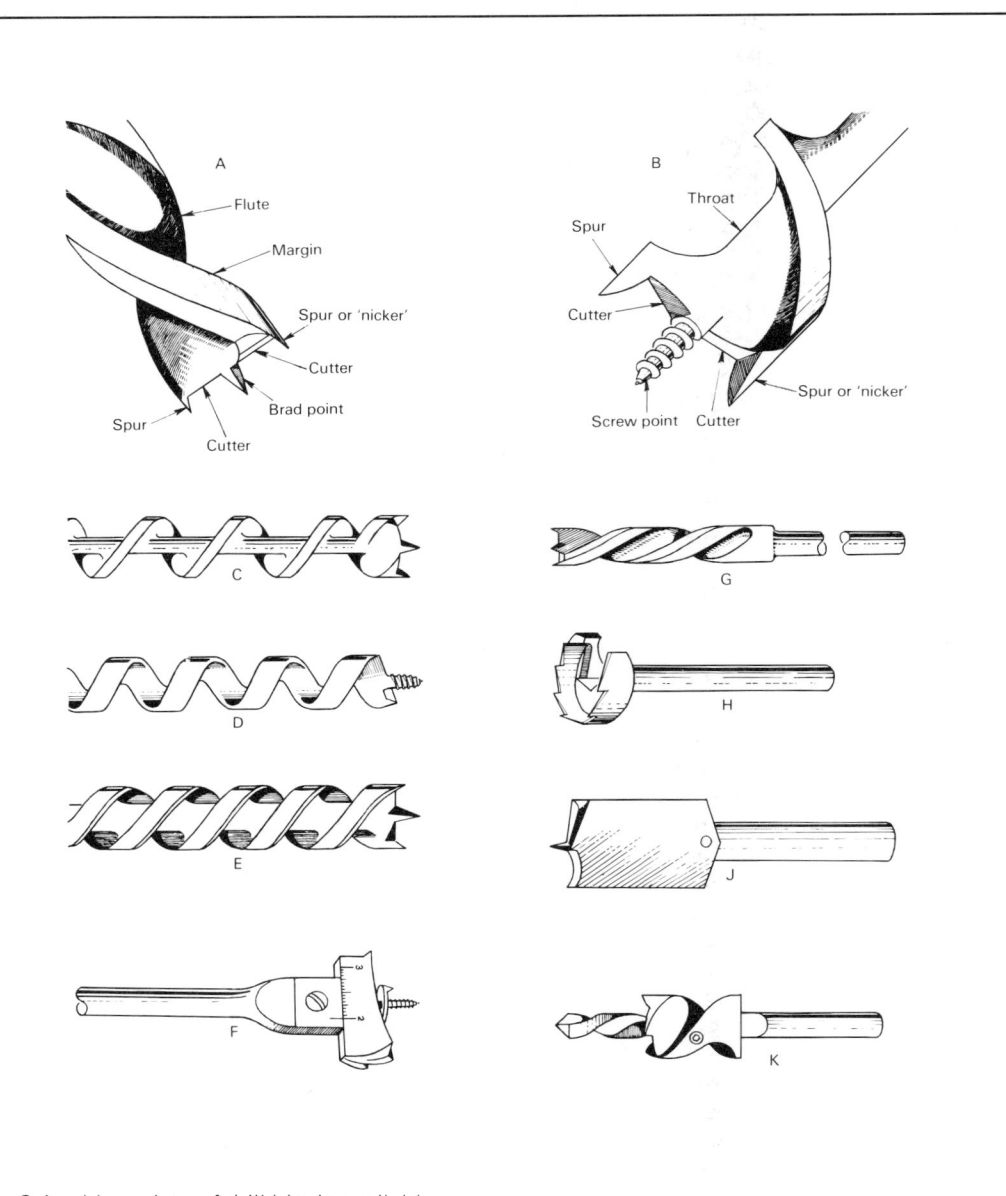

Fig. 2 A wide variety of drill bits is available for the pillar drill, some are shown here. The type shown at **F** are not to be used on any powered machine unless held in a brace.

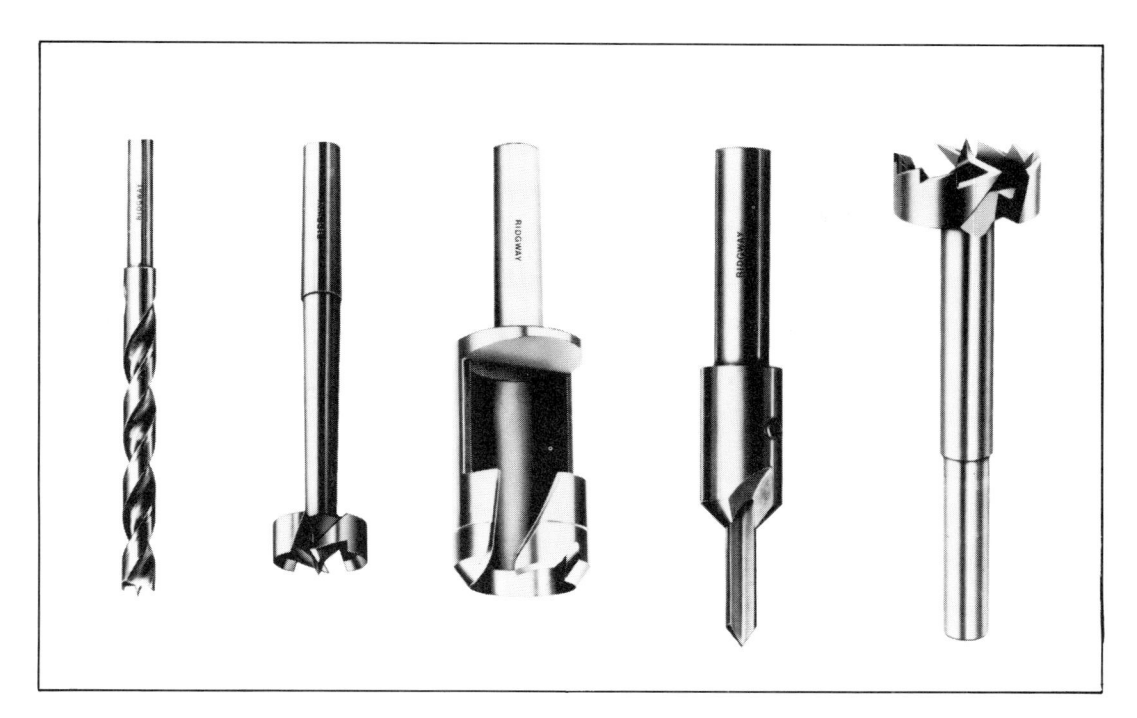

Left to right:
Fast-cutting twist bit for machine work.

Forstner pattern bit has knife edge and radial blades to remove waste.

A plug cutter. When used in a vertical drill press it will produce wooden plugs with cross grain for hiding sunken screws.

This cutter pre-drills for screws, and produces countersink for screw heads.

Saw tooth bit. The teeth cut a circular trench and the radial blades remove the central area.

use of small sanding drums. These can be set so that they are rotating just above the table surface and are extremely useful for sanding the edges of curved work moved along against them.

Using the pillar drill
There is nothing critical about the speed at which this machine is run for drilling timber but it must be borne in mind that high speeds will create considerable friction when large cutters are in use and since large cutters are extremely expensive it is as well to use the lowest satisfactory speed in order to lessen any risk of softening of the metal through excess of heat. Most workers tend to use a wooden table clamped in position across the metal table of the machine so that it is not necessary to have the drill centred exactly over the hole in the metal table. The wooden table can be bolted in position, the heads of the bolts being dropped below the working surface and passed through the slits in the table of the machine itself.

Accuracy is very important in marking out work for drilling and provided the wood which is being drilled has sufficient support from the wooden table there should be no trouble with splintering when the cutter

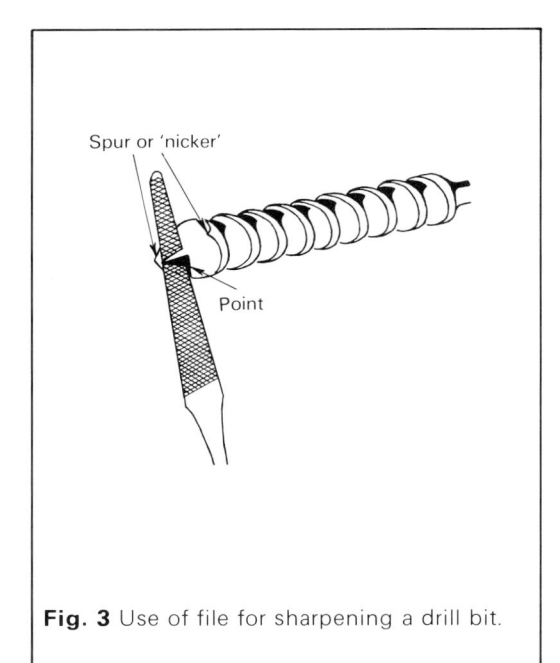

Fig. 3 Use of file for sharpening a drill bit.

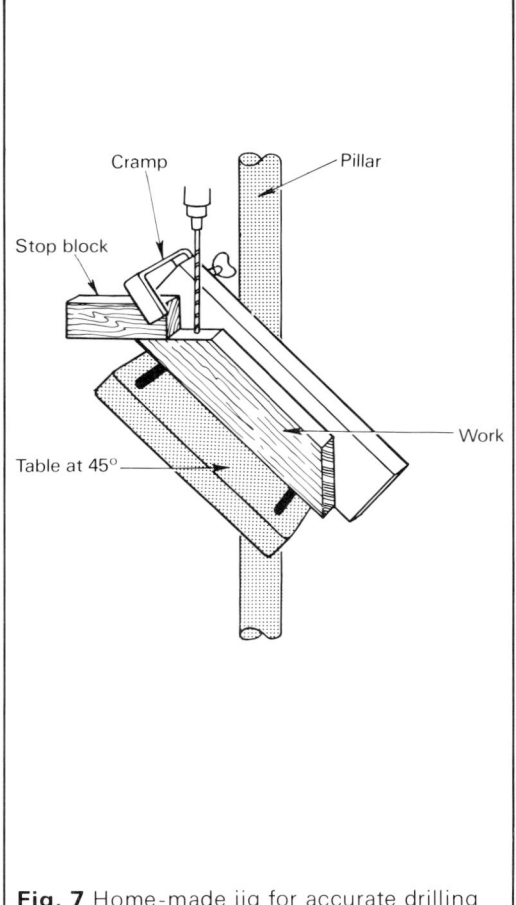

Fig. 7 Home-made jig for accurate drilling of mitred joints.

emerges. In some cases it is possible to reverse the position of the wood after drilling half-way through, and to complete the cut from the other side which will make certain that the edges are clean. Very small holes up to 12mm ($\frac{1}{2}$in) are normally drilled with a twist bit as used in electric drills.

As is the case with bandsaws or circular saws, drilling of circular workpieces can present problems. One common requirement is the drilling of radial holes in cylindrical workpieces and if these are not drilled accurately the resulting job can look very bad indeed. To ensure that the holes being drilled pass exactly through the centre of the wood, or are radial to the workpiece, a block of wood is clamped to the drilling table with a suitable sized V groove cut in it. The block of wood is positioned so that when the drill is brought down its point will come exactly to the centre of the V groove. A circular workpiece laid in this groove will obviously be drilled correctly and there is no danger of the work suddenly twisting.

A similar system can be employed when it is necessary to drill into the edge of a disc, as for example when drilling a hole through a base of a table lamp to permit the passage of the flex. For this purpose, an L-shaped wooden jig is made, to the

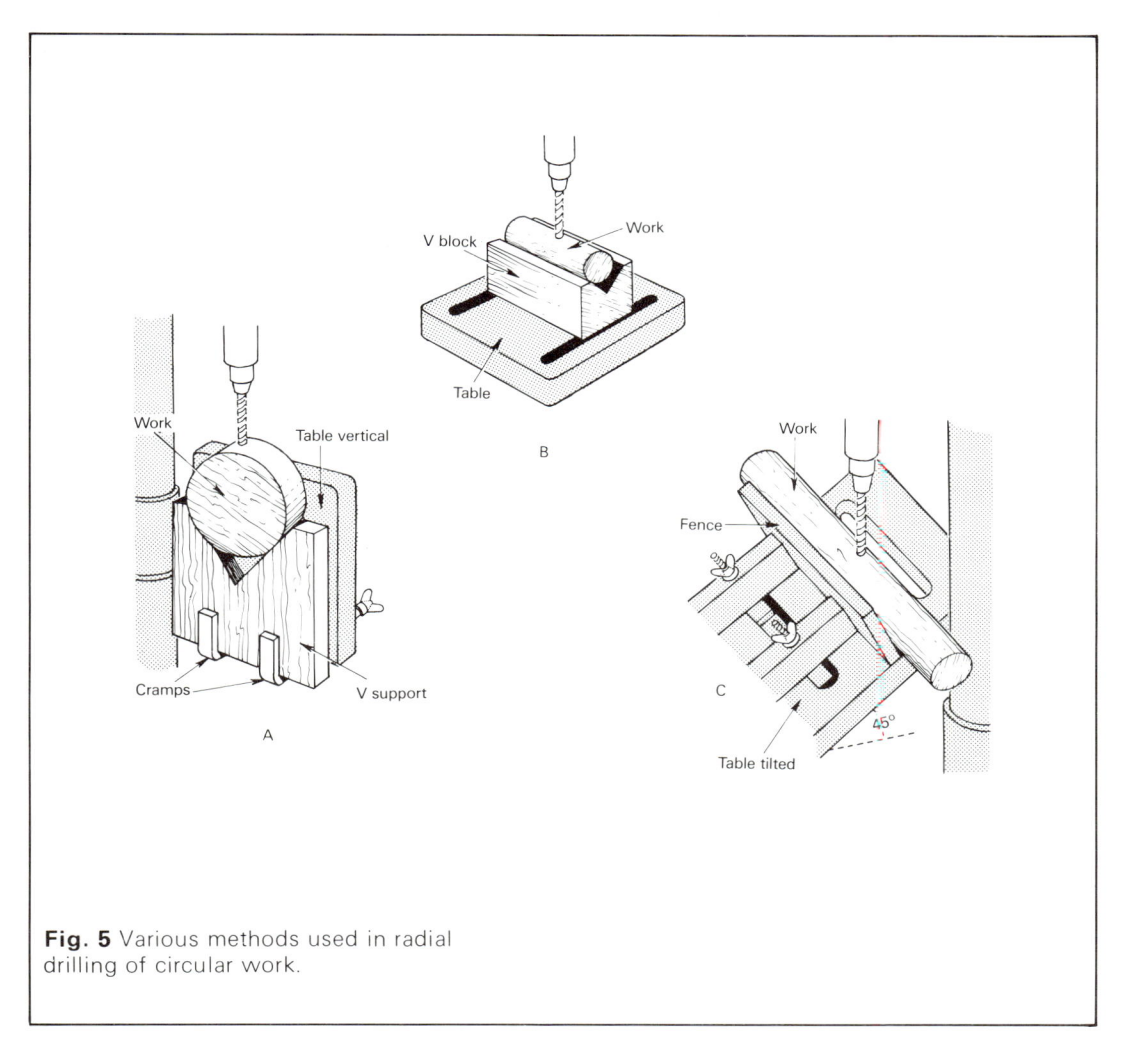

Fig. 5 Various methods used in radial drilling of circular work.

front face of which is attached a board with a large V-shaped cutout. The disc is dropped into the V and can be clamped by means of a G cramp to the upright section. Again, before the jig is used a check should be made to see that the point of the drill is lined up exactly with the centre of the V. Care must be taken in all forms of drilling to ensure that a cutter which is fluted is not taken into the wood beyond the upper ends of the flutes. If it is there will be no method by which the chips can escape and the tool will rapidly become very hot indeed.

In the drilling of holes up to 37mm (1½in) in diameter the torque produced is relatively insignificant; in using larger cutters than these, however, the workpiece should be clamped firmly to the table or it may suddenly twist, with the attendant possibility of injury to the worker's hand.

83

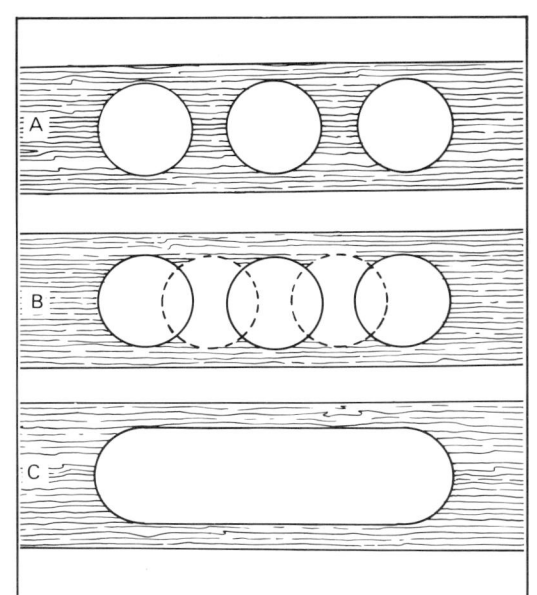

Fig. 6 Stages in boring out a mortice on a pillar drill.

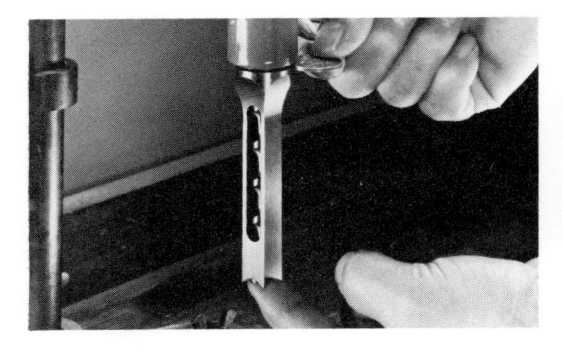

Setting up chisel and bit in a Wolf mortiser; cutter and bit are set level with coin in place, then bit is secured, coin removed and chisel pushed fully home to give correct clearance.

For the purpose of assembling many woodworking projects it will be necessary to use woodscrews and if the holes for these are to be pre-drilled in the correct manner the process is rather time consuming. It can in fact all be done in one operation by using the extremely useful Stanley Screwmates as described on page 67.

Some projects will require the drilling of quite a large number of holes, equally spaced, along a workpiece. This can be done by marking out each hole carefully by means of a pencil and a rule but the operation can be greatly speeded up by using a simple spacing pin technique. For this purpose a batten can be clamped along the back of the wooden sub-table to act as a fence. A small nail can be driven into the sub-table at the required distance from the drill itself and when one hole has been drilled it can be placed over the small nail and the second one drilled. If this process is repeated the holes will be equally spaced along the job. A simple method of establishing the correct position for the nail is to mark the positions of the first two holes on the first workpiece and drill them both. With the drill itself left in position in the second hole it then becomes a simple matter to pass the nail through the first hole and tap it firmly home.

The drilling machine can be used for very satisfactory mortising, most of these tools do in fact have mortising attachments available as optional extras. The exact procedure for mortising is discussed on page 122 but it should be noted that quite good mortising can be produced with a pillar drill simply by marking the mortise out and removing most of the waste with an ordinary drill bit, finishing by hand with a sharp chisel.

Chapter six

The Portable Router

Routers are fascinating tools, but probably the least well understood of all woodworking machines in amateur hands. In recent years a great deal of work has been done to improve this and more and more woodworkers are discovering the tremendous versatility of the tool. It would probably be much quicker to explain what cannot be done with a router rather than to go into full detail as to what can be achieved and there is no doubt that the more ingenious the worker, the more benefit he will derive from a machine of this nature.

The router has a very high-speed electric motor, on the shaft of which is mounted a chuck to hold small cutting tools. The motor is mounted in what is, in effect, a sophisticated jig which enables accurate depth-setting and positioning of cutter relative to the work. These machines are used widely in light industry for the cutting of plastics and metal and many of the applications of a router enable a small commercial enterprise to step up its production considerably. Although a router may seem to be quite a complicated machine, particularly to anyone who has never used it, very little skill is required to produce first-class work. The use of a router is in fact more common sense than anything else and an inventive turn of mind used in the designing and construction of wooden jigs will extend the capacity of the machine. The incredible versatility of a router means the range of applications to which they can be put is perhaps wider than any other power tool.

There is insufficient space available to go into all the possibilities open to the owner of a router so the most sensible approach will be to take a look at one specific

Elu plunging router. Depth of cut can be accurately set, and the plunging action is controlled by the lever (lower left of name plate).

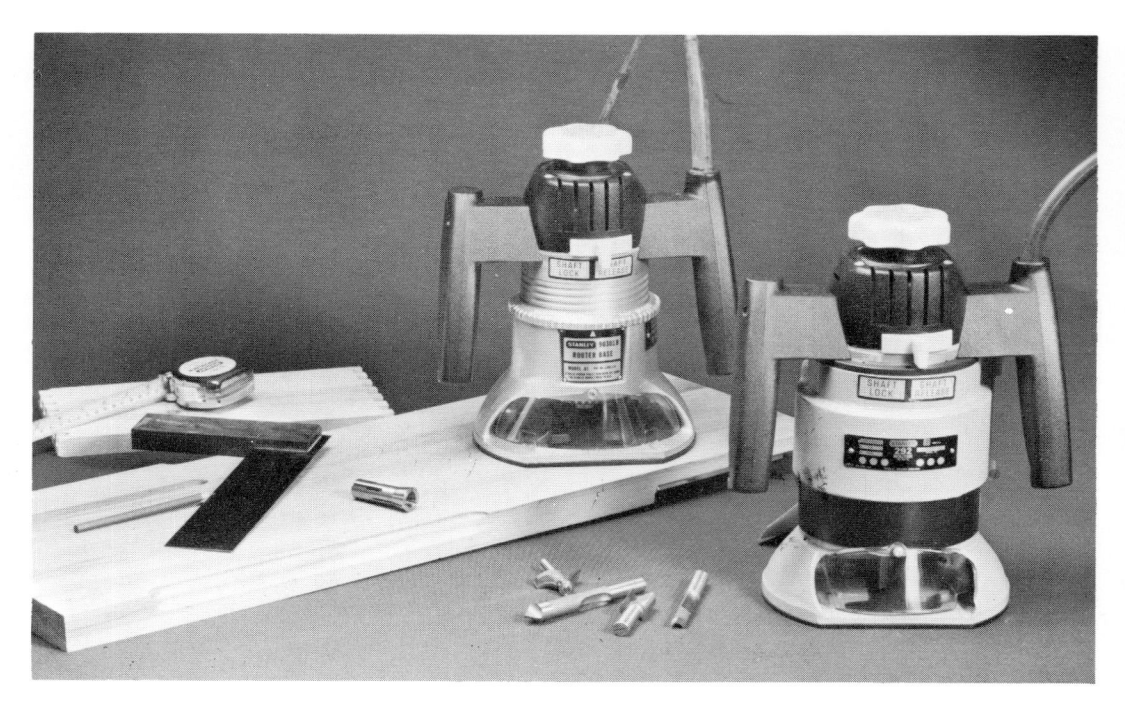

Heavy-duty production router from Stanley. These are capable of continuous use and heavy cuts.

machine and some of the more normal applications in which it excels. The machine I have chosen for this purpose is the Elu model MOF96 plunging router, which is frequently chosen by home workers. Those who envisage long periods of use or heavy cutting requirements would be well advised to purchase the MOF31 which is a heavier machine.

The Elu MOF96 router is beautifully made and has a double insulated electric motor. This system has found considerable popularity with portable power tools over recent years and, for the benefit of those who are not familiar with it, I should perhaps explain that it removes the necessity for an earth wire and offers a very high degree of protection for the user against electric shock. The machine also has a thermal overload protection system to prevent the burning out of the armature in situations of high overload. An important feature from the point of view of safety is that the router, when operated as a portable machine, is so designed as to have its cutter projecting below the base *only when actually cutting*. The design gives very good visibility, which is an important point in the use of a router and the plunging system permits the cutter to be fed into the work and retracted from it at right-angles to the work surface.

Cutters can be changed in a few moments using two spanners which are provided with the machine, one holds the spindle and prevents it rotating whilst the other operates the collet chuck. The MOF96 is supplied with a 6mm ($\frac{1}{4}$in) collet and it should be noted that cutters with large shanks such as 10mm or 12mm ($\frac{3}{8}$in or $\frac{1}{2}$in) diameter cannot be used in this

This simple but highly efficient attachment for the trimming of laminates is available for the Stanley router. The normal plastic sub-base of the router is removed and the unit shown here is fitted in its place.

Stanley 263 Laminate Trimmer. Not the sort of tool which is likely to be found in a home workshop, but very useful for the commercial user. Will rapidly trim overhangs of laminate flush to the surface.

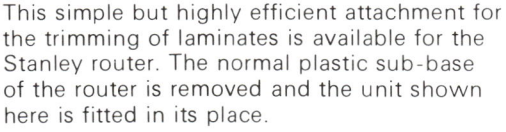

machine. They can, however, be used in the industrial models. The machine referred to here is supplied with collet nut and collet, adjustable side fence with guide rods, guide bush follower, straight flute cutter 19mm ($\frac{3}{4}$in) diameter with 19mm ($\frac{3}{4}$in) shank and straight flute cutter 12mm ($\frac{1}{2}$in) diameter with 19mm ($\frac{3}{4}$in) shank.

When the cutter has been fitted securely into the collet the machine is placed on a flat surface and depressed until the tip of the cutter is resting on the surface. The plunging movement is controlled by a turn to the left or to the right of one of the two guide knobs, or grip handles. The router is locked in this position simply by turning the knob clockwise a quarter of a turn. The required depth of cut can now be set by moving the depth bolt to the desired position and securing it there by means of the thumb screw. The distance between the head of the screw on the rotary turret and the bottom of the depth bar is now the depth to which the cutter will plunge.

The side fence is extremely useful and is fitted to the base of the router by sliding the rods into the holes and securing them by means of the thumb screws. If the machine has been set up as described above to a pre-set plunging depth it can now be placed on the work with the motor running, depressed to its full extent, and locked in that position by means of the handle.

When cutting is finished the cutter can be retracted before lifting the machine from the work. Routers, when working along the edge of timber, should always be fed in the opposite direction to the cutter rotation, as illustrated on page 93.

Using the router
Because of the very high speed of the motor, something in the order of 20,000 rpm or more, the noise factor has to be taken into consideration. Routers emit a high-pitched noise and many operators wear a pair of ear defenders in order to avoid side effects, such as headaches. For the amateur who uses a router occasionally in his home workshop this point is not perhaps of great significance, but anyone who is expected to use one all day and every day, must certainly give it a thought.

The difference between a plunging router and the non-plunging variety, is that with the latter the desired projection of cutter from the base of the machine must be made, the machine then being taken to the job. This means that on many occasions the cutter will be rotating below the router base when it is not actually in the wood, and this is potentially dangerous. With the plunging type of router the cutter is above the base at all times except when cutting, and so gives greater protection to the operator. Standard types of router which do not have a plunging facility are, in general, excellent tools capable of very good work. There is no doubt, however, that the plunging facility is well worth the extra cost.

Another point which must be borne in mind is that with a plunging router the depth of cut can be pre-set, the machine taken to the work and placed upon it, the carriage then being pushed down so that the cutter enters the material to the desired depth. Not only is the operator certain of achieving this depth, but he can also be sure that the cutter will enter the work at exactly 90° without damaging the surface in any way, both when starting the cut and when finishing it.

The design of the Elu router enables the operator to have an excellent view of what he is doing at all times, the lower part of the machine being uncluttered. This particular router is also fitted with turret stops with screws projecting from them which can be set to given distances, so that when the router is plunged into the work its downward progress will be arrested by the head of the particular screw which is lined up with the depth-setting rod. One advantage of this is that when a fairly deep cut is to be undertaken it can be done in two or three stages, rather than in one heavy cut. The turret is set to give the depth for the first cut, which is completed. The turret is then rotated so that the correct depth for the second cut is provided and so on. This means that the router does not have to be taken away from the job in order to reset the cutter depth.

As with many other woodworking machines, the intending purchaser should consider the power of the tool with some care. It is most important for every woodworking machine to have adequate power, and the power which should be considered is the output rather than the input. Some machines are listed as being one horsepower or one and a half horsepower, but investigation will frequently reveal that this is the input power and that the power actually delivered is considerably less. This should be checked when a router is purchased since routers do require a fairly high amount of power for some operations. It is also very important that the motor is of high quality with an armature properly engineered to withstand the heat generated in operation.

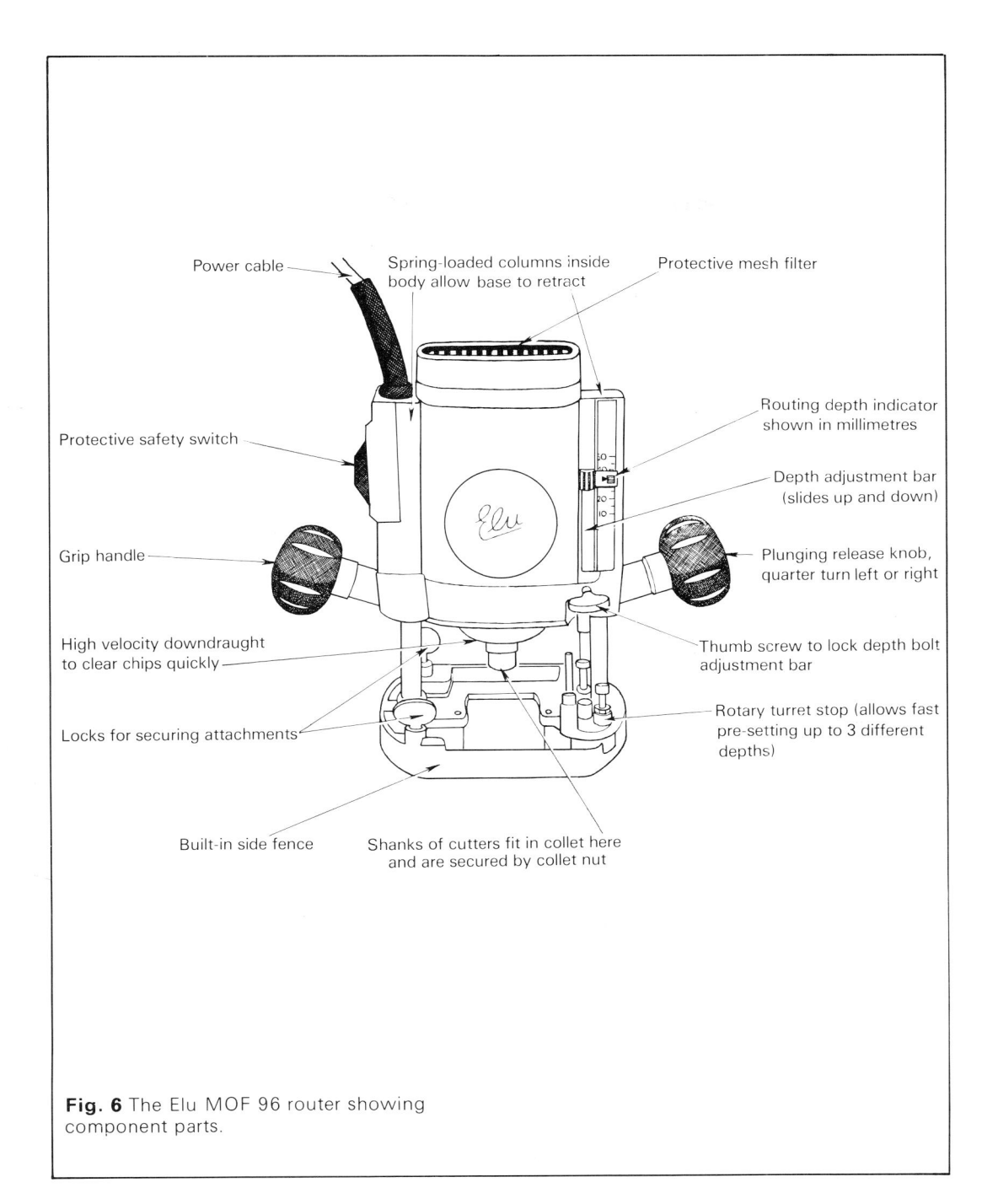

Fig. 6 The Elu MOF 96 router showing component parts.

The most common abuse of portable routers is the overloading of the motor through taking heavy cuts, or through the use of blunt cutters. The manufacturers of the Elu router state that a blunt cutter may overload a motor by as much as 400 per cent and I see no reason to doubt this. It would be a great pity to buy a relatively expensive piece of machinery which is quite capable of lasting for many years and giving good service and then to overload it in this way, when all that is needed is a few moments to sharpen the cutter. By the same token, when cuts of any reasonable depth are required it is important that these are done in two or three stages rather than in one pass. The cutting of grooves or routing out of areas which are quite deep by setting the router to cut the full depth at once will also result in overloading the motor as well as overheating the cutter and softening the metal. In fact, to rout out an area with a cutter which is set too deep is wasting time rather than saving it, since if the job is done in two or three easy stages it can be completed at a much greater speed. The operator should at all times listen to the note of the router motor, from which he can judge whether or not the machine is being overloaded. This may at first seem to be a trifle difficult, but with practice it becomes instinctive. The third way of overloading the motor is the too rapid rate of feed which is sometimes employed. This is where experienced judgement is required since if the rate of feed to a router cutter is too slow there will be too much friction and the cutter may be softened and ruined, often indicated by the burning of both the cutter and the wood. If, on the other hand, the rate of feed is too high the note of the router motor will drop considerably, and the motor will become overheated. It should be remembered that it is the output of power when the machine is under load which is the real test of a router, rather than the theoretically available power when the machine is running free.

It is very important with any woodworking machine that when making adjustments, or changing cutters, the plug should be *removed from the mains socket*. It is not sufficient just to switch the machine off. The plug *must* always be removed from the socket.

One item which may be extremely useful to the new owner of a router, if he has enough money left over to purchase it, is the routing machine table manufactured by Elu for use with its routers. This is an extremely well-made table, into which the router can be inserted from below, effectively turning the unit into a small spindle moulder. More details of this appear on page 91.

Cutting out shapes

Shaped work can be carried out effectively on a bandsaw but it does mean that the edges have to receive quite a lot of attention with abrasives in order to get them finished smoothly enough. The use of a router for this kind of job leaves the work with really silken edges requiring no further attention, thereby speeding up the whole process considerably. A router with a plunging facility would be even more advantageous. The procedure for cutting out shapes, be they apertures in doors, or for windows, or shapes such as I have just referred to, is as follows.

The material to be cut is placed securely on supports on the bench so that it is clear of the bench surface and unable to move during the cutting. With a suitable cutter fitted in the machine, having sufficient length to penetrate the material being cut, the router is placed flat on the material to be cut, the plunge lever is

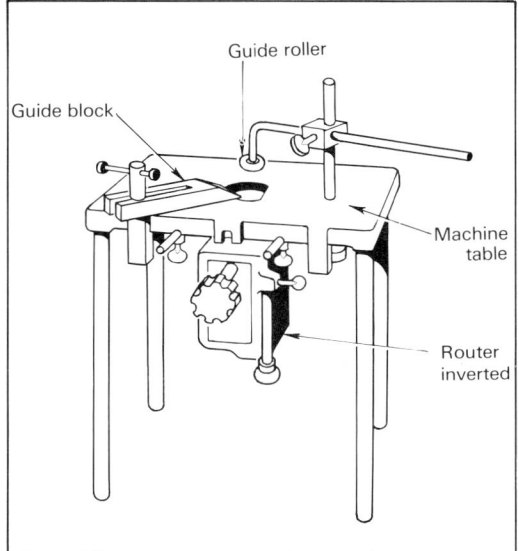

Fig. 2 The router, when inverted into a suitable table, can be used with a guide roller bearing for circular work.

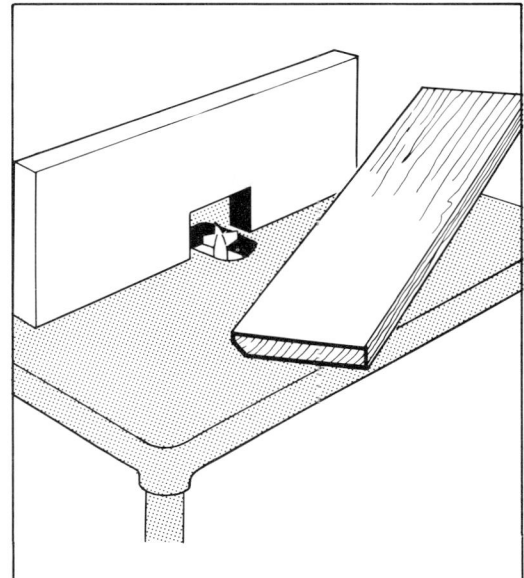

Fig. 3 When fitted to a suitable table, the router becomes a small spindle moulder.

depressed and the carriage pushed down until the cutter touches the workpiece whereupon the lever is released, locking the router in that position. A turret stop with three heads on it means the cutting out of a shape can be performed in three stages. The longest screw is set to permit penetration of the timber by a third of its thickness. The second screw, or medium screw as it is normally described, is set to allow the cutter to penetrate by twice the depth of the first cut, and the short screw is adjusted so that the cutter will penetrate the material, emerging by about 1·5mm ($\frac{1}{16}$in). The router is now switched on and is plunged to the depth permitted by the long screw, the lever then being released to lock it in that position. The first cut is made around the design, until it meets its starting point, whereupon the turret is rotated to allow the medium screw to come under the stop rod, the lever is depressed and the router is plunged to the depth of the stop, the cut then being repeated. The same process will be followed for the third cut, rotating the turret once more and plunging the router so that the cutter will in fact penetrate the material and the piece which is being cut out will drop through on to the bench top as the cut is completed. The lever is now depressed, which will allow the router carriage to move back to its original position, the cutter being above the router base where it is safe. The motor can now be switched off. This system can be applied to cutting out all manner of shapes with a router which is a very intriguing pastime.

Note that when a router cutter is working completely in the material, as when cutting out a shape, it can be moved from left to right, or right to left, without any great difference being obvious. When it is cutting along the edge of a piece of material, however, it is important to move the

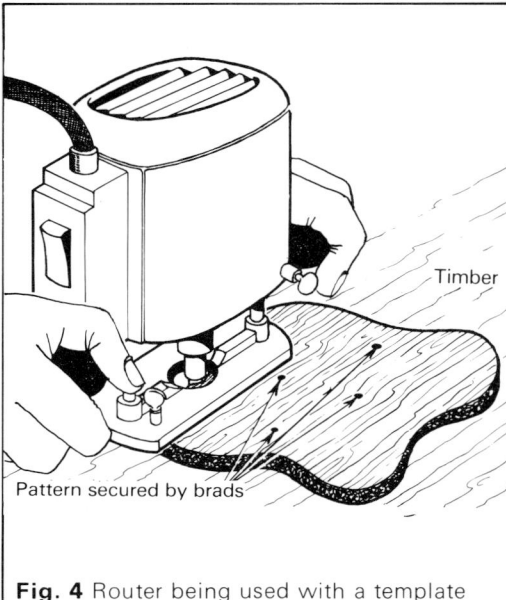

Fig. 4 Router being used with a template guide to cut out shapes.

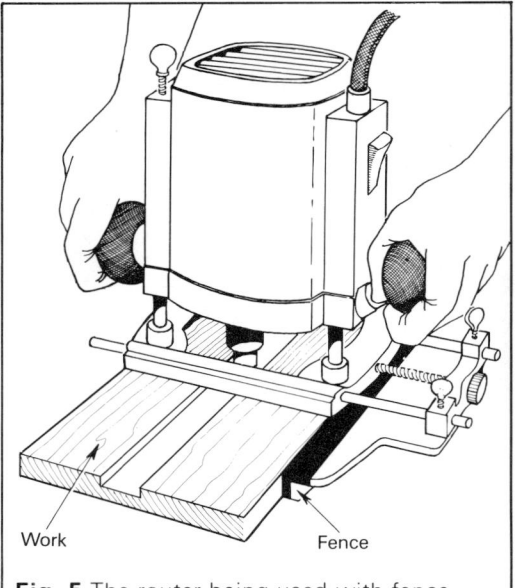

Fig. 5 The router being used with fence to cut the groove for a drawer side.

router so that the rotation of the cutter is into the direction of the movement. Routers cut very well indeed, and most cuts can be made at a satisfactory speed. Great care, however, must be taken to see that they are not overloaded or the motor will suffer in the long run.

Cutting grooves
One of the common functions of a router is the cutting of grooves and housings which are used in the making of cabinets and the fitting of shelves. When a groove has to be cut along the length of a workpiece the guide fence provided with the router can be fitted. This runs along the edge of the material being routed and can be positioned so that the cutter is in the desired place. Provided that the fence is kept firmly against the work throughout the cut, complete accuracy is ensured, but if the groove to be routed is of any real depth it will again be best to cut it in two or three passes. There will be numerous instances where housings or stopped housings have to be cut in timber at points where the guide fence cannot be employed. This is not too much of a problem since a piece of straight-edged batten can be placed across the wood at exactly 90° and clamped into position so that the router, when riding against it, will have its cutter exactly where it is needed. This type of sub-fence can be used for quite a lot of operations. A router which has a sharp cutter and is used correctly will produce a magnificent finish by virtue of the high speed of its cutter. If the finish being produced is poor the cutter should be sharpened and the operator should check that the rate of feed is correct.

Mouldings
The router can also be used for the production of mouldings along the edge of workpieces as, perhaps, in putting a

A router cutting a housing, note the use of the adjustable side fence.

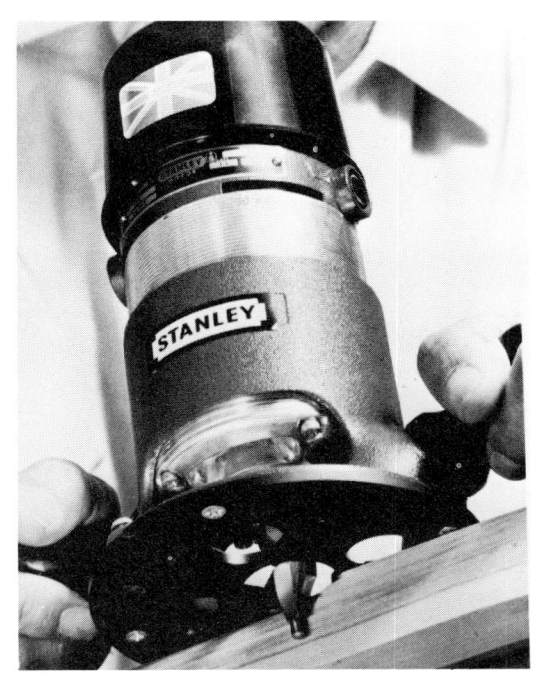

The production of a moulding along the edge of a workpiece. The router guide fence is not being used since the machine is guided by the small pin which projects below the cutter and over-cutting is impossible.

small ovolo around the top of a table. This type of cut does not require the use of a guide fence but it does call for a cutter which has a guide pin. The illustrations will show clearly what is meant here. If this type of cutter is set up precisely the correct depth it is impossible for it to overcut since the guide is running against the edge of the material to be moulded. Again, the direction of feed should be in the opposite direction to the rotation of the cutter and the rate of feed must be watched carefully. The operator should also note that the edge of a workpiece which is to be treated in this manner must be absolutely smooth since any bump or ridge will be reproduced by the machine.

It must be noted that when using a cutter which has a pilot, about 3mm ($\frac{1}{8}$in) of the edge which is to be moulded must be left for the pilot to run against. If the router is rotating in a clockwise direction, when viewed from above in a working position, the movement of the tool along the edge of the workpiece should be from left to right.

When a moulding is to be cut around the edge of a square or rectangular workpiece the cuts across the ends should be made first. In the event of any timber being split away by the cutter at the extreme end of the cut, the following cuts which run with the grain will clear up the damage.

When producing a moulding around a piece of timber which has a straight edge the job can be carried out without a cutter which has a pilot, using a batten clamped to the workpiece as a guide for the router.

Template routing
Template routing is extremely useful for production work in the cutting out of shapes or the routing of specific areas. A template is a pattern and if it is accurately made the results produced with it will be entirely satisfactory. It is necessary to use the correct type of cutter and to fit the router with a template guide, which is a small collar fitted to the base of the router so that it projects slightly and can run against the edge of the template. It is important to note that it is necessary for a template to be made either slightly smaller or slightly larger than the desired shape. If the shape to be cut out is to be made by working on the inside of the template then the template will need to be larger than the finished article. On the other hand, if working around the outside edge of a template it will need to be smaller. This, as will be clear from Fig. 5, is necessary in order to position the router cutter itself in precisely the right place. Templates can be made from good quality plywood, hardboard, or Masonite, which are quite strong and sufficiently durable materials.

Routers are used quite widely by woodturners for the beading and fluting of turnings. A lathe with a dividing head is used so that the work can be divided up into exactly the required number of beads

A moulding produced with a router. The high speed of rotation and sharp cutters produce a very good surface.

The Elu router in use with a template for stair stringing. This operation cuts recesses for the treads and risers of stairs.

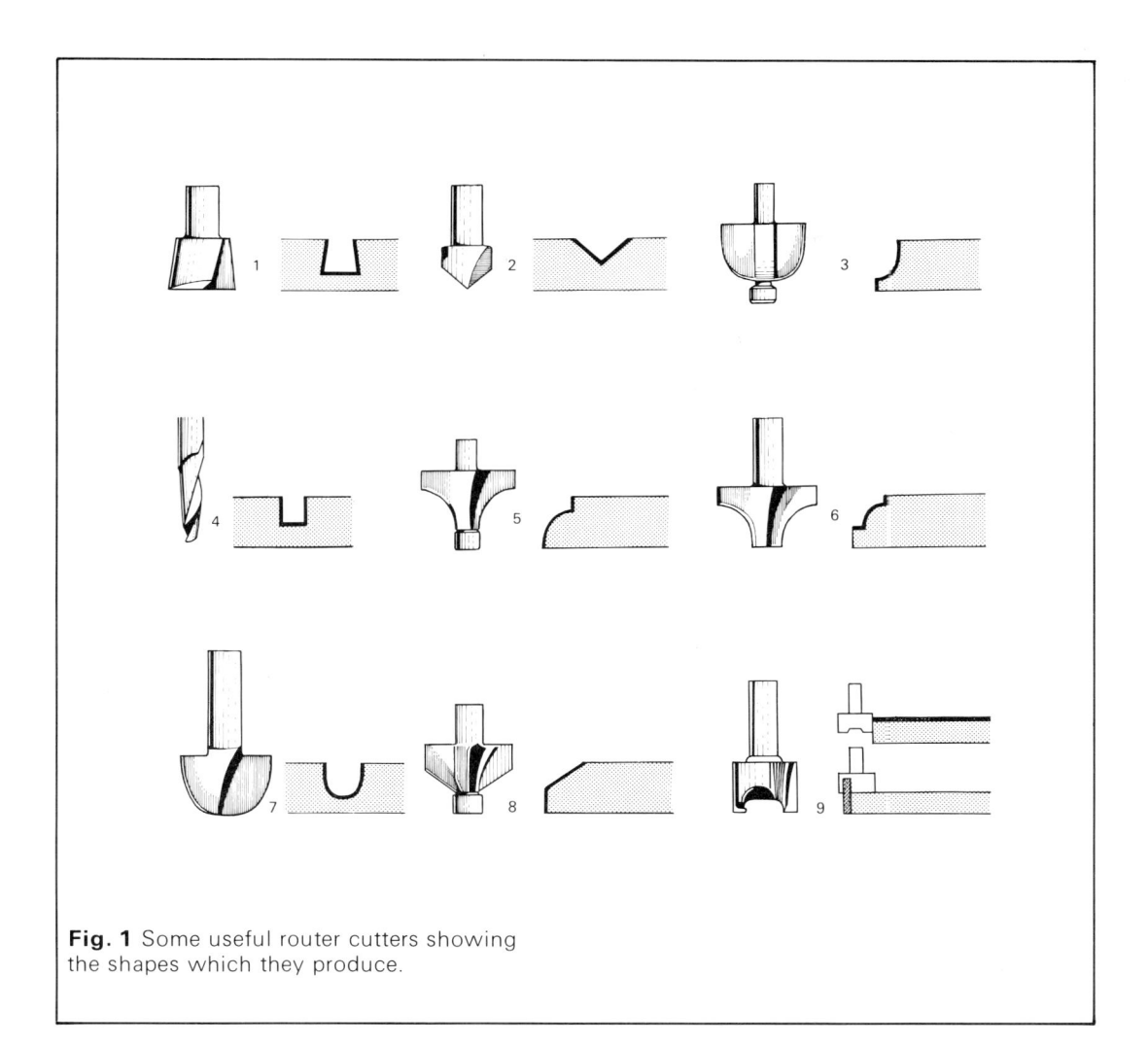

Fig. 1 Some useful router cutters showing the shapes which they produce.

or flutes and a jig is made in the workshop to hold the router so that the depth of cut can be maintained along the workpiece, which remains in the lathe during the process.

Freehand routing
With a little practice it becomes surprisingly easy to use the router freehand having first marked out the required design on the surface of the material with a black felt pen.

Chapter seven

Spindle Moulders and Disc Sanders

Spindle moulders

The spindle which carries the moulding block is horizontal, whereas in the case of a spindle moulder the spindle is vertical, and this makes the tool more versatile. The machine is simple enough in that the vertical spindle projects through the top of the table and can be raised or lowered. A fence is provided so that wood can be passed along it to the cutters in much the same way as is done on the sawbench. The height of the shaped cutters can be varied, as can their projection through the fence, and a great many interesting and useful mouldings can be produced with this tool.

In the past mouldings around the edges of furniture were produced by means of a scratch stock and later with special moulding planes. These are still used today but they are extremely slow by comparison with the spindle moulder which relies on a high speed of rotation, together with sharp cutters, to produce a satisfactory finish both with and across the grain. Anyone who has tried to use shaping cutters with ordinary electric drills will have discovered that the finishes so produced are very poor. This is due to the low speed of the drill, combined with the small diameter of the cutter, producing a situation where the relative speed between the cutter and the material is low.

These tools do have a bad reputation in respect of injuries to hands. At the same time, of course, it is not the machine which reaches out to grab the hand — injuries are caused by operators placing their hands too close to the cutters. Great care must always be exercised when using a spindle moulder. The safest method of operation is to pass the timber along the fence to the cutter. The timber must never

The Sheppach HF30 spindle moulder with optional sliding carriage.

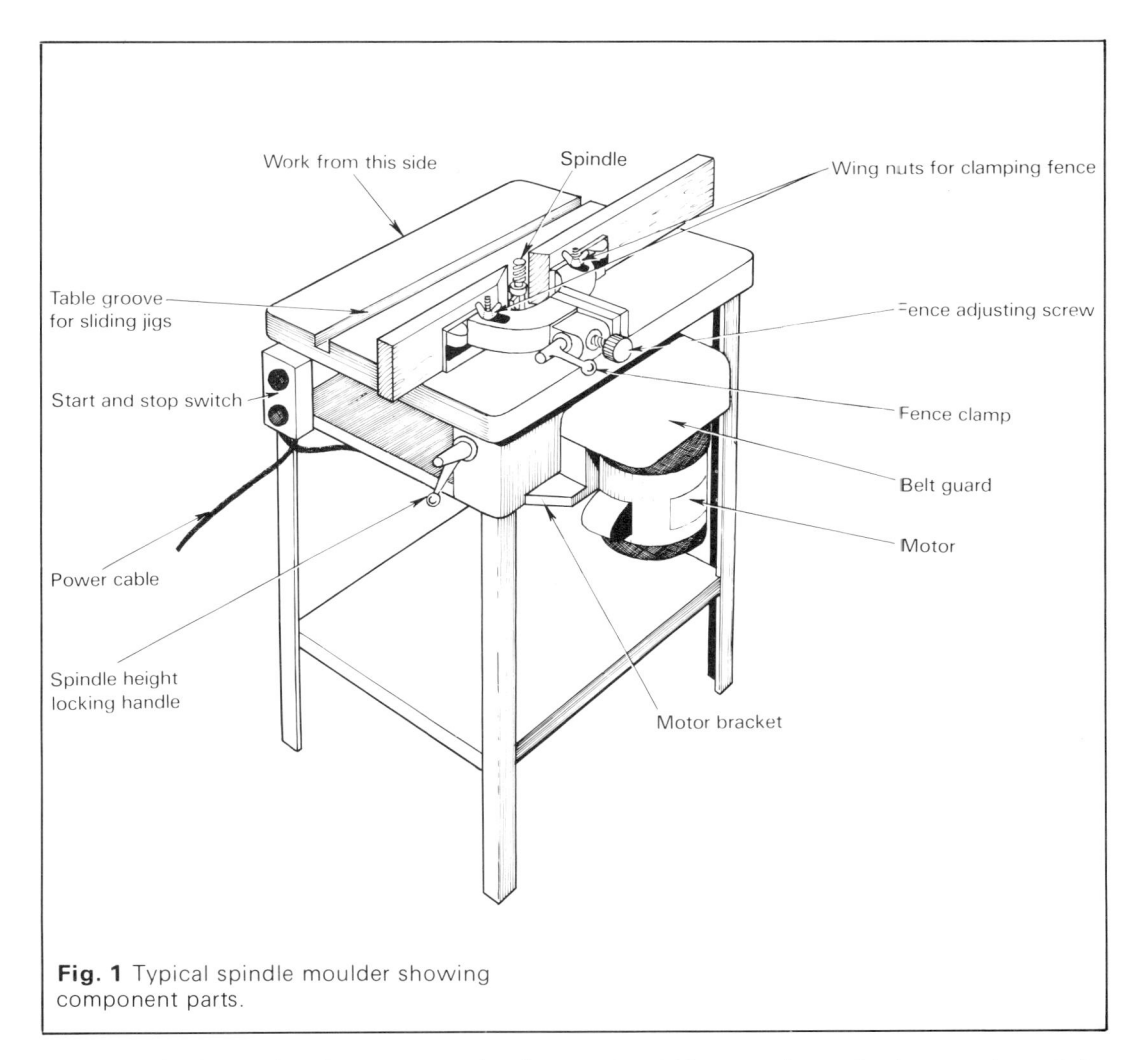

Fig. 1 Typical spindle moulder showing component parts.

be passed along the fence towards the cutters so that the direction of rotation of the cutter block is the same as the movement of the timber. The two should be opposite, or the timber may well be snatched from the operator's hands.

There are some operations where the cutter knives run along the top edge of the work, and again extreme care must be exercised. Wherever possible the cutters should be run along the lower edge of the work so that they are masked by the wood and cannot reach the operator's fingers. As when using a circular saw, it is always a good idea to try to anchor the feed hand, by hooking a finger around some part of the workpiece. Feed rate, as with other woodworking machinery, should be fairly steady so that the tool is not overloaded and a push stick should always be used to finish off the cut. It is

97

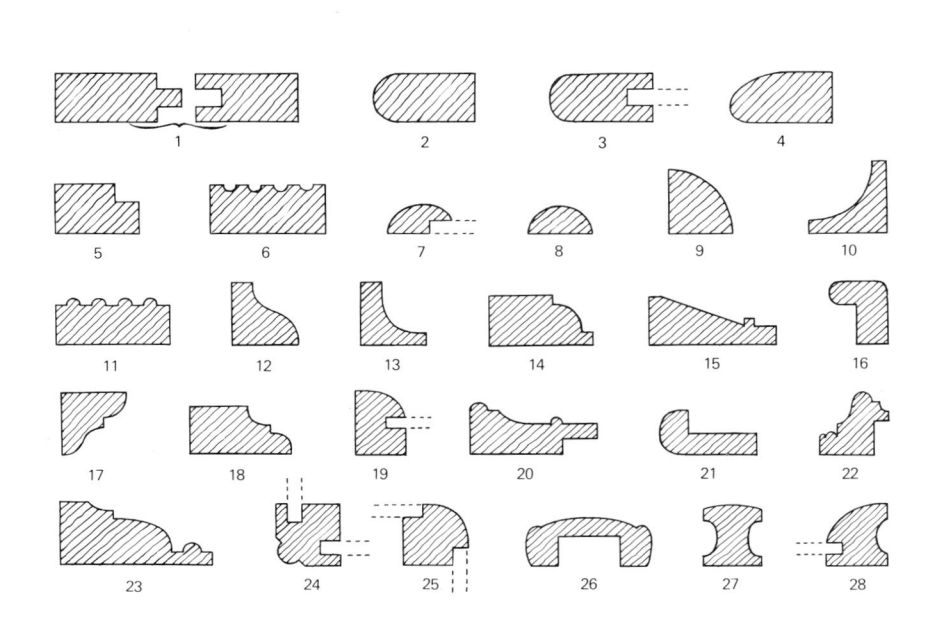

Fig. 7 Sectional view of mouldings commonly produced on spindle moulders.

1 Tongue and groove
2 Plain bead
3 Grooved bead
4 Thumb
5 Rabbetted
6 Fluted
7 Rabbetted half round
8 Half round
9 Quadrant
10 Scotia
11 Beaded
12 Ogee
13 Cove
14 Ovolo
15 Box picture frame
16 Cushion
17 Bead and ogee
18 Cove and bead
19 Drawer slip
20 Spoon picture frame
21 Hockey stick
22 Rabbetted, ogee and astragal
23 Architrave
24 Box corner
25 Rabbetted corner
26 Cable cover
27 Handle
28 Tray

not necessary to be afraid of woodworking machinery but it must be respected.

A great many different patterns of spindle moulder cutter are available but the average worker will probably select half a dozen shapes which will cope with all the work he is likely to perform. It should be borne in mind, in relation to this, that many interesting shapes can be produced by making several passes along a piece of wood moving the cutters slightly for each one. Moulding cutters are not cheap and there is no necessity to buy a complete set. The spindle itself is normally provided with a selection of tubular collars and washers which can be moved around to give extra versatility to the machine in the raising or lowering of the block itself. In varying the shape produced with a medium cutter, three adjustments can usually be made. One is the height of the cutter block in relation to the table, another is the depth of cut, and on many machines there is a third which is the angle at which the cutter itself is set into the block. Quite apart from the standard cutter patterns which are available, it is possible to buy hard or soft blanks which can be ground or filed to suitable shapes for special operations. Small rubber-backed drum sanders can be obtained for use with spindle moulders and these are useful for sanding curved workpieces along their edges. The speed of rotation of the machine is high, so light pressure must be used and the timber should be moved along fairly quickly.

Most workers will be familiar with what is commonly known as the drop leaf table joint, or rule joint. This can be produced very easily by means of a spindle moulder since pairs of cutters are available to form both halves of the joint. Spindle moulders can also be used to produce tongued and grooved boards and most are adaptable with special saw blades for the production of tenons. In operations of this kind there is usually a sliding carriage which will hold the timber securely by means of a clamp as it is passed through the cutters. Attention should be paid to the question of holding the material down to the table and firmly against the fence. Often with large workpieces hand pressure will be quite sufficient, but when smaller pieces of timber are being processed there is considerable danger unless spring clamps of some kind are used.

When working on a very small piece of timber it is best to pass it through a rebated block of timber which is clamped against the fence. If this is not done the timber may be smashed up by the fast-moving cutters and injury to the operator is also quite likely. A great deal of work can be carried out on a

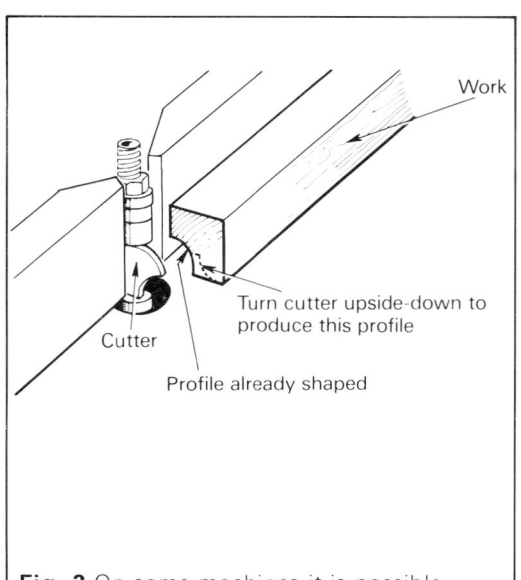

Fig. 2 On some machines it is possible to invert the cutters to produce mouldings as shown here.

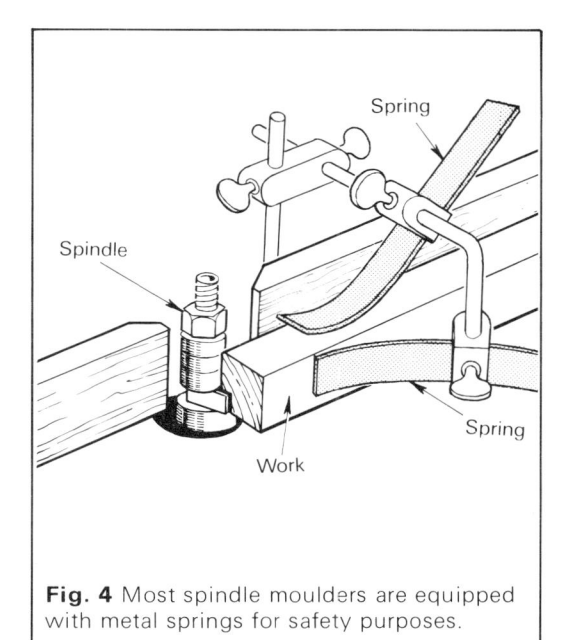

Fig. 4 Most spindle moulders are equipped with metal springs for safety purposes.

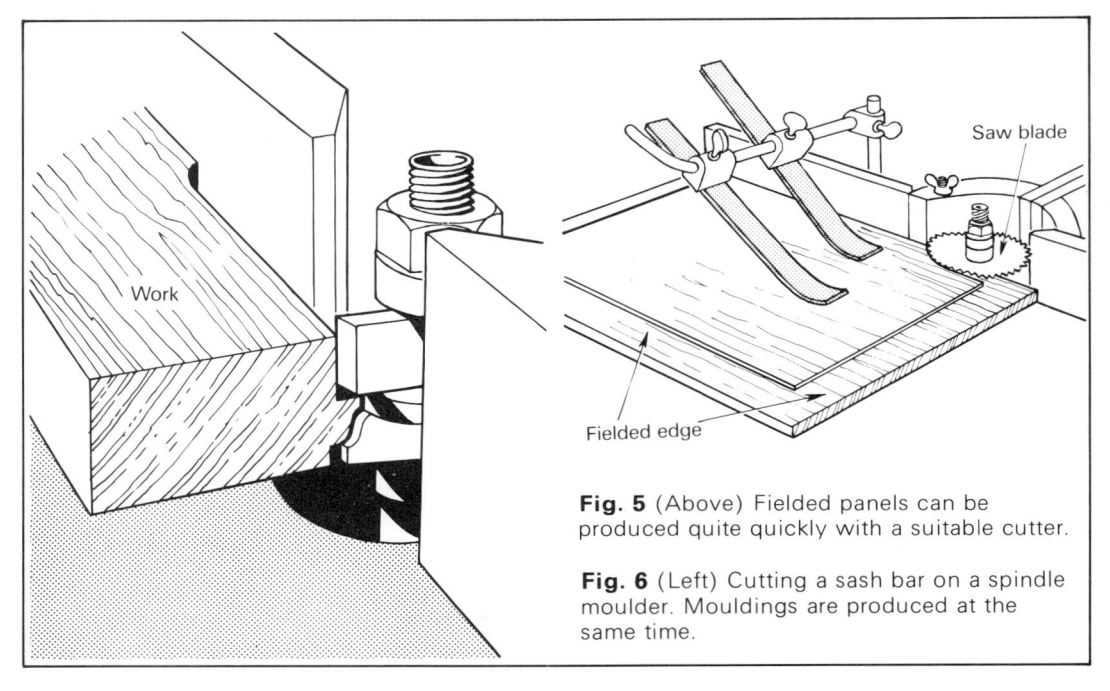

Fig. 5 (Above) Fielded panels can be produced quite quickly with a suitable cutter.

Fig. 6 (Left) Cutting a sash bar on a spindle moulder. Mouldings are produced at the same time.

spindle moulder by means of a ring fence. This runs against the timber, the cutters projecting the required distance beyond it. As when using a router the precise rate of feed is important. If the wood is not moved fast enough the rapidly rotating cutters will become overheated and, in the process, will burn the edge. If the timber is moved too quickly the resulting finish will be poor. The pressure used in holding the wood to the table and against the fence should not be varied during the cut. If it is there may be variations in the pattern produced. If the surface produced on a workpiece is not sufficiently smooth this can be due to cutter edges which are not sharp, cutters which have been set too deeply, too fast a feed rate, cutting against the grain of the timber or even too low a speed if the particular machine has a variable speed.

Disc sanders

A disc sander is a simple tool which is not particularly useful for finishing purposes but is valuable in the sanding of end grain and for shaping purposes. The disc is mounted in the vertical plane and a table is provided so that material can be held at right-angles to the faceplate. On some tables provision is made for tilting so that angled sanding can be carried out. Certain disadvantages will immediately become evident to the user of a disc sander. The speed at any given point across the face of the disc will vary, the outside edge will, of course, be travelling considerably faster than a point nearer the centre. This is not critical, but it does mean that a great deal of sanding tends to take place at a point somewhere near the outside edge.

It will also be noted that whilst one side of the disc is travelling downward in relation to the table, the other side is travelling upwards. Sanding, therefore, needs to be done on the side which is

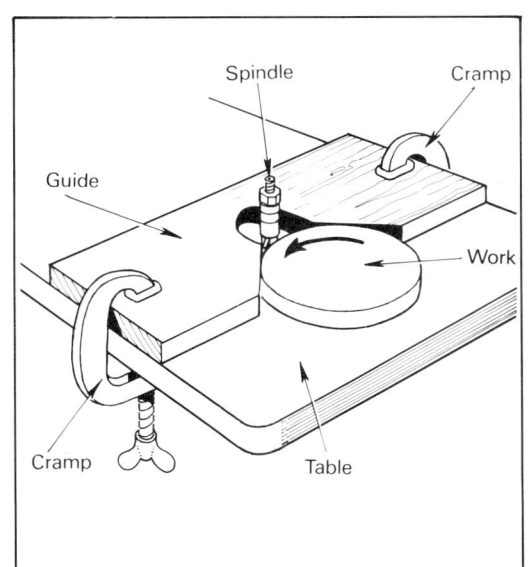

Fig. 3 In the absence of a ring fence, circular work can be moulded by means of a home-made jig.

travelling downwards so that the wood is held firmly against the table. If the other side of the sander is used, the material will be lifted. In connection with this, if a facility for reversing the direction of rotation of the motor is available, it is sometimes a good idea to run the disc in the opposite direction which will help to clean the clogged dust from the surface. Another quick way to do this, with the machine travelling in its normal direction, is to use a piece of fairly stiff garden hose. Place this firmly on the table and run it across the disc several times. This has a very marked effect and cleans the disc extremely well.

The discs of abrasive paper which are used with disc sanders should not be attached by means of glue as great difficulty will be experienced in removing them. Special preparations are marketed for this purpose, though many workers do

Above: End grain sanding of a large workpiece. Pressure against the disc sander must be light or the material will be scorched.

Below: The mortises produced by most modern mortiser attachments are round-ended. These can be trimmed square with a chisel or the tenon shoulders can be rounded over on a disc sander as shown here.

in fact use ordinary rubber solution. This should be coated over both disc and plate, allowed to become touch dry and then the two surfaces brought carefully together. If any difficulty is experienced in removing the disc a little heat will help. There are also special adhesive sticks of solid material which can be applied to the sanding plate whilst it is rotating. First rub a piece of scrap timber across the disc for a few moments so that the friction heats up the disc. The stick is then traversed a few times across the face of the disc, the machine switched off and the abrasive paper applied.

Industrial heavy-duty sanding machine with both disc and belt facilities.

Many workers find that it is advantageous to build up a number of discs on the plate and then remove them all at once. When one disc has become too worn for further use, rubber solution can be applied over it and the next disc placed in position. If this method is adopted, it will be quite easy to remove several layers of them at once without tearing.

Care must be taken using the disc sander to see that burning does not occur; this is far more likely on end grain than elsewhere and the answer is to use light pressure against the disc, even if the operation takes a little longer. Disc sanders are quite efficient for sanding edges but they are not much good for producing a finish on a flat piece of timber. The reason for this, of course, is that by the very nature of the sander the grains must cross the grain of the wood. In the case of a belt sander this is not so and it is not difficult to arrange for the granules to run with the grain of the timber, so producing a far better surface. A disc sander is, however, very good for rapid stock removal after a workpiece has been cut out on the bandsaw.

Abrasive operations

The abrasives most commonly used in woodworking machinery nowadays are garnet and aluminium oxide. Both of these are very tough long-wearing abrasive materials which will stand up to machine use. Sandpaper of the type used in hand work would be completely unsuitable for such operations. Silicon carbide has also come into its own and is used for certain types of sander and although it is an expensive material its life is considerably longer than that of the other two.

Garnet, which is orange in colour, is the

A considerable step forward in the application of the belt sander principle from Willow Tools. Note the large table with adjustable angle cut. The table has provision for tilting.

Although somewhat bizarre in appearance, the Sheppach dust extractor unit is powerful and efficient. It is shown here connected to a Sheppach Prima HM planer/thicknesser.

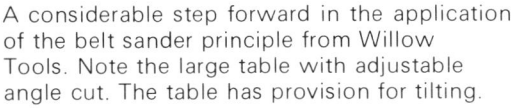

most popular medium, and the choice must be made between open or closed coat sheets or belts. Closed coat paper works extremely well on hard woods for actual finishing processing, but open coat is more widely used since the interstices between the granules do not become clogged with dust quite as rapidly. Unfortunately, manufacturers of abrasive paper do not seem to have standardised completely their methods of describing the grit size which is used. For woodworking purposes grades from 80 to about 320 are commonly employed. 80 grit is coarse whereas 320 is extremely fine. The numbers are in fact a reference to the number of holes per square inch in the mesh through which the granules have been sifted.

Consideration of abrasive machinery immediately brings to mind the fact that vast quantities of dust can be produced. This dust is mixed with fine particles of abrasive material and is injurious to the lungs. Masks can be worn, which will greatly minimise the danger, but some form of dust extraction unit is by far the best approach. An excellent unit is available from the Kity Co. Ltd., designed for use with their own machinery, but adaptable for use with machines of other makes.

Most of the dust extractors available before this unit was produced suffered from one disadvantage which was that the suction power of the machine reduced as the dust bag filled up, and it was usually

103

advisable to empty the dust bag when about two thirds full. The design of the Kity machine renders this unnecessary, full suction power being available right up to the point where the bag is full. A transparent plastic bag is used to enable an easy check to be kept on the level.

Diagrammatic view of the Octopus-type dust extractor system from Kity, which can be connected to various machines. The dust extractor uses an upper air bag in addition to the normal dust section to give full efficiency at all times.

Chapter eight

Planers

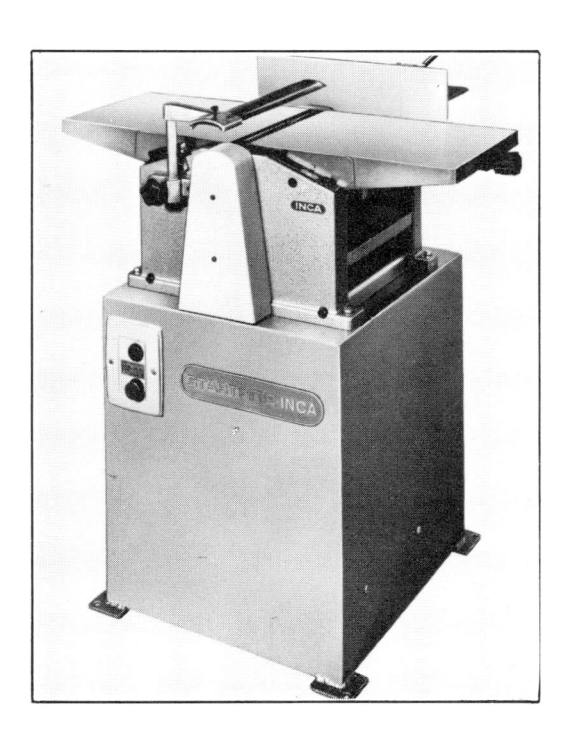

A good quality planing machine must always come high on the list of priorities when setting up a home or commercial workshop. Timber which has been sawn must be planed in most cases, and there is little point in saving time and effort in the first operation if both are to be wasted in the second. A good surface planer, with or without a thicknessing attachment, or a planer/thicknesser will provide accuracy, produce excellent surface finishes and greatly reduce the time needed to complete a project. Surface planers are considerably less expensive than planer/thicknessers and in most cases thicknessing attachments can be purchased separately to fit them, the timber being fed through manually by the operator. Small surface planers are sometimes referred to as jointers, this being the American word for the machine. A planer/thicknesser, however, is power fed, the machine itself drawing the timber through the thicknesser and in this case the rate of feed is accurately controlled to give the optimum surface finish.

If one goes purely by statistics, planing machines must be accepted as potentially more dangerous than circular saws, and rather less dangerous than spindle moulders. There is, however, no reason to fear any woodworking machine if a healthy respect for the equipment is combined with a sensible approach to its use based on a period of instruction or careful study of handbooks dealing with the use of such tools. One of the main causes of accidents is blunt cutters. Razor sharp planer or moulding knives, and saw blades, will remove wood as anticipated by the operator, who can keep his hands well clear. When cutter edges are blunt, however,

Startrite Inca planer/thicknesser with cast iron tables. Now a popular machine in home workshops.

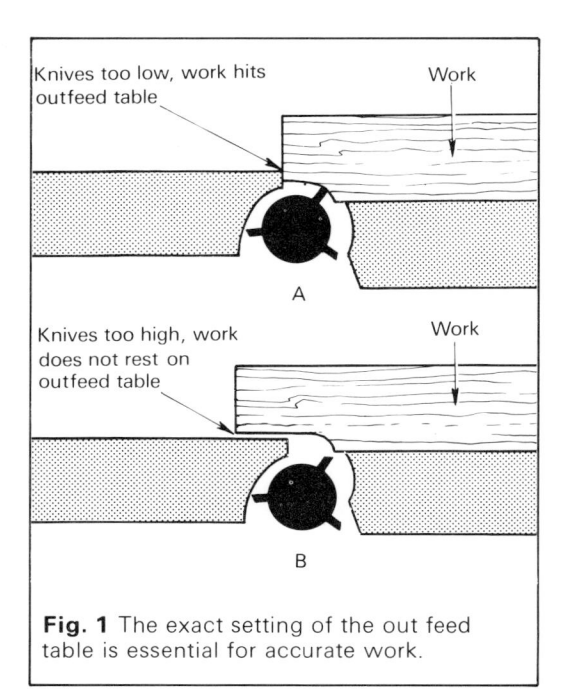

Fig. 1 The exact setting of the out feed table is essential for accurate work.

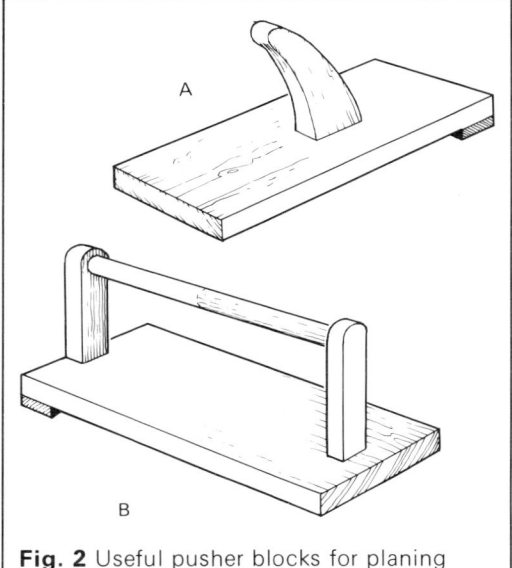

Fig. 2 Useful pusher blocks for planing operations can easily be made in the home workshop.

timber can be rejected forcibly by the machine, entirely without warning, and an accident can easily result.

Surface planers
For the purposes of this book the type of machine being considered is up to about 300mm (12in) in length of knife. Planers used in home workshops are likely to be 200 mm or 250mm (8in or 10in) which is quite adequate for most purposes. One major difference between surfacers and planer/thicknessers is the fact that surfacers can be used for the cutting of rebates up to about 12mm ($\frac{1}{2}$in) deep. Whilst this is extremely useful in the home workshop it should be noted that rebating on surface planers is now illegal in industry where the process is normally dealt with on spindle moulders.

Planing machines have finely-balanced cylindrical cutter blocks mounted crosswise at the centre, usually carrying either two or three matched knives, and the efficiency of the machine will depend to a large extent upon the accuracy with which the projection of these knives from the block is set. Some machines are supplied with special setting devices which work very well but, in fact, the operation can be carried out quite satisfactorily by means of a straight piece of wood, one edge of which has been rubbed with chalk. This is placed with its chalked edge downwards upon the rear or take-off table, projecting over the cutters. The knives are set in turn so that they will just disturb the chalk without moving the wood when the cutter block is turned by hand. This check is made at each end of each knife. If the operation is carried out carefully, very accurate results can be obtained.

The way in which the knives are secured in the block will vary from one machine to another, and in most cases some form of

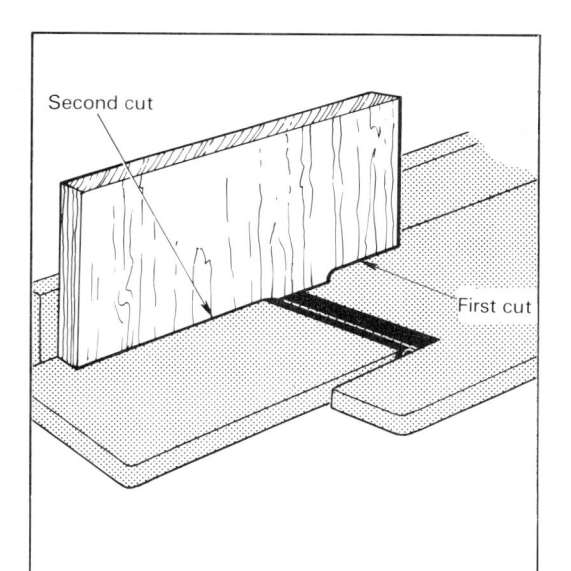

Fig. 3 Planing across the end of a board can be carried out as shown here to avoid splitting.

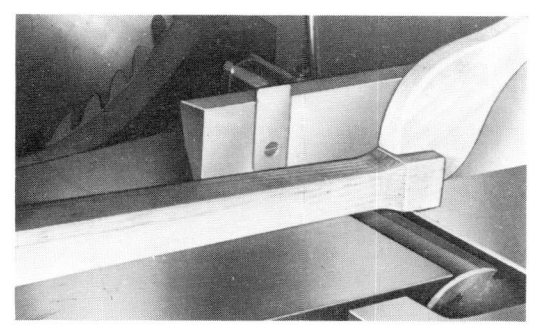

Above: Stopped chamfers can be produced quickly and accurately by means of a moulding block with 45° angled cutters.

Below: Tapered furniture legs can be produced on a small surface planer. Note use of a push stick.

adjusting device is provided to enable the knives to be moved with precision.

Some surface planers have provision for the raising and lowering of both front and rear tables so that the machine can be used for cutting stopped chamfers (chamfers which do not run the full length of the material). This is becoming less common due to the increase in the use of spindle moulders, and once the knives have been set correctly to the rear table it is as well not to alter the table height unless it is absolutely essential.

The operation of a surface planer is quite straightforward but use should be made of some form of push stick or wooden pusher block or an accident to the fingers is quite probable. It is also a good idea to get into the habit of never passing either hand over the cutter block. The depth of cut is set by altering the height of the front or feed table and best results are obtained by removing up to 1·5mm ($\frac{1}{16}$in) of wood per pass; heavy cuts will tear the surface of the wood. It is necessary to become accustomed to the rate of feed over the knives which results in a good finish and this will vary slightly among different types of timber. Too fast a feed rate will give rise to a rippled surface which can be most annoying.

Surface planers are fitted with fences against which the wood moves, like the rip fence on a sawbench. For normal planing purposes the fence is set at 90° to the

107

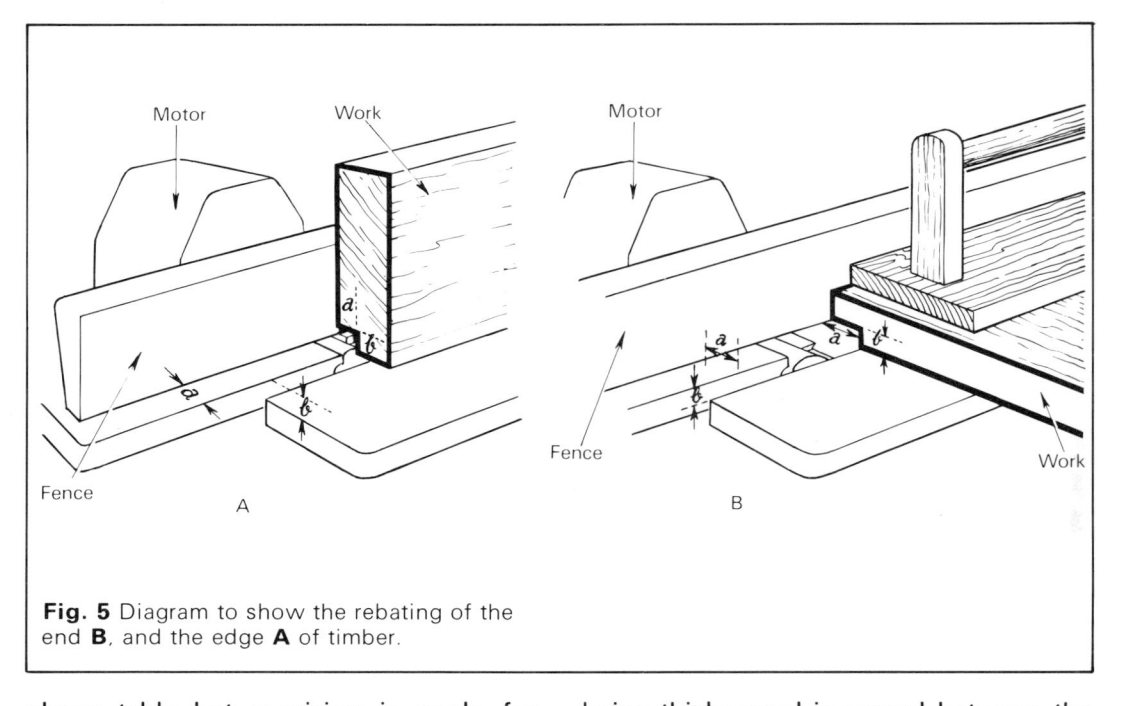

Fig. 5 Diagram to show the rebating of the end **B**, and the edge **A** of timber.

planer table but provision is made for tilting it to facilitate angled cuts. On planers of this nature the production of a piece of timber which has 90° corners is simplicity itself but the planer fence must be carefully set to a right-angle with the table. On most machines the indicator provided is not reliable and the use of a carpenter's square should preclude any possibility of error. If one face of the wood is planed it can be kept firmly against the fence while the next pass is made. If the wood is badly out of true more than one pass may be required to plane the full width of the second side, but an exact 90° angle will result. If this process is repeated on the other two sides the timber will end up smooth and with right-angled corners.

Thicknessing attachments for surface planers are made to bolt on over the machine. The feed table of the planer is lowered as far as it will go and the timber being thicknessed is passed between the planer and the overhead thicknessing plate, against which it is pressed by metal springs. The front or feed table is not used in this operation and the finished thickness of the wood is equal to the distance between the take-off table and the overhead plate. A scale is normally provided which should be set to read zero when the thicknesser plate is lowered to touch the take-off table. Once this scale has been set, it will accurately read the thicknessing setting required.

The production of a number of workpieces of identical thickness is often required, in which case one piece can be prepared to the finished size by normal planing methods, and then used to set up the thicknesser. The prepared piece is laid on the rear table and the plate is lowered on to it, the clamp which secures it then being tightened. The remaining timber when passed through the

108

Above: A small jig, as shown here, will enable right-angled strip mouldings to be produced by rebating on the planer.

Below: Planing a wide board on a narrow planer. The timber is passed through once and then reversed and passed through again. This system gives reasonable results but there will always be a small ridge where the two cuts meet which can be sanded smooth.

thicknesser will be of the same thickness. These attachments are surprisingly accurate and can even produce strips of veneer.

Planer/thicknessers
A planer/thicknesser is a surface planer which has provision for timber to be passed under the cutter block on an adjustable table and fed through mechanically by rotating rollers. The power feed device and the gearing which raises and lowers the table are fairly complex so machines of this

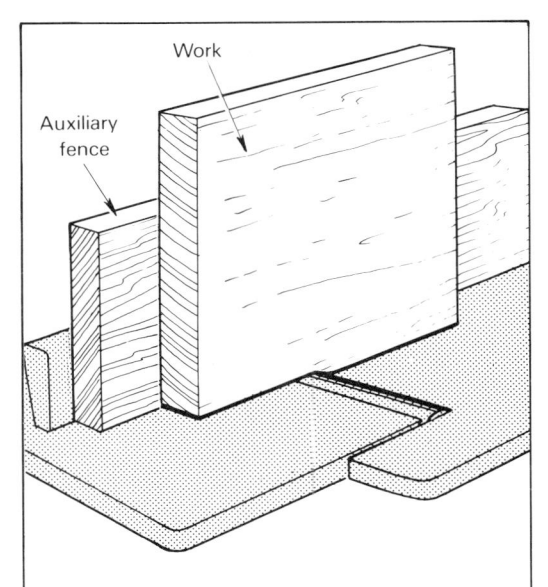

Fig. 4 Planing the edges of wide boards requires the use of auxilliary fences.

kind are relatively expensive. Where large quantities of timber are likely to be processed they are well worth their price and will perform well over long periods with surprising accuracy. Most planer/thicknessers are equipped with anti-kickback fingers, which hang in a row on a bar and trail on the timber as it passes through. They prevent the material from being thrown back at the operator.

Many machines use two types of roller for the feed mechanism; the front roller which feeds the timber to the knives being of ribbed metal, and the rear, or take-off roller, of neoprene or rubber. This is because the ribbed metal roller, which gives the more positive drive, can mark the surface of the material, particularly when soft timbers are processed. The marks so made are, of course, removed in the planing process, and the planed surface then passes to the soft roller which does

109

The Sheppach Prima HM1 planer/thicknesser. This machine with its 2·2 horsepower output motor is well-engineered and capable of driving various attachments.

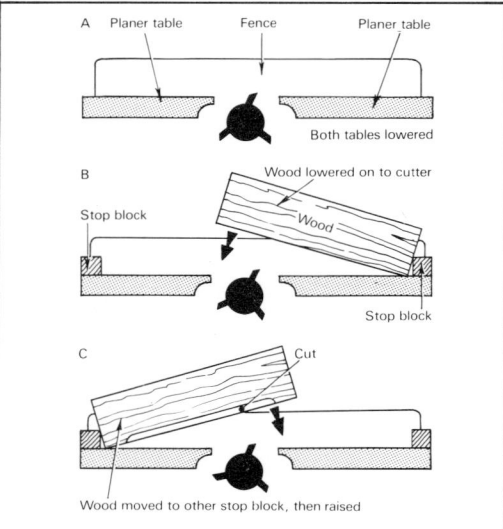

Fig. 6 Stopped chamfers. The wood is placed against the forward block, lowered on to the rotating knives, then moved forward to the rear block.

not cause the same problems. On soft timbers some marking is inevitable due to small chips of wood which are pressed against the planed surface by the take-off roller but such marks are easily sanded out. The problem does not, of course, arise with hard timbers.

When a planer/thicknesser is used, the common approach to the production of a perfectly square workpiece — a piece which has exact 90° corners — is to plane one side and one edge of the material on the planer with the fence accurately set to 90°. When this has been done the remaining surfaces are planed through the thicknesser which ensures that faces and edges are parallel.

There is now a wide variety of surface planers and planer/thicknessers since these machines have become normal equipment for the home workshop, and the choice can be difficult. It is best, as with most machines, to buy from a specialist woodwork machinery supplier who has no particular bias and is able to explain and demonstrate the finer points.

One controversial issue is that of the material used for the planer tables. Many people will swear by cast-iron tables, which are heavy and can break if they receive a severe blow. They are considered to be more accurate than other types and this is true if the castings have been weathered correctly. Casting should be left in the open air for long periods, many months in fact, before finally being milled to true flat surfaces. In these times, however, castings are often not weathered sufficiently and they can warp and twist.

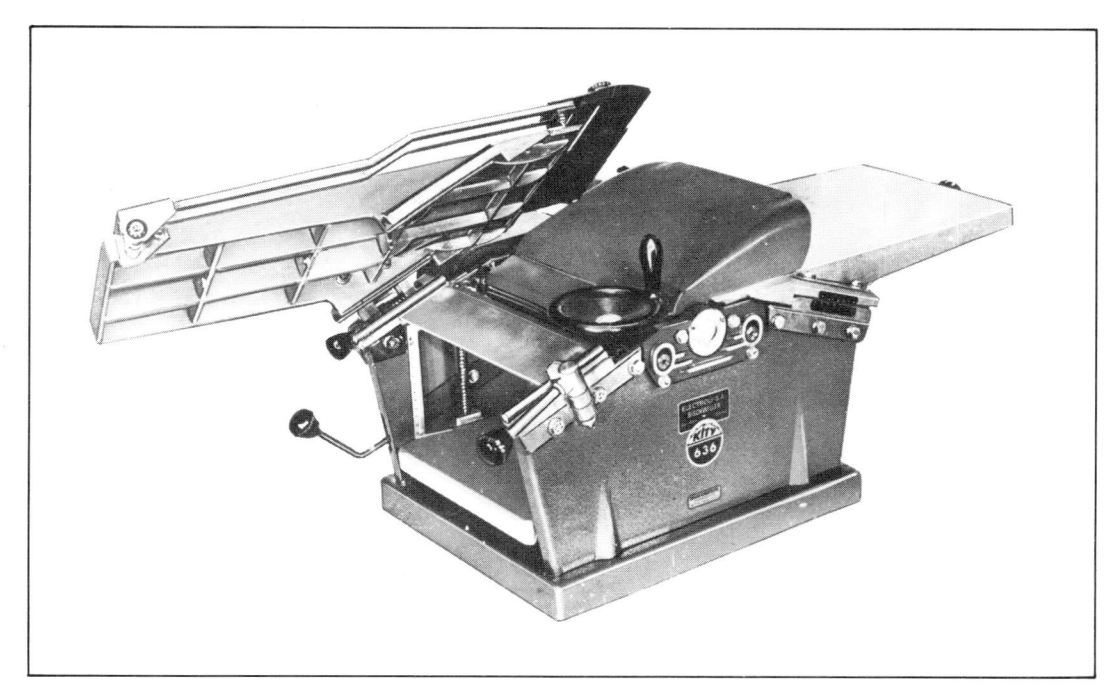

The Kity 250mm × 150mm (10in × 6in) planer/thicknesser. For thicknessing purposes the outfeed table is raised and a chip deflector/guard is fitted to cover the cutter block. Note the lever (lower left) which engages or disengages the drive for the thicknesser section of the machine.

Sheet metal tables were frowned upon when they first appeared, but my experience is that if the metal is of sufficiently heavy gauge, and the design is such as to provide strength where it is needed, tables of this kind do a very good job. Rust is a major problem with both types and precautions must be taken to avoid it.

Die-cast tables, made from various aluminium alloys, have now become very popular and have proved to be serviceable in every way. They are light and extremely strong and stand up well to normal wear and tear.

Most surface planers and planer/thicknessers are capable of taking roller extensions which provide extra support off the rear table for the machining of long workpieces. These are provided by the manufacturers as optional extras and are worth purchasing where the planing of long timbers is to be common practice.

Planers of any kind are considered to be dangerous, but one must accept that it is the use of such machines by inexperienced operators that causes accidents which can be avoided by the use of common sense. It is also worthwhile to study the manufacturer's instruction book well before using the equipment. Used with care, a good planer is a tremendous asset in any workshop.

Chapter nine

Combination Machines

One of the first points which strikes those who set out to create a workshop, either for commercial or hobby purposes, is that there are a number of approaches to be considered. Given sufficient space there is little doubt that individual machines strategically positioned in the workshop will be more satisfactory than the combination or universal machines. Many people, however, do not have this amount of space to spare, nor indeed the amount of cash required if a motor and a stand is to be purchased for every machine, and serious thought must be given to the question of whether or not there is a machine in the universal category which will be suitable

A well-designed and engineered example of a composite woodworking machine. The Zinken ZC21 offers circular saw, spindle moulder, planer/thicknesser and mortiser in one package. Each unit is selected as required by a lever at the front of the unit which can be locked for safety purposes.

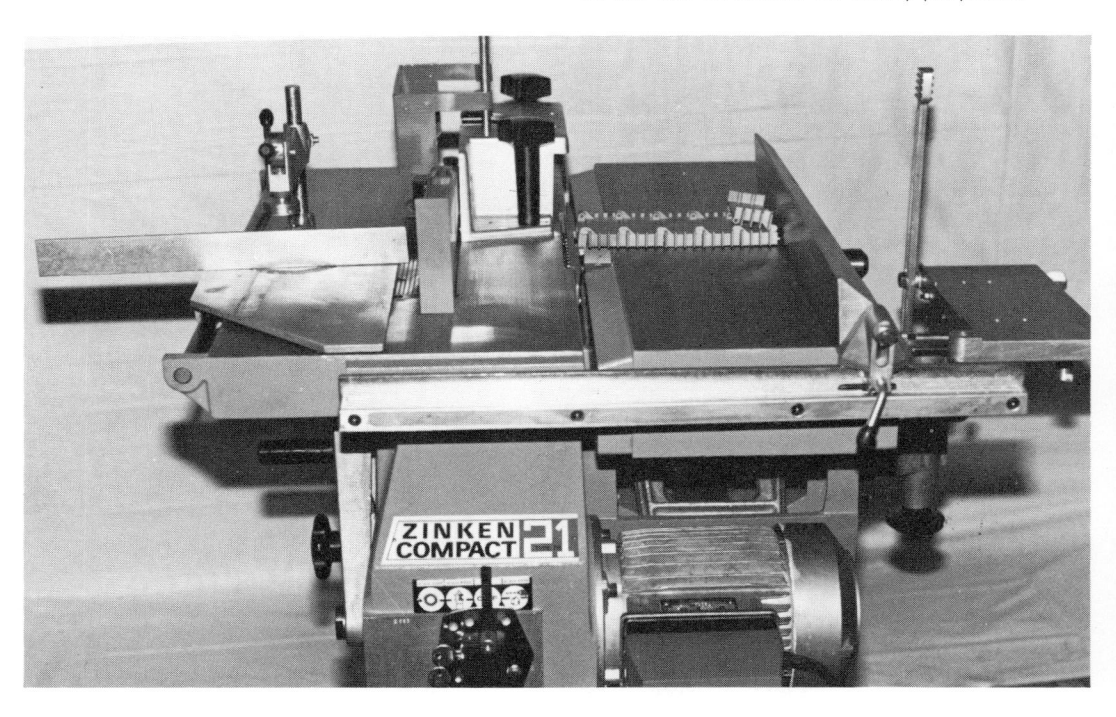

for the intended purpose. Woodworking machinery has changed considerably in recent years, and it may be helpful if certain specific types of composite machine are dealt with in this chapter.

In an attempt to clarify the situation, this range of machinery which is of excellent quality and design has relative merits and demerits which can be given some serious thought by those who are intending to start a workshop. The cost of setting up a workshop today is quite considerable and mistakes made in the early stages can be expensive. The equipment described in this section is, in my opinion, suitable for the hobbyist who is trying to make his hobby pay, or for the small commercial operator. The choice is taken from English and Continental machines all of which are built to a high standard of quality and accuracy. They all have their virtues but, as I have explained, the final choice will be very much affected by the type of work which is to be undertaken.

Kity machinery

My initial reaction to the Kity range of machinery was adversely affected by the bright colours in which the machines are painted and by the fact that they are composed partly of sheet metal and partly of cast alloy. Such a reaction, of course, must be qualified by actually using the machines, rather than looking at them and when I subsequently had an opportunity to try this range thoroughly, I was pleased with the results of my tests. The colour scheme is green and red, but the red paint is not used just to make the machines look pretty. Red indicates danger and it will be noted that the red paint is generally applied

The Susemihl SU 260 universal woodworker comparable to the Zinken 21.

to parts of the machine where there is potential danger, such as the guards.

Regarding sheet metal construction, it has to be borne in mind that there is nothing wrong with sheet metal in the construction of woodworking machinery provided that the gauge is sufficient to give the required strength and rigidity. In the case of the Kity range it most certainly is and these tools are a great deal tougher than they may first appear.

Those who are not accustomed to using modern woodworking machinery are sometimes put off by the use of cast and machined alloy tables for spindle moulders, circular saws, planers, etc, on the grounds that this type of metal is soft and will wear very quickly. Having used alloy tables for some years I do not find this to be the case. Obviously, if one does not look after machinery it will suffer, but if a little common sense is employed in the use of saws and planers and so forth, there will be no appreciable problems. The more old-fashioned types of machine which have cast-iron tables and even cast-iron construction throughout, are extremely heavy and very expensive. For a large permanent workshop where machines are normally running from a three-phase electricity supply and are bolted permanently into position, this is not too much of a problem, but the average hobbyist or small commercial operator frequently requires to move machines around in the workshop in order to create extra space for the assembly of projects, and so forth, and provided that a machine made in sheet metal with an alloy table possesses the required rigidity and strength its lightness is an advantage rather than a disadvantage.

The term universal as applied to woodworking machines is, to my mind, rather misleading and I do feel that composite or combination machines might be a better description. The word universal tends to suggest that the machine will do anything you care to think of, and I have not, as yet, discovered a machine which deserves such a description! Composite, however, whilst putting over the fact that a number of functions can be achieved with a given machine, does not suggest that it is omnipotent. There are merits and demerits and the most obvious drawback is that different types of machine require different heights in order to be in the most satisfactory position for any given user. These heights are not, however, absolutely critical and reasonable compromises can be achieved.

Another problem, particularly in the case of the small commercial workshop, is that it is sometimes desirable to have two operators working at the same time, perhaps one sawing while the other is planing. This can be achieved on some composite machines but it is not always desirable or even safe, and for such purposes there is little doubt that the use of independent machines will give far better results.

One big advantage which the Kity range offers over some others is that the complete composite unit is made up of precisely the same machines as are sold separately mounted with motors on individual stands. The point here, of course, is that there is no compromise in the machines themselves. They are individual machines grouped around a one and a half horsepower motor, and no modifications have been made to any of the machines in order for them to fit together on the large table. It is, therefore, perfectly possible to start with a composite machine of this kind and then to separate the machines at a later date by purchasing more motors and some stands. The large table upon which the machines were originally mounted is sturdy and very useful as a bench or assembly table for various projects.

Some composite machines tend to be rather heavy, in fact most of them are very heavy. Such a machine, once positioned in a private workshop or in the small commercial workshop, is difficult for one man to move. Since most people buy machines of this kind because they are already restricted for space this can be a problem. The Kity machinery, however, when assembled on the large table does not present problems of this nature since an optional extra is a system of wheels which will enable one man to move the entire unit around the workshop without

Kity combination system which groups a number of independent machines around a central power source. Shown here is the manufacturer's table with circular saw, planer/thicknesser, spindle moulder, mortiser and grinding unit.

any real effort at all. The idea is simple enough consisting of two wheels fitted to two of the legs of the table with a jockey wheel at the other end which can be raised or lowered. If the jockey wheel is lowered, thereby lifting two of the machine table legs clear of the ground, the machine can be wheeled about quite easily. When the equipment is in use the jockey wheel is raised so that the machine remains perfectly stable.

It is not absolutely necessary to buy the large table offered by the manufacturers, since a perfectly good table could be constructed in the workshop. The table which is offered is extremely well made and is precision drilled so that any or all of the units can be dropped into place and bolted down without any problems.

The one and a half horsepower motor which is used as a common driving

115

source is mounted more or less in the centre of the table. This is a double-ended motor, delivering adequate power and using a system of a flat belts. The use of flat belting is often queried by those who are accustomed to A or V belts anticipating considerable belt slippage. This, in fact, is not the case. These flat belts drive with great efficiency, do not wear, in my experience, any faster than an A or V belt, and offer one advantage over the other types of drive belt in that they can be twisted, so permitting machines to be driven in the required direction. The sort of composite unit in this range which will be found to be most popular consists of the large table with the double-ended motor carrying the saw bench, the spindle moulder and a 200mm or 250mm (8in or 10in) planer/thicknesser and a mortiser. A

A mortise cut with a slot miller bit has rounded ends.

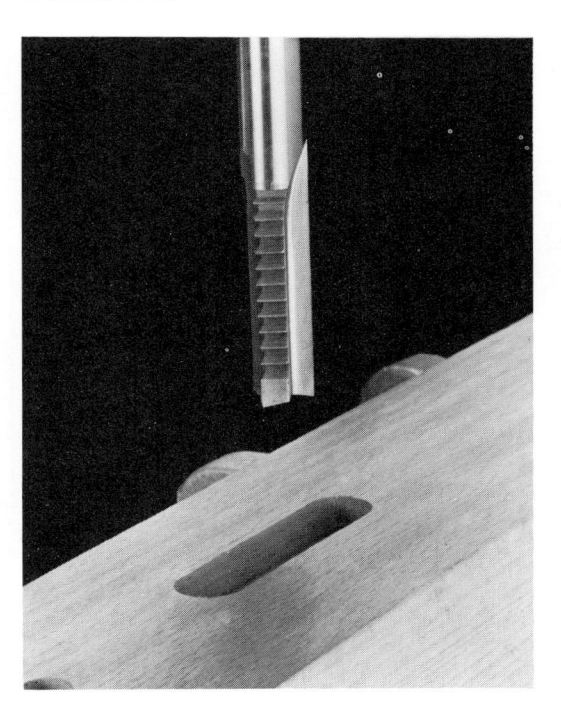

unit such as this will take almost all the hard work out of woodworking and the production rate can be stepped up immediately. Provided, of course, that it is kept in correct adjustment by the operator in accordance with the instructions given in the handbook, a composite unit will enable a very wide range of work to be done with speed and accuracy once the operator has become familiar with the unit.

The circular saw will cut timber to required sizes, cut joints such as tenons, half laps, etc, perform box combing operations for the construction of finger jointed boxes or drawers and will cut rebates, grooves, or housings. The Kity saw bench is supplied with a pair of wobble washers which enable the saw blade to oscillate whilst rotating, the amount of oscillation being pre-set by the operator so that a groove or channel of a given width is produced.

The planer will enable timber which has been prepared on the saw bench to be planed up precisely to size with a smooth finish and perfect right-angles in its corners. The thicknesser will enable the operator to produce timber which is all precisely the same thickness so that if joints are to be cut there will be no discrepancies when the work is assembled. It is also possible to produce veneers on a thicknesser of this kind if the knives are really sharp. The spindle moulder, apart from its obvious function for the production of shaped mouldings of many kinds, can also produce tongued and grooved board, tenons, rebates, stopped chamfers and many other requirements.

The mortiser uses a slot miller bit which cuts very fast and is extremely accurate. The mortises will have round ends which can be trimmed out with a very sharp chisel. Alternatively, the tenon can have its corners rounded over on a disc sander, or by means of a woodworking rasp or Surform. It is capable of adjustment for height and has stops so that the length of the mortise and its depth can accurately be pre-set.

For those who already possess a circular saw, it may be worth considering the fact that a Kity bandsaw can be set up on this large table assembly instead of the circular saw. In normal circumstances a bandsaw is a machine which is at its best when individually mounted but set up on this particular unit it does work very well. It is, in any event, a very good bandsaw having the advantage of a one and a half horsepower motor. There is a further advantage in that a steel tube runs up the back of the machine and across the top effectively stiffening the whole structure and preventing any movement between the upper and lower parts of the bandsaw casing when heavy timbers are being machined. It will take blades from 6mm–25mm ($\frac{1}{4}$in–1in) width.

For those whose capital will not run to the cost of a unit of this nature, and whose requirements are for the production of small articles in wood rather than large ones, there is a miniature version of this equipment, known as the Mini-Kity. This is built to the same high standards of quality and accuracy and is capable of excellent work. It is, of course, considerably cheaper, and there would appear to be little point in buying the large unit if the small one would do the job.

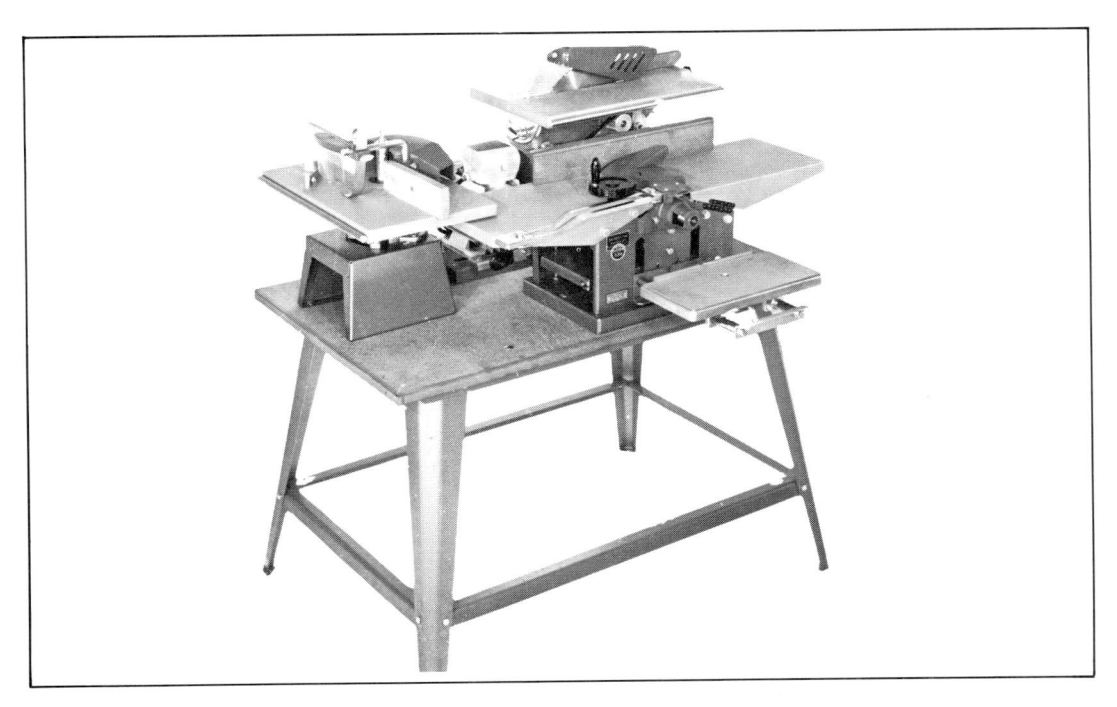

Mini-Kity combination system is scaled down in size to suit those who work in smaller dimensions of timber.

The Sheppach Prima HM1 10" × 6" planer/thicknesser

In its basic form this machine is a straightforward planer/thicknesser of rugged construction. It is of interest in this section of the book because it has an ingenious system whereby attachments can be fitted. This puts it into the class of composite machines although, unlike the Kity machine described earlier, it will run only one additional machine at a time, this being in the form of an attachment rather than a number of individual machines operating from one motor, as was the case with the Kity. The Sheppach is a German machine constructed in sheet steel, and when seen for the first time is apt to give the impression of being very much lighter in construction than is, in fact, the case. The tables, like the rest of the machine, are constructed from heavy gauge sheet steel and are more than adequate for the purpose for which they are intended.

In common with many woodworking machines today, the Prima HM1 can be purchased with either a single or three-phase motor. The most commonly used unit is the one with a two horsepower single-phase motor, since the majority of people do not have a three-phase power available on their premises, and it is extremely expensive to put in. With the two horse-power single-phase motor, the two horse-power is actual output, so there is obviously a great deal of power available. This makes the machine extremely useful for driving an attachment of one kind or another and indeed the attachments available for the Prima are very good. The basic unit, which is the planer/thicknesser itself, can be fitted with two universal adaptors, so that attachments can be fixed on. Very little time is taken up in fitting an attachment since it drops into place and is held by two circular clips. In its basic form as a planer/thicknesser, it has a 250mm (10in) cutter block which carries two blades and will produce magnificent finishes on hard or soft timbers. The thicknessing part of the machine will accept timbers up to 250mm (10in) wide by 150mm (6in) in thickness and the machine has sufficient power both to propel these large pieces of material and to cut them. It will be appreciated that most planer/thicknessers do in fact feed the timber through by means of rollers using the power of the motor. The rollers fitted to the Sheppach Prima are of thick rubber which has the advantage of not marking the surface of the timber which is being planed. The attachments available for this machine are as follows.

Circular saw bench

This is a large heavy duty bench which takes a 305mm (12in) diameter saw blade and will give approximately 100mm (4in) depth of cut. With the two horsepower output motor there is ample power for the purpose. This saw table comes with a rip fence but there is no slot for a mitre guide. Large saw benches of this kind are normally used for the ripping of fairly large timbers, so that a mitre guide is perhaps not as necessary as would be the case on a bench designed for the precision cutting of lighter workpieces. It is, in any case, not a difficult matter to manufacture in the workshop a mitre-cutting jig which will permit the cutting of mitres or other angles with complete accuracy. There is provision for rise and fall and tilt of the table which is relatively inexpensive and quite a useful adjunct to this machine.

Spindle moulder

The spindle moulder attachment for the Prima has a large table, which can be a great asset, and an excellent overhead roller system which acts as a guard keeping the material firmly down on the table and up against the guide fence while it is being processed. The cost of ready-made mouldings is high and large numbers of woodworkers are turning to spindle moulders of some kind to make their own.

Mortiser

An excellent mortiser is available and, in view of the large amount of power being supplied to a relatively small cutter, the tool is fast, extremely efficient and a delight to use. It is as accurate as the person who sets it, and considerable care should be given at all times to the accurate and correct setting of any woodworking machine in accordance with the manufacturers handbook. This mortiser, like most others, has clamps to hold the timber, levers for forward and cross feed and provision for rise and fall to position the timber correctly in relation to the cutter.

Lathe attachment

I am not greatly in favour of lathes which are attachments for other machines. Woodturning is a specialized craft and there is no doubt in my mind that for the best possible results, an independent lathe is essential. This does not mean that good woodturning cannot be done on an attachment but where woodturning forms a large part of the general woodworking operations, an independent lathe should be considered. When woodturning is, perhaps, no more than an amusement indulged in from time to time a machine capable of accepting a lathe attachment will be adequate. A great deal of fun is possible and it is certainly an excellent way of introducing oneself to the craft.

The outlay is not high, and a separate lathe can be purchased at a later date.

Disc sanding attachment

A disc sander is a very useful item in any workshop, especially if some form of dust extraction is available, and the attachment for the Sheppach is very good indeed. It is quite simple, having a table to support the timber and the usual rotating disc to carry the abrasive paper.

The Coronet range

Coronet machinery has earned a very good reputation. It is very solidly constructed and it is difficult to see how anyone could wear out one of these machines within his lifetime. With certain exceptions, which I will deal with later, the Coronet Universal or composite machines are based on a lathe. The range has become rather complex, and is not particularly easy to describe.

The best known of the Coronet machines is undoubtedly the Major which is now available in two forms, as either the CM500 or the CMB600B. The Coronet Major was changed slightly in 1977 as were several other machines in the range and the well-known maroon paint disappeared giving way to a blue crackle finish. The original Majors had a range of three speeds available through stepped pulleys, and for situations where it was necessary to obtain speeds lower than those available, there was a gear box. The gear box has now been withdrawn and the new machines have five speeds through stepped pulleys. The belt drive system was also changed to a flat poly-V belt instead of the original A belt. The size of the spindle nose on the Major was reduced to the same size as that on the Minor, presumably to make production easier, since prior to this change it had been necessary to manufacture the various chucks and fittings in two different thread sizes.

For the purpose of this section of the book it is the CM500 which will be discussed since this is the machine which is capable of taking quite a wide range of attach-

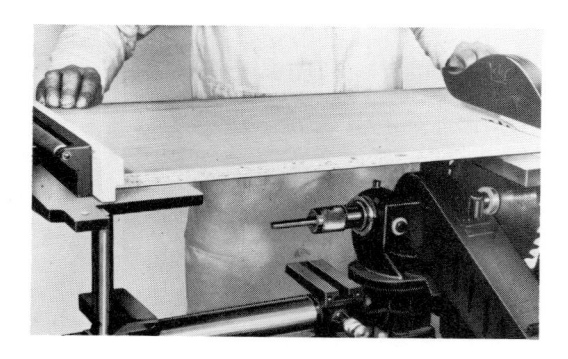

Above: Panel cutting on a Coronet Major universal machine. Note the use of the combination table (left) and the piece of rebated timber which is attached to the table fence to keep the material level.

Below: When ripping large workpieces on a Coronet saw table, the headstock is rotated and the combination table is positioned so that the material is supported by the fence roller.

ments. Before going into this, however, a few words on the CM600B will not be out of place. This is a Coronet Major, the basis of which is exactly the same as for the CM500, but the machine is intended purely for woodturning purposes. It is fitted with a very useful grinding unit on the left-hand end of the drive spindle, complete with guard. The other important difference between this machine and the CM500 is the motor speed. The CM600B is fitted with a three quarter horsepower, 1,420 rpm, Brook Gryphon, totally enclosed induction motor, as against the one horsepower, 2,850 rpm version fitted to the universal machine. The 1,420 rmp motor working through the five pulley blocks gives a very good range of speeds for woodturning but does not provide sufficient speed for a circular saw, mortiser or moulding block. If the purchaser of the CM600B should subsequently decide that he wishes to purchase the various attachments it will be necessary for him to dispose of the motor and to replace it with one which runs at 2,850 rpm. The grinding unit will also become redundant.

The CM500 is a very interesting machine indeed, extremely popular and in use in many parts of the world. The unique feature of these Coronet machines is the swivelling headstock which is popularly supposed by woodturners to have been introduced for the purpose of bowl turning but which, in fact, is of far greater value when using the machine for general purpose woodwork. It should be emphasised that the CM500 with its 2,850 rpm motor is still a complete lathe and capable of perfectly good woodturning. The main attachments available for this unit are as follows.

Circular saw

This is a heavy cast unit which fits to the left of the lathe headstock, the blade being mounted between special washers on the end of the headstock spindle. The table can be tilted to 45° and is provided with a mechanical rise and fall mechanism. If the steel insert in the centre of the table is removed and replaced by another of the correct shape it is possible to use a moulding block and cutters in the saw bench. Given the correct cutting projection through the surface of the table together with the correct positioning of the rip fence one can pass the material along the fence to produce an accurate and finely finished moulding. A wobble saw can also be used to cut grooves and housings of pre-set dimensions. Like many other sawbenches on the market today this has a rip fence which goes only part way across the table. It would be a great improvement if it were carried right to the back edge of the table and secured both at the back and the front but the operator can arrange this for himself by screwing a batten to the rip fence and clamping it at the far end by means of a G cramp. If this is not done there is a slight tendency for the fence to move when heavy workpieces are passed across the table. Micrometer adjustment is provided for the position of the rip fence which can be slid to the approximate position required and then adjusted by means of the micrometer feed. This refinement is very useful.

Planer
If a saw bench alone is purchased for fitting to a CM500 a short 50mm (2in) diameter stub bar is provided to carry the bench. If a planer is subsequently purchased, a longer bar is provided and the original short one can be removed so that both planer and circular saw bench can be mounted on the one long bar. The motor which drives the machine is double-ended so there are, in fact, two belt drives, one driving the headstock spindle, the other the planer. By this means the rpm of the cutter block on the planer is pre-set at 6,000 rpm giving a cutting speed of 12,000 cuts per minute, which is correct.

The planer attachment has a 115mm (4½ in) cutter block which may seem rather narrow, but it is astonishing how much work can be done on a small planer of this type. The planer is of the variety which is known as a surfacer, as distinct from a planer/thicknesser, and as with many surfacers it is possible to carry out rapid and accurate

Above: If accurately set and correctly used a thicknesser attachment of the type shown here can produce excellent veneers.

Below: Tenoning on a 115mm (4½in) planer attachment with the aid of a pusher block. Best results will be obtained if the shoulders are first cut on a circular saw.

rebating of workpieces. This is done by lowering the front or feed table of the planer to the desired depth of rebate and positioning the planer fence at the correct distance to provide the rebate width. It should, however, be noted that small-sized rebates can be produced in one pass but if a rebate is to be fairly wide it is far better to take it to depth by two or three stages. If one accepts the limitations of the cutter block width, this is an excellent little machine capable of really first-class work. A thicknessing attachment is available as an optional extra and this fits over the top of the planer, timber passed through

121

Mortising with a Coronet attachment using a hollow square chisel and bit. Note the special tool holder which is clamped to one of the lathe saddles.

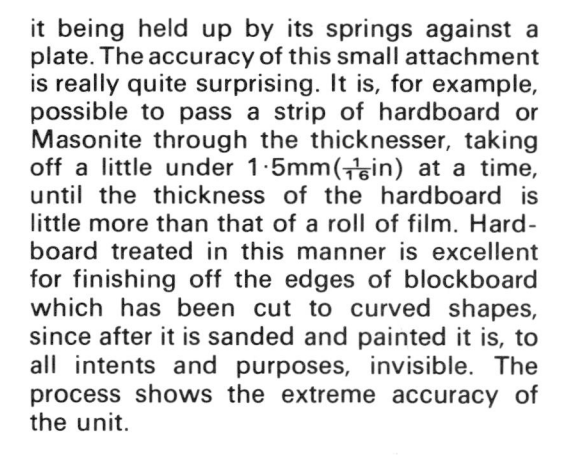

Mortiser on a Coronet Major in use.

it being held up by its springs against a plate. The accuracy of this small attachment is really quite surprising. It is, for example, possible to pass a strip of hardboard or Masonite through the thicknesser, taking off a little under 1·5mm ($\frac{1}{16}$in) at a time, until the thickness of the hardboard is little more than that of a roll of film. Hardboard treated in this manner is excellent for finishing off the edges of blockboard which has been cut to curved shapes, since after it is sanded and painted it is, to all intents and purposes, invisible. The process shows the extreme accuracy of the unit.

Mortiser
The mortising attachment is really quite a work of art. It is very heavily and ruggedly constructed, operating on dovetail slides, with an amazing number of small adjusting screws which can be employed as and when required to take up any wear which may develop. The mortising unit can be fitted in a few moments since it slides into one of the lathe saddles and is secured by one nut. Two pins which project from the bottom of the mortiser ensure that it is set up at right-angles to the lathe bed. The unit is provided with levers for forward feed and traverse and with a control which raises or lowers the work table of the mortiser to position the timber correctly in relation to the cutter. There are also stops which can be set with considerable accuracy to ensure the correct depth and length of a mortise.

Most users now run these attachments with a slot miller bit mounted in a chuck on the headstock spindle which, as in the case of the Kity mortiser described on page 116, and that of the Sheppach, will produce mortises which have rounded ends. The Coronet Major mortiser can, however, be used with the hollow square chisel and auger, which will produce square-ended mortises. Unfortunately, the cutters for this type of operation are now extremely expensive, and a certain amount of fine adjustment is necessary in order to set them correctly. If the projection of the auger from the end of the chisel is not set accurately there is a danger that the two will meet, creating considerable heat and damaging the temper of the steel in both of them. If the projection is too great the size of the chips will be too much for the correct operation of the cutter and the chips will jam inside the chisel. It should also be noted that in the case of large mortisers considerable effort is needed on the

Coronet Major universal machine with belt sander in position. The curved ends of this machine are invaluable for the sanding of curved workpieces.

forward feed lever in order to force the chisel into the timber. This is particularly so in the case of hard timbers such as oak, and the strain on the machine is perhaps undesirable.

Belt sander
The belt sander used on the Coronet Major is normally 150mm (6in) wide. It fits on to one of the lathe saddles in the same way as the mortiser and is driven by means of a short belt from a special pulley which is screwed on to the headstock spindle. The small fence provided enables timber to be sanded exactly at right-angles to the surface of the sander or at any other angle pre-set by the operator. Curved objects can be sanded on the curved ends of the sanding unit. It is a useful addition to a composite machine of this kind, but should not be run too fast, particularly when sanding end grain, as there is a danger of the timber being overheated and burned. End grain of timber can also crack if subjected to severe local heat in this manner.

Changing of belts on this sander is a quick and simple operation, and it will provide an excellent finish on a workpiece since this is the only type of sander in which the abrasive grains travel along the fibres of the wood rather than across them. All sanders create fairly large quantities of dust, and the belt sander does this rather more than most. Some form of dust extractor is advisable if long periods of sanding are envisaged, see page 103.

The attachments described above are the main ones for this machine. There is also a disc sanding attachment which can be equipped with a tilting table, the sanding disc being screwed on to the spindle of the lathe, and the table then being mounted in one of the lathe saddles.

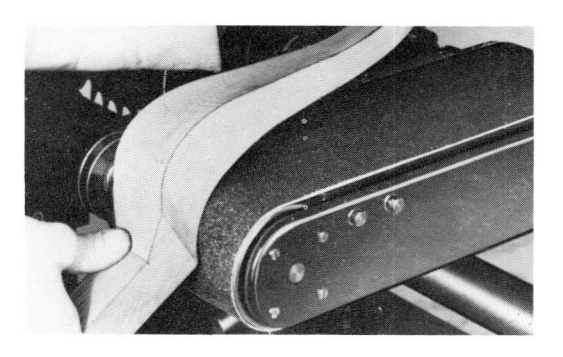

One attachment which tends to be overlooked by a number of purchasers is the combination table. This unit has a number of functions all of which are of interest to the woodworker. The combination table is attached to one of the lathe saddles by means of a bracket and is supported by a round rod which passes through the bracket. This means the height of the table in relation to the lathe bed can be varied at will and clamped in any desired position. The table itself is equipped with a fence, attached in the way the table is attached to the machine. In other words, there is a round rod passing through a bracket. This means that the fence can be positioned anywhere across the table and clamped firmly in position by means of a small lever. The fence itself carries a roller on its upper surface which can be of great value to the worker.

Returning to the swivelling headstock, it will be appreciated that in many cases machines of this nature have to be located in a garage, usually against a wall. Use can, therefore, be made of the swivelling headstock when long workpieces have to be planed or sawn. Without the swivelling headstock, it would be necessary to pull the machine away from the wall, but when the headstock is turned the planer, the circular saw and the motor will all move. It is possible to swing the headstock round in either direction so that long workpieces can be dealt with in a direction parallel to the lathe bed, rather than at 90° to it. If the headstock is swung so that the saw table is facing down the lathe bed the combination table can be set up so that in the ripping of a heavy plank, which is a difficult and somewhat dangerous operation for one person working alone, the timber will pass over the roller on the combination table, which has been pre-set to the correct height to receive it. The worker can, therefore, rip the plank along its length, finishing the operation off with a push stick, then walk round to the other end of the machine and lift the timber clear.

Many workers use the combination table as a sanding table instead of purchasing the tilting one which is available as an extra. If no sanding disc as such is available the faceplate of the lathe can be used, a circle of blockboard or plywood being screwed to this, with a disc of abrasive paper glued to it. It is also possible to use the combination table for dowelling purposes.

One of the operations for which the combination table will be found to be essential is the cutting of large sheets of plywood, chipboard or blockboard, the operation being known as panel cutting. When the machine is to be set up for this operation the first job is to set the table at a height which will give the desired projection of the saw blade. Once this has been done, and the table firmly clamped in position, the combination table is raised to the same height. This is best achieved by moving the combination table along so that it is as close as possible to the saw table and slightly above it. The combination table fence is then brought over until it is above the saw table and the combination table is lowered until its fence is resting on the saw table. The combination table is now clamped and the rip fence of the saw table is brought over until it touches the fence of the combination table. This should now be checked to make certain that the two fences contact along the full length. If they do not then the combination table can be swung slightly in its mounting until they do. If the saw table is correctly set, so that the rip fence is parallel to the blade, it now follows that the fence of the combination table is also parallel to the blade and since it is resting on the saw table, it is equally obvious that it is at the same height. The clamps can now be tightened and the combination table can be moved away from the saw-blade to give the required length of cut-off. In using this table for panel cutting many workers fix a strip of timber to the combination table fence which is fractionally higher than the table than the thickness of the wood to be processed. This means that the panel is trapped under this piece of wood and cannot lift from the table as it is cut. When cutting a panel using this method it is not necessary to watch the saw blade. No more projection of blade than is necessary should be given and the guard should be dropped down until it touches the workpiece. There is, therefore, no danger from that end and the worker's concentration can be applied entirely to keeping the timber correctly in contact with the fence of the combination table as it is pushed forward. If the setting up has been done correctly, and this procedure is carried out as it should be, extremely accurate work will result.

It will be seen that this type of machine is capable of a very wide range of woodworking operations and whilst it is very

Above: Large diameter jobs such as this built-up tub can be handled effectively on a Coronet machine if the headstock is rotated through 90°.

Below: Pummel of a stool leg being turned between centres on a Coronet Major lathe.

popular with the hobbyist, it is also suitable for small commercial enterprises.

In the original range of Coronet machines the Coronet Minor, a smaller version of the Major and slightly less sophisticated, could also be equipped with a range of attachments, very similar to those used on its larger brother. With the introduction of the Consort saw bench, however, this was discontinued since the Consort is capable of accepting the attachments, including a lathe, which were originally designed for the Coronet Minor.

The Minor is now the Minor M6 lathe, a smaller version of the CM600B, with a grindstone fixed on the left hand end of the spindle and a motor of a speed suitable for woodturning. The Consort saw bench gives approximately 50mm (2in) depth of cut with provision for rise and fall and tilt of the table. The attachments available for this machine are similar to those used on the Coronet Major, scaled down a little in some cases. The lathe attachment for the Consort is capable of quite serious work but for anyone whose main interest is woodturning this would not be the best choice since the Consort was designed for those whose main interest is in woodworking, rather than in turning. The swivelling facility of the headstock is missing and it is necessary to dismantle the machine to some extent for bowl turning — the lathe attachment needs to be removed from the machine for this operation.

Coronet also produce as an independent self-motorised machine, the Capitol 175mm (7in) surface planer, for which a thicknessing attachment is available, which has an optional extra, a rebating table which can be fitted to the side of the machine. There is also a bandsaw in the range, marketed under the name of Imp. This is a three-wheeled machine, motorised and capable of quite serious work.

Chapter ten

The Woodturning Lathe

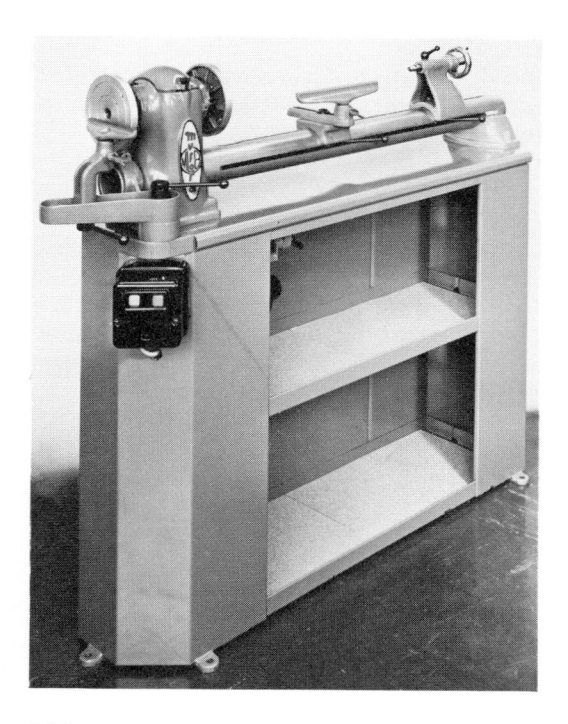

A tremendous rise in popularity has been achieved by the woodturning lathe over the past ten or twelve years and there is no doubt that this tool, which at one time looked as though it might disappear from the market, has now established a place among the leading types of woodworking machine.

The essential difference between a lathe and other woodwork machines is that this tool merely rotates the timber so that it can be shaped by means of cutting tools and good woodturning calls for a very high degree of manipulative skill. The proper use of such a machine, therefore, calls for a great deal of practice and this practice must be along the right lines.

There are two approaches to the shaping of wood in a lathe, these being respectively scraping and cutting. The scraping method is employed by many lathe owners because of its simplicity and the fact that it requires no real skill. Unfortunately, the use of scrapers where cutting tools should really be employed produces a very rough surface finish which requires a great deal of time to be spent in sanding, thus producing a great deal of unnecessary dust, and tends to blur the outline of a turning so that it lacks that crispness which distinguishes the work of a skilled turner. No matter how highly skilled a woodturner may be there will still be occasions when he will find it necessary to use scraping techniques but these should always be restricted to situations where there is no alternative, because it would either be difficult or dangerous to continue to use cutting tools, such as chisels or gouges. When scraping techniques are employed it is absolutely vital that the

Myford ML8 woodturning lathe-mounted on the manufacturer's cabinet, a very popular tool with home users.

scrapers be correctly sharpened so that they will, in fact, remove shavings from the wood rather than dust.

The purchase of a lathe of any description will represent a reasonable outlay, therefore care should be taken to ensure that something suitable is purchased. Lightweight lathes are, in general, unsatisfactory and what is required is a lathe of reasonable weight, sturdily and accurately constructed, with bearings which can be adjusted easily by the worker as wear takes place and which is solid enough to absorb vibration created by the turning of work which is off balance. New makes of lathe appear on the market from time to time and some of these disappear again fairly quickly. The prospective woodturner would be well advised to ensure that the machine purchased is likely to be available for some time to come and that spares and accessories will present no difficulty.

Once a decision has been made as to the type of lathe to purchase, it is necessary to decide whether or not to mount this on the cabinet stand offered by the manufacturer. Some of these are good, others are rickety and quite unsatisfactory. Anyone already quite happily established in woodwork may prefer to construct a solid wooden bench on which to mount the lathe. If such a bench is well made from timber of sufficient dimensions, it will assist in absorbing vibrations and render the learning of the craft considerably easier. A woodturning lathe should, if possible, be mounted so that its drive and tailstock centres are at elbow height for the operator. If the lathe is mounted on a bench which is too low the turner will be working with his back slightly bent and this can lead to considerable discomfort.

Woodturning lathes are usually provided with facilities for running at more than one

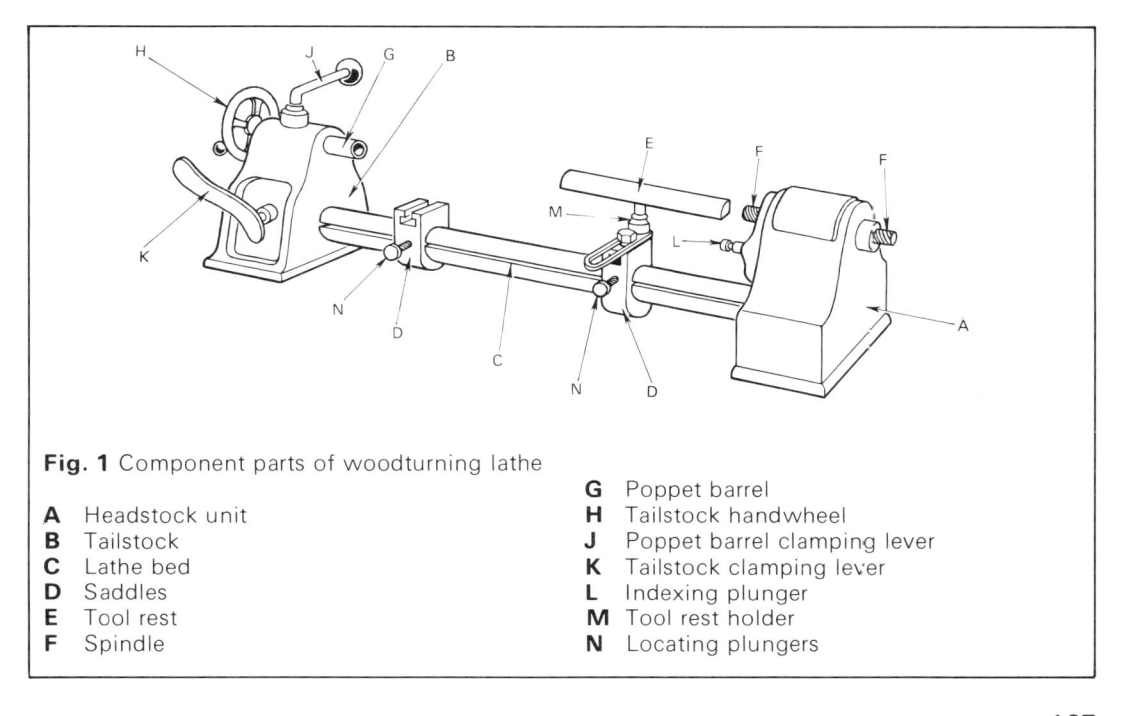

Fig. 1 Component parts of woodturning lathe

- **A** Headstock unit
- **B** Tailstock
- **C** Lathe bed
- **D** Saddles
- **E** Tool rest
- **F** Spindle
- **G** Poppet barrel
- **H** Tailstock handwheel
- **J** Poppet barrel clamping lever
- **K** Tailstock clamping lever
- **L** Indexing plunger
- **M** Tool rest holder
- **N** Locating plungers

speed. The question of speed in woodturning is, however, often over emphasised and it will be found in practice that a great deal of turning of varying diameters can be done at a standard speed. For the beginner a speed of between 1,000 and 1,500 rpm will be comfortable for normal spindle turning. It will be necessary to reduce this speed to as little as 500 or 600 rpm for the turning of large diameter discs and it may be advantageous to increase it to 3,000 or even 3,500 rpm when turning very small articles, such as chess men or tiny knobs for furniture. It should be borne in mind that excessive speed is not an advantage, since it leads to overheating of the tools through considerable friction and does not produce the smooth cut which is the object of the exercise.

The majority of lathes on the market at

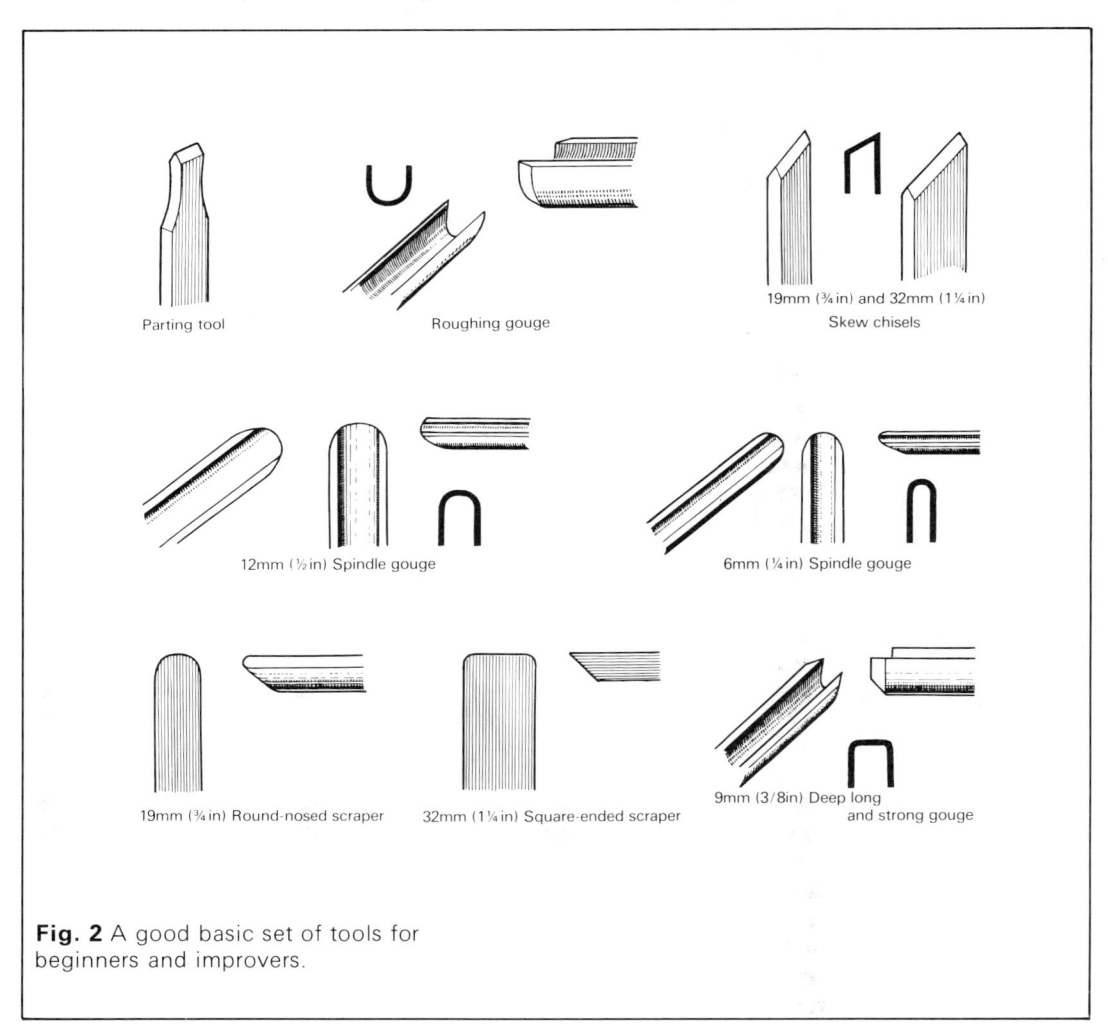

Parting tool

Roughing gouge

19mm (¾in) and 32mm (1¼in) Skew chisels

12mm (½in) Spindle gouge

6mm (¼in) Spindle gouge

19mm (¾in) Round-nosed scraper

32mm (1¼in) Square-ended scraper

9mm (3/8in) Deep long and strong gouge

Fig. 2 A good basic set of tools for beginners and improvers.

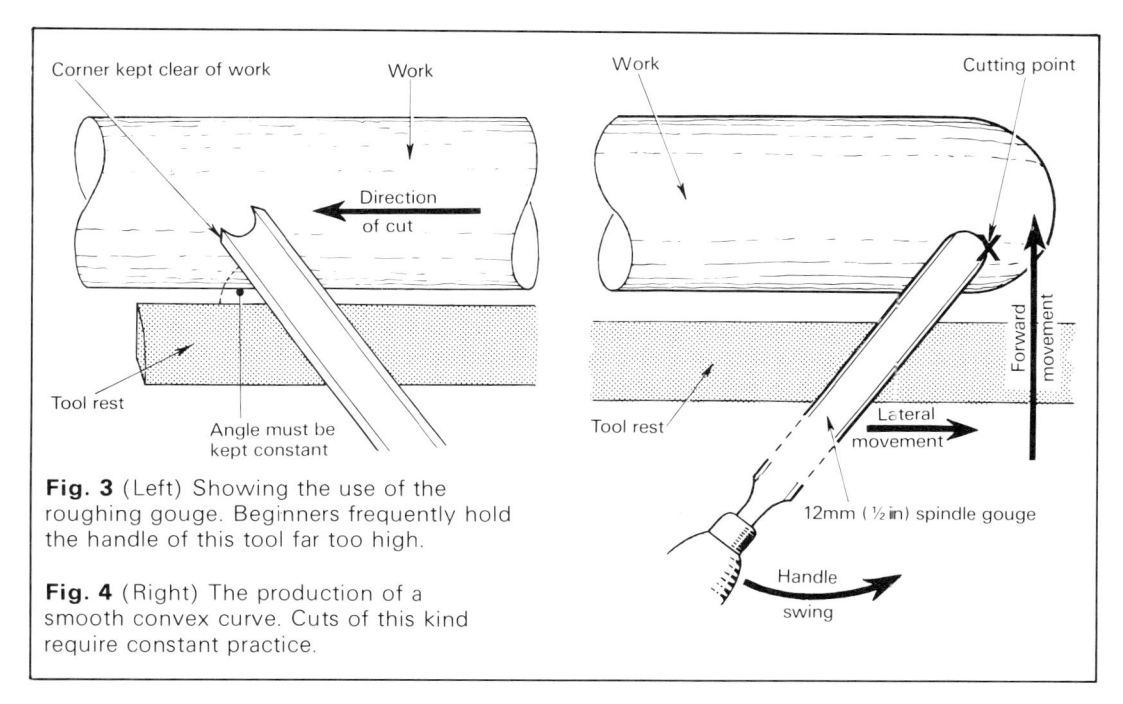

Fig. 3 (Left) Showing the use of the roughing gouge. Beginners frequently hold the handle of this tool far too high.

Fig. 4 (Right) The production of a smooth convex curve. Cuts of this kind require constant practice.

the present time will accommodate a piece of timber approximately 76cm (2ft 6in) in length between centres and this will be found to be adequate for the majority of woodturning projects. Items which are longer than this are generally manufactured in two parts being joined together by means of a pin at some point where the design changes.

Suitable lighting must be arranged for the lathe and over a period of more than thirty years I have found that an ordinary electric light bulb gives better results for this particular operation than does the neon tube which tends to cast a flat light over the work and does throw up the shadows which are so essential to reveal imperfections in the surface.

Lathe tools
It is not necessary for a beginner in woodturning to spend vast sums of money on tools. The purchase of too many tools will simply serve to confuse rather than to help and it is better to work with about nine or ten tools until they can be handled with reasonable skill, before purchasing others. Cutting tools required for a medium-sized lathe would be as follows.

Gouges 19mm ($\frac{3}{4}$in) roughing gouge (trade description half round) for reducing squares of wood which are to be turned between centres, or on a chuck, to cylindrical form.

Spindle gouge 12mm or 19mm ($\frac{1}{2}$in or $\frac{3}{4}$in) for cutting convex or concave curves.

Bowl gouge Used in the turning of any form of disc. It is a deep fluted tool available in sizes from 6mm–25mm ($\frac{1}{4}$in–1in); 10mm ($\frac{3}{8}$in) gouge is recommended for beginners. This particular

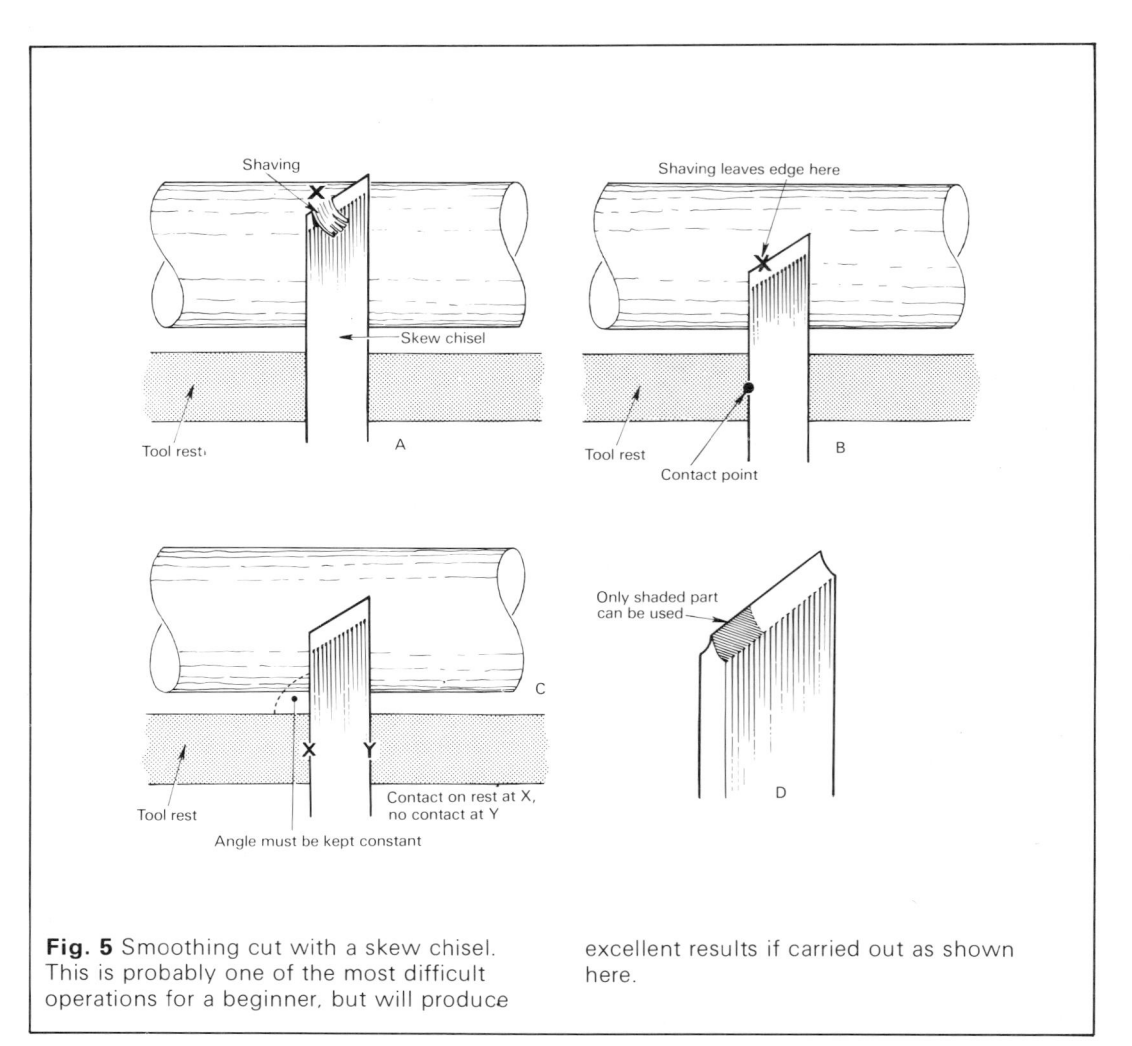

Fig. 5 Smoothing cut with a skew chisel. This is probably one of the most difficult operations for a beginner, but will produce excellent results if carried out as shown here.

gouge is longer and heavier in section that the others.

Skew chisels For smoothing and for the cutting of details such as beads, and the trimming of end grain surfaces. One 19mm ($\frac{3}{4}$in) and one 32mm ($1\frac{1}{4}$in) should serve quite well.

Parting Tool For cutting right through pieces of wood, for setting out furniture legs and similar items, recessing for the letting in of tiles in cheese boards, etc.

Spindle gouge 6mm ($\frac{1}{4}$in) can be used where the 12mm or 19mm ($\frac{1}{2}$in or $\frac{3}{4}$in) spindle gouge is too large to go comfortably but is mainly useful for the initial hollowing of vases, pots, egg cups, etc.

Round- and square-ended scrapers A round-ended scraper is necessary for

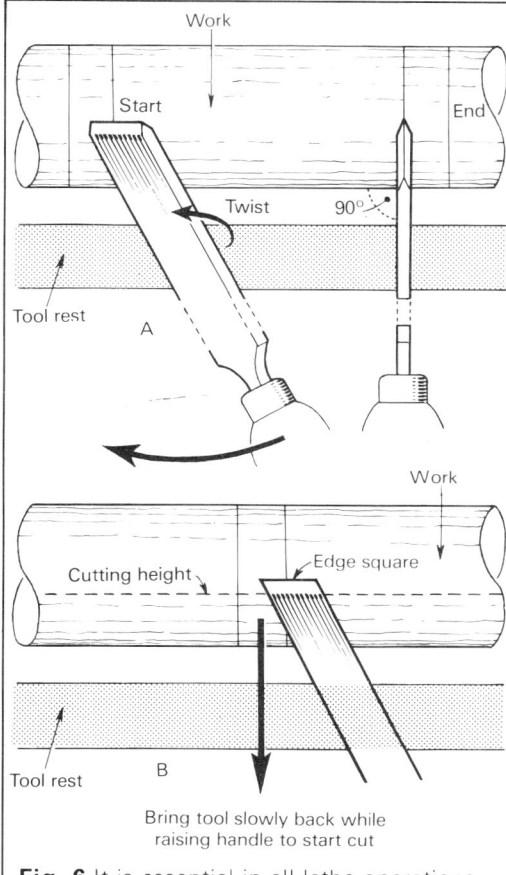

Fig. 6 It is essential in all lathe operations for the tool to be correctly positioned at the start of the cut. Position of chisel for the start of a bead cut is shown here.

Fig. 9 Sketch showing components of long hole boring kit.

finishing inside bowls and other objects which have to be hollowed out. A scraper with a square end and a straight edge is useful for final levelling of recessed areas.

The set of tools as described above should be quite sufficient to enable a beginner to work for a year or two and would be suitable for the production of a very wide range of objects on the woodturning lathe.

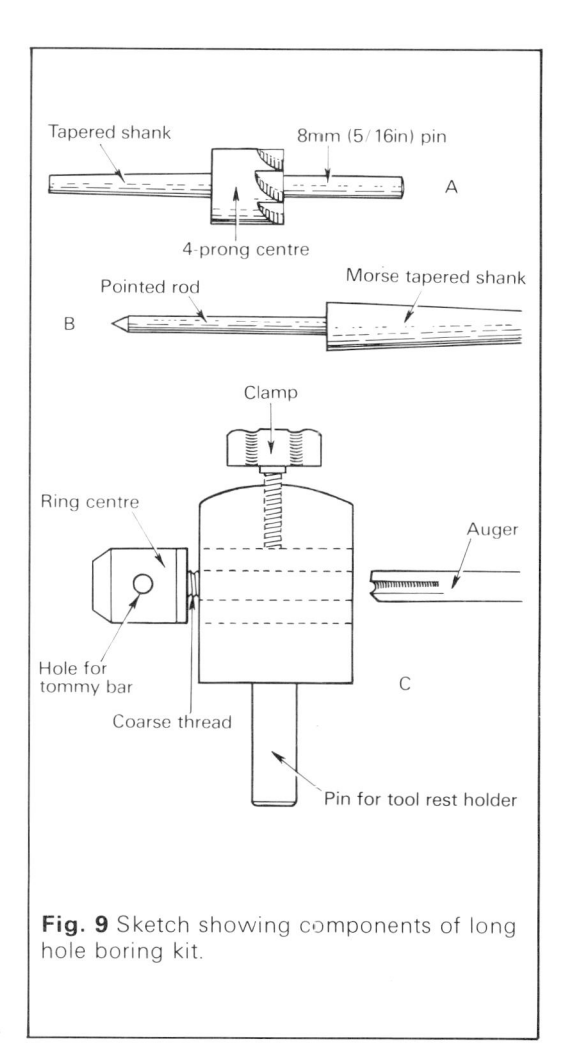

A few words on the subject of grinding the cutting tools should perhaps be included. Those who are not used to woodturning lathes should appreciate that the relative speed between the timber and the cutting edge of the tool is many times higher than in any other form of woodwork in which tools are held in the hand. This means that the edges receive a severe hammering from the hard timbers in a very short space of time, and one

131

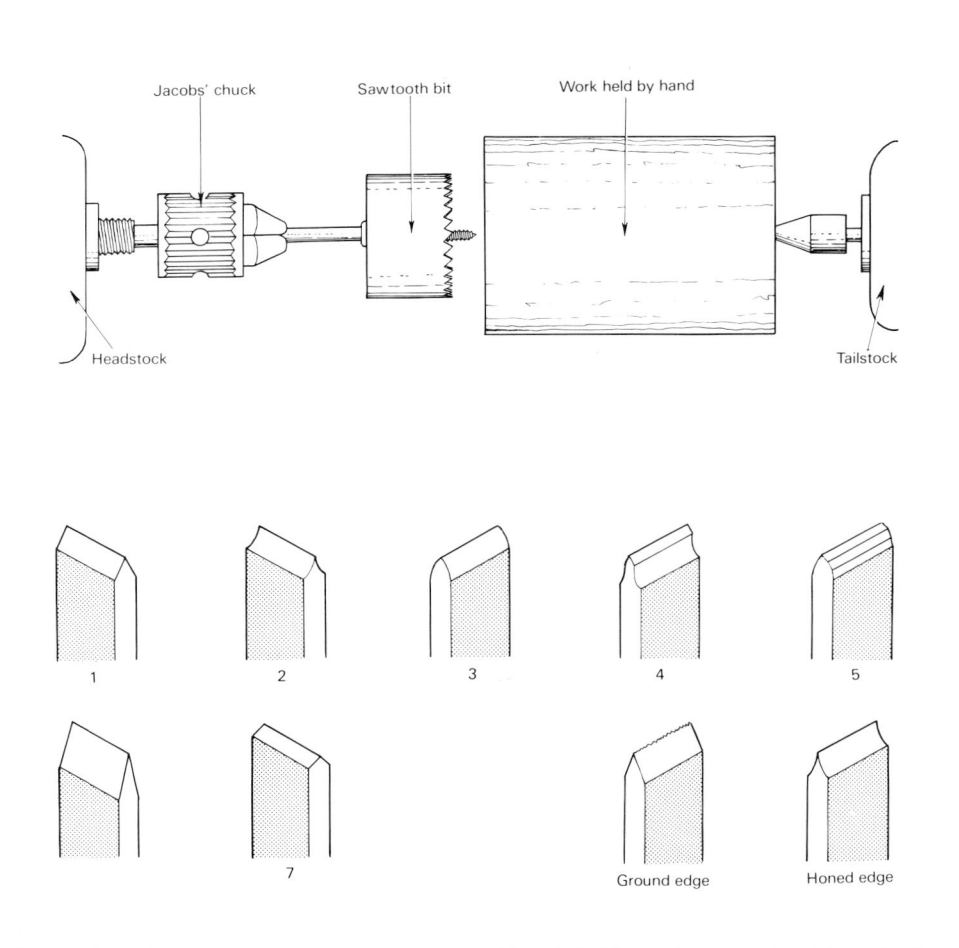

Fig. 7 Sketches of tool shapes.
1 Bevel ground on side of wheel.
2 Bevel ground on face of wheel.
3 Convex bevel.
4 Second bevel formed by bad oilstoning.
5 Series of facets, caused by removal from stone and incorrect replacement.
6 Long bevel, too weak.
7 Short bevel, strong but will not cut.

Fig. 8 Drilling of end grain objects in the lathe, as for opening up blanks for vases etc. Lathe speed should be very slow. The work is held firmly by hand and pushed on to the cutter by means of the tailstock.

Fig. 10 Showing drilling of end grain objects and use of tool rest inside workpiece.

Fig. 11 Box construction on a woodturning lathe is fascinating, but difficult unless carried out as indicated here.

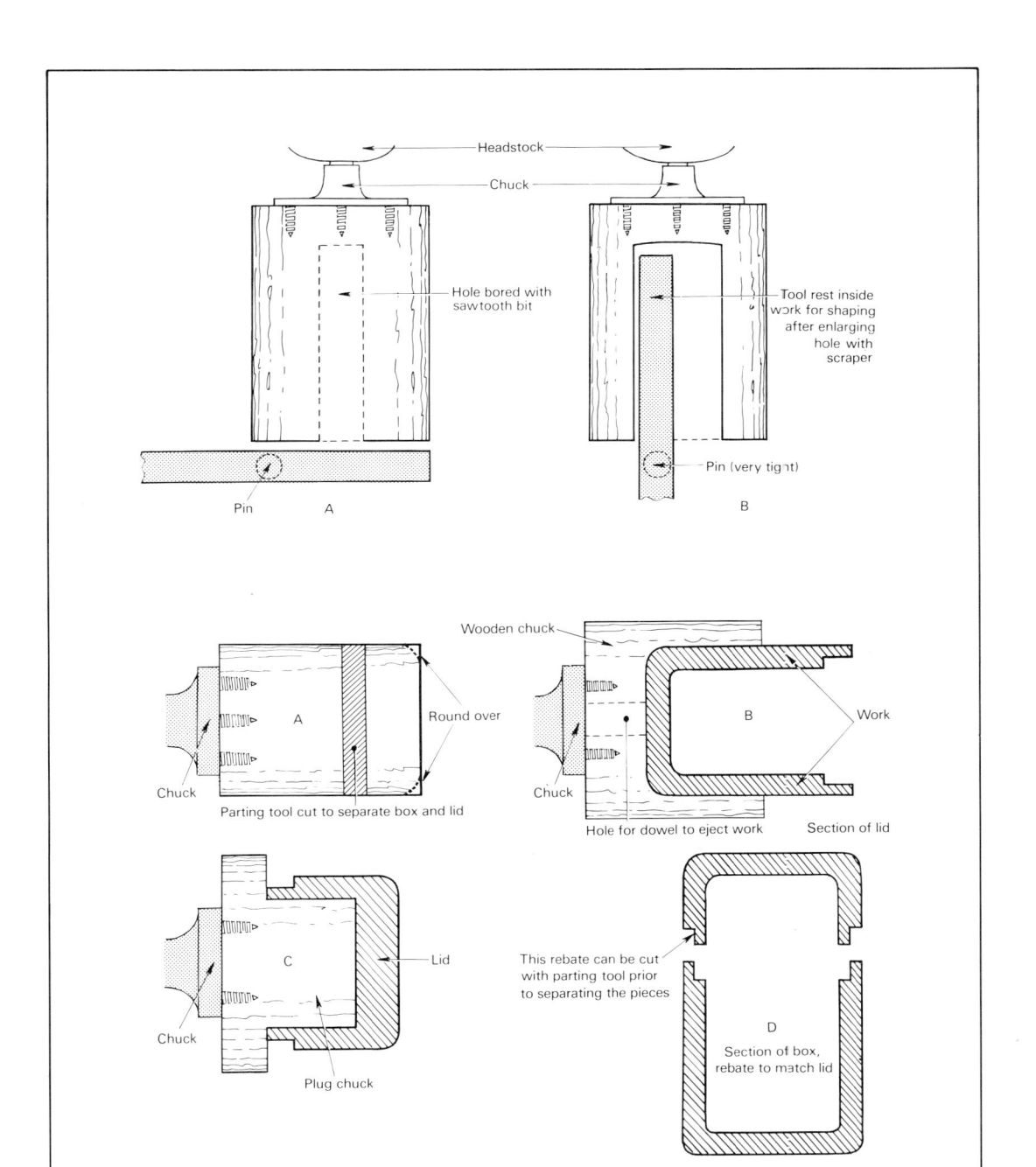

Headstock
Chuck
Hole bored with sawtooth bit
Tool rest inside work for shaping after enlarging hole with scraper
Pin (very tight)
Pin
A
B

Wooden chuck
Round over
Chuck
A
Chuck
B
Work
Parting tool cut to separate box and lid
Hole for dowel to eject work
Section of lid

Chuck
C
Lid
Plug chuck

This rebate can be cut with parting tool prior to separating the pieces
D
Section of box, rebate to match lid

133

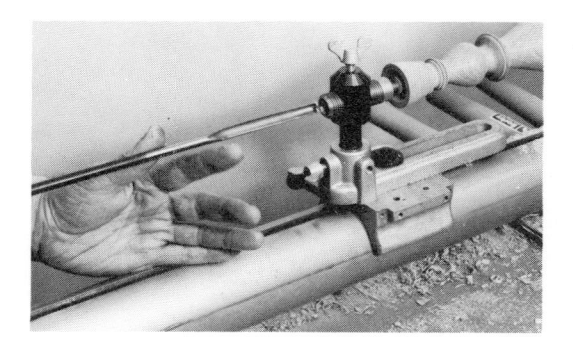

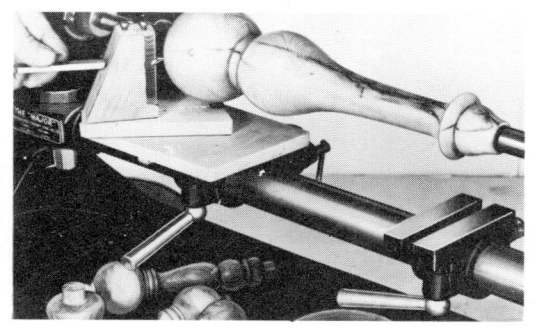

Above left: Commencement of drilling operation on table lamp. This system although rather crude is surprisingly efficient.

Above right: This copying device is well made, but the scraping action produces rough finishes.

Below left: Home-made jigs are often very useful. This illustration shows a simple jig to hold a scraper, permitting the tool to be moved in a perfect arc to trim the roughly-turned ball.

Below right: Boring on wood lathe with saw tooth bit, run at slow speed.

must also allow for the fairly high level of frictional heat produced as the bevels of the cutting tools rub against the wood. The combination of these two factors will cause the edges of woodturning tools to become blunt in a relatively short space of time. If considerable time and trouble is expended in honing and stropping tools for turning the resulting fine edges will not be suitable for the job, being far too fragile.

If grindstones are kept in sharp and good condition by the judicious use of a dressing stone, and as little pressure as possible is used when presenting the tools to its surface, there should be no problem and the knack of sharpening turning tools can be acquired fairly quickly by practising with pieces of scrap steel similar in shape to the tools. If the stone is not sharpened and cleaned, or too much pressure is applied in the grinding, the temperature of the steel will be raised to a point where its temper is destroyed, after which it will not be possible to hold a cutting edge.

The burr which is formed on the cutting edge as the tool is ground can, in most circumstances, be ignored since it will rapidly be removed by the timber. Some workers do not feel happy until they have removed this burr by means of an oilstone.

Chapter eleven

Workshop Layout

I am frequently asked to assist with the layout of workshops for commercial or hobby purposes, and in situations where the size and shape of the workshop and the machinery which is to be located within the available area is known this is not difficult at all. To generalise on this subject in a book, however, is by no means a simple matter. There will be some fortunate people with a considerable amount of money to spare, and a large workshop which will easily accommodate the machines which they intend to use. On the other hand a great many people have to make do with fewer machines than they would like, to be located in very small workshops. The important points regarding workshop layout for power tool work are adequate lighting over any given machine and adequate space around it so that workpieces of reasonable size can be processed without any difficulty. Certain points are fairly obvious, as for example the fact that a circular saw bench must be situated in the centre of the workshop since long pieces of timber cannot be processed on it if it is placed with its back to the wall. The situation is totally different if a radial arm saw is in use since this can be placed against the wall and long workpieces will be processed parallel to the wall itself.

Considerable thought must be given to the location of the electric power points. It is highly undesirable to have lengths of cable trailing on the floor as the worker may easily trip on them and in falling put his hand into a machine. In addition, electric cables which are lying around on the floor will undoubtedly be trodden on quite frequently, and the internal insulation may well be damaged. Should this happen there is every possibility of a short circuit and possibly a fire. Since the longer the cable, the greater is the resistance to the flow of electric current, such cables should be kept as short as possible and sited where they will not be damaged or cause any form of accident. A sufficient number of electric plug sockets is essential since it is most inadvisable to run numerous machines from one plug point using adaptors. This will overload the wiring system and again could result in a fire.

It is also most important to make certain that offcuts of timber are not left lying around on the floor close to machines since it is possible that the operator will trip on one of these and, again, an accident could result. Most of this, of course, is nothing more than common sense but it is surprising how many people fail to notice quite obvious points.

Some thought must be given to the finishing processes involved in woodworking. If there is to be the use of polyurethane or lacquer then dust is a major enemy. If the workshop area is large it may be possible to reserve one section of it purely for finishing and to put up a hardboard or plywood wall which will completely separate this from the workshop proper. If this can be done the finishing area can be kept dust free without too much trouble. If the workshop is not large enough for this then finishing methods which are susceptible to dust need to be carried out elsewhere.

Some thought must also be given to the heating of the workshop since it is extremely uncomfortable to work in a workshop which is not adequately heated in winter. The heat source which is provided should be sufficient to maintain a reasonable level of temperature without producing moisture. For instance, if paraffin heating is chosen this is likely to cause rust since a considerable amount of water is given off by paraffin heaters. There are some excellent woodburning stoves designed for workshop heating which, in fact, consume sawdust or shavings. These are perfectly safe in operation, give off a very satisfactory heat and little or no smoke, once they have been correctly lit. If the workshop itself does not produce sufficient sawdust to feed such a stove, sacks of sawdust can often be obtained from local sawyers at a very nominal charge. Electric heating is quite satisfactory but some note must be taken of the current which is being drawn since the machines themselves will absorb a fair amount. If the workshop is to be heated by electricity, then an expert should be consulted — unless the operator himself is qualified.

The problem of rust in workshops is not normally very great, except in the cases of those tidy-minded individuals who sweep up thoroughly after each session and remove all the shavings. Wood shavings and sawdust are hygroscopic by nature and will absorb large quantities of water from the atmosphere. Since I am by nature extremely untidy and sweep up only when I have to, I have never been troubled by rust in any of my workshops! It is also a good idea to keep metal surfaces wiped over with an oily rag.

Those who are setting up their first workshop must appreciate that there is no shame whatsoever in working with safety visors, or at least goggles to protect the face. It is quite easy for a small chip of metal or timber to embed itself in the eye, with results which do not bear thinking about. This can be prevented simply and efficiently without any undue expense by the purchase of a suitable visor or good pair of goggles. There are goggles on the market which are, in fact, built to government specification for use in industry, which will slip over a pair of spectacles and are quite comfortable in use. They must, of course, be kept clean since one does need to see clearly what is going on when using the machinery.

Although I am untidy by nature, in areas where I use machinery I do try to be a little more sensible. It is a big mistake to lay tools, etc. on top of machines since frequently these machines will be started without a check to see if the blades or cutters are clear and items which have been left lying on them can be flung quite some distance with considerable force. Tidiness in this respect should therefore be cultivated from the outset. Another safety point is that all machinery should be checked occasionally right through to see that all nuts and screws, etc are tight. Where trouble is experienced with nuts or screws, which become loose due to vibration in operation the use of a substance known as Loctite, which can be obtained

Mobile dust extractor unit by DeWalt. This unit is easily moved from one machine to another and its powerful motor is very efficient.

from good tool stores, will cure the trouble.

A little of this substance is smeared on to the thread of the nut or screw which then will not loosen through vibrations. It can, however, be easily removed by normal methods when required.

Chapter twelve

Grinding and Sharpening

It is sometimes said that the difference between an amateur and a professional woodworker is that the former tends to regard the sharpening of tools as a waste of time, whereas the latter regards any attempt to go on using a cutting edge which has become blunt in the same light. In my experience most keen amateur woodworkers are well aware of the necessity for sharp cutting edges. A blunt edge takes more power from the machine, is much less efficient in operation and can be dangerous because the increased feed pressure which is required may lead to a hand slipping into a rotating saw blade or cutter. Blunt saw blades and cutters will cause motors to overheat and, in the case of a circular saw blade, there is far greater chance of a kick-back which may reject the material being processed and hurl it towards the operator. This latter point is also very important where planing machines are being used since blunt planer knives are very prone to kick the material back towards the worker.

In the case of tools for woodturning the grinding process is normally all that is required but where the tools are to be used for joinery or carving there is a necessity for subsequent honing with an oilstone and possibly stropping on a prepared leather strop. Some workers use grindstones mounted on the universal type of machine and if the necessity for the use of the grindstone is infrequent this system can work extremely well. It is, however, extremely dangerous to operate a modern man-made grinding stone without proper guards and the fitting up of the grindstone and its guard on such a machine can take quite a lot of time.

Most workers now tend to use double-ended grinders such as the Wolf or Elu, which are extremely efficient and do not interfere with the operation of other machines.

A general purpose stone for use on such a machine would be about sixty or eighty grit and usually 150mm or 180mm (6in or 7in) in diameter and about 25mm (1in) in thickness. Care must be taken with such stones as they are rather brittle. In use on a grinding machine they are perfectly safe but they must not be subjected to sharp knocks and a stone which has been dropped on the floor should be regarded as suspect. If internal cracks should develop in a stone of this kind it is possible for it to disintegrate under power and this could cause a serious accident. When a grinding stone is purchased thick paper washers will be found on either side of it. These should under no circumstances be removed, since they offer some degree of resilience when the nut is tightened. The nut itself should be pulled up so that it secures the stone, but should not be pulled up really tight. It is self-tightening, due to the direction of rotation of the spindle, and overtightening may crack the stone.

Many people advise the use of a pot of water for cooling the tools during the grinding process. This is a curative measure which is not often employed by competent grindstone operators since it is far better not to bring the metal to a temperature where it requires cooling in water.

The older type of grinding stone was a large natural stone wheel 300mm–450mm (12in–18in) in diameter by 75mm–100mm (3in–4in) in thickness which rotated slowly in a trough of water. The surface of the stone was at all times covered in water which cooled the blade and the slow speed of rotation did not produce excessive frictional heat. This type of stone is no longer in general use and although motorised versions of it are available they are relatively expensive. Modern man-made grinding stones are very efficient if cared for in the proper manner; these stones are made up of millions of extremely hard particles bonded together with a special bonding agent. The grit size quoted for a grinding stone relates to the number of holes per square inch in the sieve in which the granules have been sifted before handling.

When instructing students in my workshop I frequently compare the stone to a very large number of fine, circular saw blades jammed tightly together on the same spindle. This is because the stone has a vast number of what should be extremely sharp cutting points with gaps between them, just as a circular saw blade has a fairly large number of sharp points with gullets to separate them. If the teeth of a circular saw blade are allowed to fill up with resin, dust and other foreign material, the cutting action is drastically impaired, frictional heat is built up and efficiency falls off at an alarming rate. Precisely the same thing can happen with a grinding stone which must be kept sharp and free from deposits of resin and so forth. If this is not done the stone ceases to cut and simply produces a very high temperature in the metal which is applied to it. Grindstone dressing tools can be purchased and these are extremely useful if the stone has to be shaped, as for example to fit the gullet of a large circular saw blade. If the intended use of the grindstone is the sharpening of tools, however, the use of a dressing tool is not recommended, since the metal washers which are mounted loosely on the spindle of the dressing tool produce a hammering effect on the surface of the stone as it rotates, and pulverise the surface, leaving it extremely coarse.

The best method of keeping such a grindstone in good condition is the use of what was known in the past as a devil stone. This is a very hard stick of carborundum, impregnated with waste from industrial diamond processing, which is many times harder than the grindstone itself and, when placed on the grinding rest and applied to the stone, will remove a fine layer from its surface, uncovering fresh sharp points and removing the unwanted material from between them. A grinding stone which is in need of attention will show this fairly clearly if it is rotated very slowly in a good light. Any glaze which is apparent on the surface indicates the necessity for the use of the devil stone. A grindstone which is to be used for sharpening tools and saw blades should never be used for grinding non-ferrous metals or other materials such as plastic, rubber, wood, etc.

When using a grinding machine *always*

wear protection over the eyes. High-impact goggles or a face vizor should be employed.

Man-made grinding stones, such as are employed on modern double-ended grinders, are mounted on their spindles between metal washers. These washers should preferably be about half the diameter of the stone, and certainly not less than one third its diameter. Normally the washer face which is intended to go against the stone is very slightly dished or has a small rim around the edge. They should not be fitted the wrong way round.

In the interests of safety it is very important that only stones which are designed for the specific grinding machine are employed. It is vital that the machine be run below its maximum recommended speed at all times, and that stones larger than those recommended by the manufacturer are not fitted to its spindles. If this is ignored, there is every possibility of a wheel bursting in use.

Anyone unaccustomed to the use of grinding wheels will find it best to support the tools on the grinding rest. Those who have become proficient in the process, however, frequently do not use the grinding rest at all, simply allowing the tool to rest against the wheel and controlling it in a free-hand manner. The reason is largely because the pressure used between the tool and the stone must be very carefully controlled. When grinding is done off the tool rest this is fairly easy, only the weight of the tool itself is resting on the stone with sufficient control to prevent bouncing. When a tool is placed on a grinding rest it is by no means as easy to judge the pressure being used, and there is more likelihood of the tool being burned by frictional heat. An exception to this would be when a precise angle has to be ground on the edge of, for example, a plane iron. This would be extremely difficult to do by free-hand methods and most workers employ some sort of home-made jig which can be fixed to the grinding rest and which will present the cutter to the stone at exactly the angle required.

The grinding of a twist drill on a grindstone of this type is an extremely difficult process if the results are to be good. The point of a twist drill must be kept absolutely central to the drill itself and the length of the cutting edges should be identical. Such drills are also ground so that they are relieved behind the cutting edge itself, reducing friction. If the length of the cutting edges is unequal, the hole produced will be larger than it is intended to be. There are some excellent jigs on the market which will enable twist drills to be sharpened by the complete novice, with virtually perfect results, and such a jig is strongly recommended.

Twist drills as such are particularly useful for metalwork though they are sometimes used for wood. Wood-boring bits are more commonly employed and these are sharpened with files. The leading manufacturers of high quality boring bits issue booklets of instructions for those who are unacquainted with the correct method.

Sharpening circular saw blades
There can be little doubt that the workshop item which causes the most difficulty in sharpening, where beginners are concerned, is the circular saw blade. Some home workers never learn to do this correctly and overcome the problem by having a number of blades so that one or two can be sent away to the local saw doctor for treatment while using others. The care and sharpening of a circular saw blade is not, however, as difficult a matter as may at first be supposed and the process is covered broadly here. The

circular saw takes a great deal of power from the motor when cutting thick hardwoods and the amount of power drawn goes up drastically as the quality of the cutting teeth deteriorates. The continued use of circular saw blades which are in a bad condition will have a harmful effect on the motor over a period of time.

Circular saws come in a wide variety of patterns but the type which mainly concerns the newcomer to power tool woodworking is the plate saw. This has a circular saw blade produced from a flat sheet of steel which has the same thickness from centre to rim, the teeth being set with alternate teeth slightly bent in opposite directions. This produces a blade which will cut a kerf in the timber wider than the thickness of the blade itself and this set must be correct.

The plate saws most likely to be used by home workers are the rip, cross-cut and general purpose patterns. A general purpose saw blade will serve very well and many do not bother to buy the other types. There is no doubt, however, that when a great deal of heavy ripping has to be done it is advantageous to have a blade designed for this purpose, since it cuts much more rapidly. Conversely, if the worker is engaged in cabinet-making where good surfaces are required on the sawn end grain, then a cross-cut blade will do a much better job. The general purpose blade will both rip and cross-cut but it does not perform either operation as well as a blade designed specifically for the job. A cross-cut blade has a large number of small triangular teeth which are usually sharpened by means of a small file, triangular in section.

The mill file which is used for the sharpening of the combination or rip blade is flat with a curved edge. A flat file which has 90° corners on it should not be used for this purpose since the corners of the file will produce small nicks in the curvature of the saw gullet which can lead to cracks and will certainly help the build-up of resin and dust.

Many operators now purchase saw blades which have their teeth tipped with tungsten carbide, which is among the hardest of metals known to man. These are very expensive, cannot be sharpened in the home workshop and should be sent to a specialist firm of saw doctors. Special equipment is needed for the sharpening of tungsten carbide tipped blades, together with the knowledge of how to use it. The tungsten carbide tipped blade has come into its own in recent years due to the wide use of

A Wolf grinding attachment, in use with the Sapphire 2-speed drill.

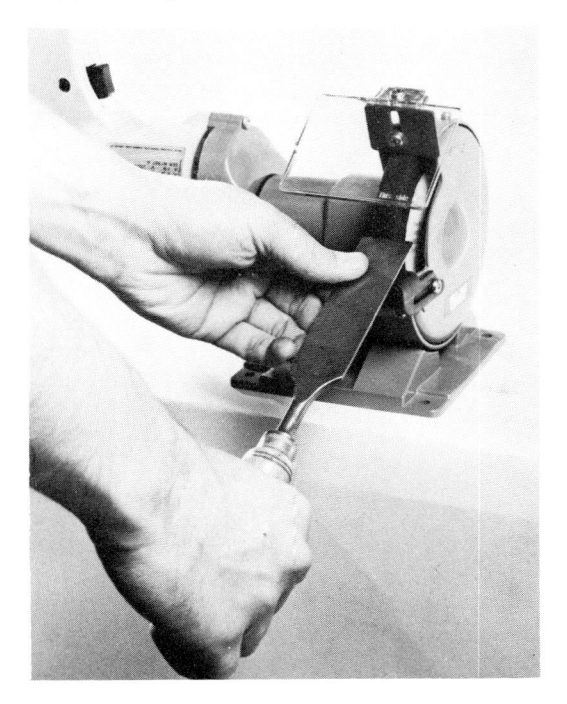

141

man-made boards, such as chipboard, blockboard and plywood. These are bonded with special bonding materials which are extremely hard and very rapidly remove the cutting edge from normal steel blades. A good quality tungsten carbide tipped saw blade will produce a very smooth sawn finish but is by no means a cheap item.

The processes involved in sharpening circular saw blades appear to have different names in different countries, and indeed at times in different parts of the same country, but the processes themselves are universal. Examination of a blunt saw blade with a powerful magnifying glass will reveal wear on the front of each tooth, close to the cutting edge and usually a humping or rounding over of the point itself. When a new circular saw blade is purchased it is a good idea to place it on a sheet of white paper and draw round it very carefully with a sharp pencil. This will provide a pattern of that particular blade when in perfect condition and is a useful guide for the operator to check after future sharpenings. The first step in sharpening is known variously as topping, stoning and ranging. The object of the exercise is to make certain that the distance from the centre of the blade to the tip of each tooth is identical. If the circular saw has a reversing switch fitted to it it should be run backwards for this process. If this facility is not available the blade should be removed from the machine and refitted with the teeth pointing backwards. Next the machine table or saw blade height should be adjusted until the teeth will just lightly mark a piece of wood which is held flat on the table. When this has been done, and the clamps of the machine have been securely tightened, an oilstone is passed over the top of the revolving blade. This process may sound extremely dangerous but it is not, provided due care is taken, and is a standard procedure. It is helpful to position the rip fence so that it will help in steadying the oilstone. When the operation has been carried out as described a check should be made to ensure that every tooth has been marked by the oilstone. If this is not the case the projection of the blade through the table should be increased very slightly and the process repeated. Once every tooth has been marked, however slightly, this part of the operation is finished. If the blade has seen a lot of hard service it may be found that a considerable amount of metal has been removed from a number of the teeth whilst others are hardly marked at all.

The next operation is filing, and this is best done with the saw blade placed between two discs of scrap timber and held firmly in a vice. An experienced worker will file the blade correctly, almost by instinct, but many inexperienced operators blacken the teeth in the smoke of a candle before starting the filing. Care must be taken when doing this to see the blade is not left too long and too close to the candle flame itself, thereby overheating the tips of the teeth.

Many people who simply want to revive a blade which has become blunt, and do not wish to spend too much time in the process, will just file the tops of the teeth. This is not a very good practice to follow, and if it is carried out too many times the depth of the gullets will be reduced to a point where the efficiency of the blade will be affected. Correct sharpening procedure, if done with a mill file with a suitable curvature for the bottom of the gullets, will help to preserve the correct shape of the blade. A mill file cuts on its wide flat faces and on its edges which are rounded and it is important to purchase one which has a suitable curvature for the type of blade being used.

When the blade has been set up between the discs of wood in the vice, the filing can begin and the object of blackening with the candle will immediately become apparent. As the first stroke is made across the face of the first tooth a check will reveal whether or not the file is being correctly applied so that it cuts right across the surface of the metal. If it is not doing so then the necessary adjustment to its angle must be made and two or three slow pushing strokes will normally be all that is required. Files should, of course, never be pushed rapidly backwards and forwards. They are meant to cut on the forward stroke, which should be slow.

Filing on the teeth of circular saw blades should be done only on those which are leaning away from the operator. This, of course, means filing alternate teeth, then reversing the blade and the supporting wooden discs in the vice to file the ones which have been missed. Any attempt to file teeth which are leaning towards the operator will result in a juddering of the tooth which will prevent the proper file action. When the filing of the fronts of the teeth has been completed, some metal being removed from the bottom of the gullet at the same time by the edge of the file, the tops of the teeth can be dealt with. This is where confusion in names comes into the matter, since sometimes this process is referred to as topping whereas to others topping seems to be applied to the ranging or jointing process. For clarity I will refer to it here as filing the tops of the teeth. Many of the teeth will have had the marks produced in the jointing process completely or partially removed when the fronts of them were filed. Any teeth which have no marks left on them from the jointing process should be left out and not touched at all in the process of filing the tops. Once again, alternate teeth, those leaning away from the operator, will be dealt with, and the saw reversed. It will be noted that the tops of the teeth are, in general, not square but have an angle of 10° or 12° on them. This angle must be maintained and the filing process, which need consist of no more than one or two slow pushes of the file, must be done with the handle lowered to allow for this.

When the processes described have been completed the saw will usually be in an efficient condition and capable of very good work. The only other aspect which needs to be considered is the question of the set, which is usually adequate and in no need of attention. If it is considered necessary to alter the set note that only the top third of each tooth is bent outwards and not by very much. I have always set my circular saw blades by laying them on top of the end grain of a block of wood and tapping them with a hammer and punch. With experience it is possible to produce very good results by this method but there are proprietary saw setting devices which can be purchased and these, if used in accordance with the manufacturer's instructions, will also produce good results. Never put extra set on a circular saw blade in the hope of making it cut more efficiently since anything more than adequate set will have precisely the opposite effect.

If the advice given above is followed faithfully the result should be very good indeed and most beginners derive tremendous satisfaction from their first sharpening of a circular saw blade which has become really blunt, since a few file strokes have quite a noticeable effect. The cost of sending blades out to be treated now is ever increasing, apart from the general inconvenience involved.